P9-CFS-601

Life Sketches

545-9000

ALSO BY JOHN HERSEY

Fling (1990)

Blues (1987)

The Call (1985)

The Walnut Door (1977)

The President (1975)

My Petition for More Space (1974)

The Writer's Craft (1974)

The Conspiracy (1972)

Letter to the Alumni (1970)

The Algiers Motel Incident (1968)

Under the Eye of the Storm (1967)

Too Far to Walk (1966)

White Lotus (1965)

Here to Stay (1963)

The Child Buyer (1960)

The War Lover (1959)

A Single Pebble (1956)

The Marmot Drive (1953)

The Wall (1950)

Hiroshima (1946; new edition, 1985)

A Bell for Adano (1944)

Into the Valley (1943)

JOHN HERSEY

Life Sketches

Vintage Books
A Division of Random House, Inc.
New York

First Vintage Books Edition, February 1991

Copyright © 1989 by John Hersey

All rights reserved under International and Pan-American
Copyright Conventions. Published in the United States by
Vintage Books, a division of Random House, Inc., New York,
and simultaneously in Canada by Random House of Canada
Limited, Toronto. Originally published in hardcover by
Alfred A. Knopf, Inc., New York in 1989.

Owing to limitations of space, acknowledgments to reprint
previously published material may be found on page 379.

Library of Congress Cataloging-in-Publication Data
Hersey, John, 1914-
Life sketches / John Hersey.—1st Vintage Books ed.
p.   cm.
Reprint. Originally published: New York: Knopf, 1989.
ISBN 0-679-73196-2
1. Biography—20th century.   2. United States—Biography.
I. Title.
[CT120.H435   1991]
920.073—dc20
[B]   90-50193
CIP

Manufactured in the United States of America
10 9 8 7 6 5 4 3 2 1

To William Shawn

Contents

Note

Harold Ross accosted me in a corridor of the nineteenth floor of *The New Yorker*'s offices, one afternoon in 1946, during a week when he and William Shawn were editing what I had written about six survivors of the first atomic bomb at Hiroshima. On the final page proof at the end of the process, when the magazine was just about to go to press, one of us, I can't remember who, had discovered a misprint of the mischievous sort that tucks itself plausibly into its context and so hides away from the most alert proofreader. "Misprints!" Ross exclaimed in his wild, half-shouting way. "Let me tell you a story about a misprint."

Ross, the founding editor of *The New Yorker*, was an odd-looking specimen. It seemed peculiar that the editor of a sophisticated city-slicker magazine—a man who, late at night, was always given the most élite table in the back room at the Stork Club, then the smartest night spot in town—should look like such a hayseed, an absolute rube. He had a wide country-man's mouth, his complexion was as coarse as the face of the moon, and he wore the hair on his biggish head cropped to about two inches in length, so it stood up in all directions. He gawked at pretty girls and shouted commonplaces to his friends. Never mind. He edited with a very keen pencil and an even keener mind. The magazine always put a piece it had bought quickly into galleys, I suppose so that its editors could measure it against *New Yorker* standards as soon as possible, and Harold Ross's way of editing was to write questions in the margins. I once counted more than fifty questions alongside an early galley of a piece of mine. Sometimes they were interrogatory howls of outrage. On the first galley of the tale about John Kennedy in this book, I had put it that toward the end of his ordeal Kennedy, encountering some natives, had given them a coconut, on which he "wrote a message." "With *what*, for God's sake?" Ross's note asked. "Blood?" He demanded clarity and exactitude. In the Hiroshima piece, I had written of "lopsided bicycles" near the epicenter of the explosion. Ross asked, impelling a change, "Can something that is two-dimensional be 'lopsided'?"

He said, that afternoon in the corridor, that he had hated misprints ever since an early issue of *The New Yorker,* but he had learned, in that green issue, to be humble in his contest with them. It seems that the magazine had bought for that issue an article by S. J. Perelman about the habits and manners of New York theater audiences. Those audiences, Perelman had written, "would laugh at the drop of a ha on the stage." Ross could see bad trouble ahead. On the very first galley he wrote in big letters: "THIS IS PERELMAN'S JOKE. DO NOT CHANGE TO 'HAT.'" Through galley after revised galley Ross nursed this line unchanged. He grew obsessed by that "ha." It became so important to him that when the magazine was finally to be run off, he actually climbed into the press, looked up at one of the rollers for the right page—he told me he had learned in his newspaper days to read cold type in its upside-down and backward state—and saw, to his relief, "ha." Not quite satisfied, he assembled the printers and told them that they must not, under any circumstances, change that word. He went happily home and slept soundly all night.

In the morning, he went to the office, opened the magazine

to the Perelman piece, and saw "hat." Then he realized that he had lectured the printers at eleven-forty-five. At midnight, a new shift had come on. A zealous artisan had seen the obvious error, stopped the presses, and made the change.

I retell this story of Ross's because I have cherished it all my life as a lesson. His story was a fable, the moral of which is: a writer, even more than an editor, should care so passionately about every word he uses that he will be willing to risk his life by climbing into a press at the last moment to make sure the words on the roller are the ones he has chosen—but, alas, he must also know that there is no way in the world for him to produce a work that is perfect in every word. He will, at some point, as Ross did, forget what time it is in all the hours of making. This lesson stands in my mind alongside the terrifying first sentence of Joseph Conrad's preface to *The Nigger of the Narcissus:* "A work that aspires, however humbly, to the condition of art should carry its justification *in every line.*" (The emphasis, God help me, is mine.) In the face of such an admonition, I feel, often, as if I am making my life sketches not with a fine pen or a sharp pencil but with a thickish piece of charcoal. The best I can hope for is that the smudged and blurred lines will lie on the page in such ways as to hint at, even if they cannot really represent, the amazingly clear pictures that I believe I have seen in my mind.

The dates of publication of the life sketches in this book are given at the foot of each title page. The pieces are not presented, however, in the chronology of their coming out in print. They appear, instead, roughly in the order in which I happened to encounter the people who are pictured. In several cases, the subjects were alive when I wrote the pieces but are not now. I have thought it best, nevertheless, to leave the texts, including the tenses of the verbs, just as they were when I wrote them.

Life Sketches

George Van Santvoord

What looms first in memory is the forehead. Up and up and up it went, incised crosswise with swooping wrinkles which seemed to be the tracks of endless thought. What a castle that long head was! In its keep there must have been brains enough for three normal men. When I first read "Kubla Khan" I could not help picturing Coleridge's "stately pleasure-dome" as George Van Santvoord's forehead.

Second in memory: our headmaster's eyes. They were as deep as the Atlantic rift. The range of temperature in those eyes was universal—from the heat of the sun to the unimaginable cold of the gaps in the galaxies. Their look could penetrate every fiction and falsehood; they could make a transparency out of a first-year student. But behind every powerful look in them, no matter how accusatory, there lurked a glint of mischief, an ember of something still boyish in the marvelous intellect, and with that glint every student, even in terror, could ally himself.

And a third memory: his right hand. It was broad, spatulate, and extraordinarily dry—as dry as papyrus. His handshake was limp, flaccid; our student awe of him was sharply height-

Memorial tribute to George Van Santvoord, Headmaster, the Hotchkiss School, Lakeville, Connecticut, May 17, 1975; *Hotchkiss Alumni Magazine,* Spring, 1975.

ened when we learned that the weakness in the hand had been caused by a grievous injury in the First World War, in which he had won the Croix de Guerre. And yet what voltage there was in those flattish long fingers! When one was idling, a bit too loudly perhaps, in the Main Corridor, and suddenly from the rear one felt the big limp shape of that hand slip into the crook of one's arm, it was as if one were being electrocuted.

The first time that happened to me was no more than a week after I had arrived at the school. The hand slithered under my elbow, and I looked up and saw the great forehead, the grim features, and Jupiter's eyes. A voice that seemed to come from a stone statue asked me a question: "What was Stradivarius's first name?" There I stood, brainless, in the dim light of the varnished wainscoting, faint with the smell of floor wax, dizzy with homesickness, and all I could force from my lips was "Uh, sir, I don't know." It was not much comfort to discover very soon that this was the standard student answer to the Duke's questions.

Within a few days, I was shocked again by the flexible hand, and this time the question was "Is it true that eeny, meeny, miney, mo is counting in Chinese?"

This time I knew the answer. "No, sir."

"Then how *do* you count in Chinese?"

I heard my cracking voice, just recently changed, intoning, *"Yi, erh, san, sz, wu, lyou, chi, ba, jyou, shr."*

"I think you are wrong," Mr. Van Santvoord gravely said. "I believe the correct way to count in Chinese"—this time he mimicked the singsong tones I had used—"is eeny, meeny, miney, mo."

My heart leaped then with fear and joy—and it still does today, remembering—because I knew that I was right and the man with the three-story forehead was wrong.

Only later did I realize that this austere personage, who had to cope with the tidal energies of three hundred and fifty mostly miscreant students, and with endless problems of bricks and mortar, and with ever-furious parents, and with towering eccentrics on the faculty like Doc Rob and Pop Jeff and Uncle Joe Estill and Howdy Edgar and John McChesney, had nevertheless been able, within the very first days of my arrival in his amazing ambit, to breathe an identity into the shapeless clod of a homesick fifteen-year-old that I was, for not only had he known my name, he had known that I had been born in China, he had known that I played the violin. And I became convinced then, and I hold the conviction today, that he knew much, much more, right down to the innermost secrets of my groping adolescent mind.

And much later still I realized that by putting me in the right and putting himself in the wrong, in the matter of Chinese numbers, he had given me my first small sand grain of self-confidence.

In this way, and in many other ways, he taught. For he was, above all, a teacher. In the First World War, as an enlisted sergeant, a former Rhodes Scholar, he was designated to lecture the officers of his battalion on military campaigns. At Hotchkiss he could step into any class in place of an indisposed teacher, whether of Greek or trigonometry or modern history or physics, and could teach there at least as well as the incumbent expert. After his retirement, he even made a kind of school of the Vermont Legislature, where, according to the *Bennington Banner,* "his colleagues listened when he spoke."

Any boy who was fortunate enough to attend the Sunday-evening open house at Mr. Van Santvoord's would be treated to one of his astonishing monologues. The first week, it would be on beekeeping; the next on Zoroastrianism; the next on the methods of construction used in building the Pyramids. We were not old enough to know how truly dazzling those performances were, products of total recall and of a gift for shaping an essay, and yet even our crude perceptions could be jogged into a kind of grudging juvenile uneasiness, the first stage perhaps of wanting to learn, by the spectacle of that beautiful mind at play in the fields of knowledge.

He was born, it may have been, two centuries too late. His mind was as large and wide-ranging and noble as those of the men who wrote *The Federalist Papers,* who designed octagonal Monticello, who tempted the charges of a thunderhead with a wired kite. "As a member of the Yale Corporation," Dick Gurney wrote in the *Lakeville Journal,* "he sat between Senator Robert Taft and Secretary of State Dean Acheson without awe or embarrassment, for the excellent reason that he probably knew more about most things than they did."

Yes, he was a man of the Enlightenment. He was a poet. He painted watercolors of wildflowers. He was an aviarist and an apiarist; a topographer and a cartographer. He was an angler who in his seventies scorned the use of rubber boots or waders in frigid Northern streams. He was a moderator of town meetings, a legislator. He was a dairy farmer, whose fine bulls gave their seed for breeding throughout the Northeast. He was a Puritan, an equestrian, a philosopher who sweetened his thought with pipe smoke.

Like a true eighteenth-century man, he was completely in tune with nature, as many a student can testify who learned woodcraft from him. He revered all creatures of the meadow and woodlot—horses, woodchucks, badgers, bears. He was a botanist. His heart was torn between the beautiful rare ducklings he raised on the hockey pond in the warm seasons and the equally beautiful owls that snatched them away for prey. He was a trainer of homing pigeons who, scorning Western Union, released the birds in Pottstown, Pennsylvania, to wing home to Hotchkiss carrying in their message capsules the scores of just completed football and baseball games against the archrival, The Hill.

Some years after I had graduated, Mr. Van Santvoord invited

GEORGE VAN SANTVOORD

"Is it true that eeny, meeny, miney, mo is counting in Chinese?"

me to give the Hotchkiss Commencement address. The day
before graduation, he was sitting on the veranda of the Headmaster's House with half a dozen pairs of parents—not his
most beloved category of humankind. He said, "Well, John,
you have an audience here. Why don't you rehearse your speech
for tomorrow?" I thanked him and said I thought one performance would be more than enough. "All right, then," he
said, "*I* have a commencement speech for them." He went into
the house and fetched a volume of short stories by the collo-
quial satirist George Ade, and he read out loud the whole of
"The Fable of the Last Day at School and the Tough Trustee's
Farewell to the Young Voyagers," a story of a small-town businessman's exceedingly practical advice to a graduating class.
Mr. Van Santvoord read in the tone of a kind father reading
his little children to sleep. I will never forget his mock solem-
nity as he read the last sentences of the story: "'I will now ask
you'—the Trustee said—'to come up and get your Sheepskins.
Take this precious Certificate home and put it in a Dark, Cool
Place. A few Years hence when you are less Experienced, it
will give you a Melancholy Pleasure to look at it and Hark
back to the Time When you knew it all. Just one word in
Parting. Always count your Change, and if you can't be Good,
be Careful.'" He looked up. There was a stunned silence. He
broke it, that little fire of mischief burning bright in the deeps
of his somber eyes, by saying, "Since you enjoyed that story so
much, I'll read another." And he read "The Horse Maniac and
What Caused the Filing of the Suit." *Then* he read "The Two
Wives Who Talked About Their Husbands." And THEN he
read "The Old-Time Pedagogue Who Came Down from the
Shelf." And after that the parents fell over each other heading
for the nearest exit. Mr. Van Santvoord looked very surprised
at their sudden departure.

Was his notorious treatment of parents mere rudeness for its
own sake? I am certain it was not. I think it was a combination

of a deep, deep shyness he had, along with a shrewd sense of alliance with the secret souls of the boys in his school, who were condemned by nature in their formative years to a helpless war with the very idea of parenthood. They could see that on this painful battlefield, as elsewhere, the Duke was on their side.

And so again and again we come back and back to that quality of mischief in him. It could be heard in his Socratic questions. His massive severity had a bubbling laughter close beneath the surface. He was a whole man, and he wanted his charges to open their eyes to the many shades of light in life. Character in a boy was more important to him than high marks. His smoking pledge had sharp teeth—students were kicked out not for their smoking but for breaking their word. But grim rectitude was not his aim for us; to be whole and healthy, a person had to see the force in human affairs of irony, of absurdity, of folly, and of fun. And so he always teased as he used his luminous mind to teach his mind that was like a display of aurora borealis on a north-wind night. He wanted a man not just to be learned, but rather to be wise, decent, humane, generous, forgiving, and light of heart in heavy days. As to all these traits, he gave us the great gift of his example.

Sinclair Lewis

One morning in May, 1937, back from a year's study at Clare College, Cambridge, I sat reading *Gone With the Wind* in the New York apartment of my former Yale roommate Chester Kerr, wondering what to try next in the job line. A hoped-for spot on *Time* had fallen through. The phone rang, and the call was for me—from another Yale classmate, Henry McKnight, who was working at the *Herald Tribune*. He said he had heard from Dorothy Thompson, then a columnist for the paper, that her husband Sinclair Lewis was looking for a secretary. Why not take a shot at that? He gave me Lewis's phone number.

The Nobel laureate himself answered my immediate call and invited me for an interview that very afternoon. He directed me to an apartment on Central Park South.

McKnight had not told me why Lewis needed a new secretary, and indeed I was not to learn the reason until many years later, when Mark Schorer, who was writing Lewis's biography, told me what it was. I was dimly aware of some of Lewis's notorious capers, such as his fisticuffs with Dreiser, but I had no idea that he was an alcoholic, and that most of his scrapes

"First Job," *Yale Review,* Spring, 1987; and, in slightly different form, "My Summer with Sinclair Lewis," *New York Times Book Review,* May 10, 1987.

were boozy. He had had to be hospitalized once, in 1935, to dry out. His drinking had ruined his marriage, and he and Dorothy Thompson had separated on April 28th, less than a month before my appointment with him. A few days after the split, a friend called Thompson to tell her that Lewis had disappeared. Experience made her fearful for him, and intuition put her right to work. She got a list of inns in Connecticut and called them one after another. Sure enough, she finally located him in Old Lyme. With him was Louis Florey, a professional stenographer whom Lewis had employed off and on for years. Son of an illiterate French-Canadian blacksmith, Florey had served, as Schorer would put it, "as drinking companion and audience, valet and bootlegger, at least as much as he served as typist." He told Thompson that Lewis had had a bad fall. She drove to Old Lyme and found Lewis in a frenzy of delirium tremens. Furious at Florey for having let things get so far out of hand, she fired him, and she drove Lewis to the Austin Riggs Center, in Stockbridge, Massachusetts. Although the sanitarium did not ordinarily treat alcoholics, they discovered he had three broken ribs and took him in. Schorer told me that Lewis was famous for swift and spectacular recoveries. Once, while drinking on a farm in the Michigan dunes with the *Chicago News* drama critic Lloyd Lewis and his wife, and Florey as well, he passed out in the midst of uttering a sentence; Florey hauled him to a bed; an hour later he reappeared, clearheaded and fresh, and picked the incomplete sentence up in the middle and finished it. And now, within days, he was back in New York, on the wagon, and—to my eyes, as I first met him—full of sparkling energy and great charm.

The first impression, as he walked ahead of me into his living room, sat down, and lit a cigarette, was of a thin man put together with connections unlike those of most human beings. All his joints seemed to be universal. His long, slender hands seemed to turn all the way around on his wrists. Wolcott

Gibbs had once described his emerging from a car—"a tall man, getting up in sections." Next, piercing pale blue eyes, the bluer for being lashed into the pink face of a redhead. Thinning light-red hair, ill-brushed and tufted, over a wide dome of a forehead. Then, in better focus, terrible cheeks, riddled, ravaged, and pitted where many precancerous keratoses had been burned away by dermatologists' electric needles. Narrow, dry lips, and a slender chin. I would have sworn that he was hideously ugly until he started to talk, when his face suddenly turned on, like a delicate, brilliant lamp.

We talked awhile about Yale. A member of the class of 1907, he had been a miserably unhappy outsider as an undergraduate. He was pleased that I remembered he had been given an honorary degree at my graduation. He asked me if I knew a classmate of mind named Brendan Gill. I certainly did—and then I recalled that Brendan had persuaded Lewis to submit a piece, along with contributions from Thornton Wilder, Archibald MacLeish, Stephen Vincent Benét, and other famous Yale writers, for a centennial issue of the *Yale Literary Magazine,* of which Gill was the editor. Lewis obliged. Gill took the article back in his own hand to Lewis in Bronxville, where both were then living, and told Lewis that the piece wasn't good enough for the *Lit.* The notoriously enrageable author, charmed by Brendan's blarney, rewrote it. I was an applicant; I refrained from bringing up this risky memory. Suddenly, Lewis broke off the interview and dismissed me—curtly, it seemed to me.

Oh my, I thought; that went badly. What next? I returned to *Gone With the Wind.*

Early the following morning, Lewis called up and asked me to come back up to see him at ten o'clock. This time we talked about England, where I'd been studying, and about the American Legion, which was just then holding a convention in New York. He told me that his wife Dorothy had said the Legion was the first manifestation of Fascism in the United States, and he had said to her, "Come on, Dorothy, this is the first chance these fellows have had to get away from their wives in years. Let them have a little fun." Lewis had put me completely at ease when, once again, he suddenly sent me away, now thoroughly puzzled.

He invited me back the next morning. He began chatting about what it was like to be married to a newspaper columnist, without any bitterness that I could detect; and went on about one thing and another. His phone rang. He answered it in his bedroom. Soon he came back, and he said, "John"—he was now calling me by my first name—"I have to shave and change for an appointment. There's a young man down in the lobby who's applying for a job as my secretary. Would you mind interviewing him for me?"

The young man, I was happy to be able to report, was hopeless.

It seemed, without anything having been said about it, that that chore had been my first task as his employee. After some more casual conversation, Lewis gave me a month to learn shorthand—he suggested either the Gregg system or speed-writing—and to switch over from hunt-and-peck to touch typing. He told me to report to him after thirty days at a house he had rented in Stockbridge. (I hadn't the faintest idea that he needed the security of being near the Riggs sanitarium, in case he should tumble off the wagon.)

The house was a small, simple, shingled, summer-resortish cottage. Lewis had settled in a ground-floor bedroom, and the whole second floor was mine. A local woman came in to cook and clean.

I had barely had time to unpack when Lewis put in my hands the typescript of a novel he had just finished and asked me to read it and tell him what I thought of it. I had no way of knowing that he had reached a critical stage in his writing life. He was fifty-two years old. He had won the Nobel Prize seven years before, at the end of a remarkably fecund decade, which had seen the appearance of *Main Street, Babbitt, Arrowsmith, Mantrap, Elmer Gantry, The Man Who Knew Coolidge,* and *Dodsworth.* He had coveted the Nobel and had lobbied for it with shocking brazenness, but the hanging of the medal around his neck in Stockholm had turned out to mark, as the *Herald Tribune* put it, "his hour of awful nakedness." The tirade of his acceptance speech on the poverty of American culture had raised such a storm back home that Calvin Coolidge felt the need to say, in one of his longer and more ornate sentences, "No necessity exists for becoming excited." Lillian Gish told Schorer that Lewis had said to her, "This is the end of me. This is fatal. I cannot live up to it." He had published two mediocre but commercially successful novels, *Ann Vickers* and *Work of Art,* and then, in the last flare-up of his astonishing creative energy in his lifetime, he had dashed off the massive, awkward, but resonant novel *It Can't Happen Here* in four months of work. That book had been published a year and a half before he hired me.

The typescript he handed me was entitled *The Prodigal Parents.* Ten years earlier, bouncing back from the revulsion of *Elmer Gantry,* Lewis had begun to plan a more positive novel with a labor leader like Eugene Debs for a hero, who lived by "the God within" him. Its theme would be: "Blessed are they which are persecuted for righteousness' sake." Again and again in the following years, he had sought out one knowledgeable informant after another, who could be for this work the sort of teacher and guide the bacteriologist Paul de Kruif had been for *Arrowsmith.* Nothing ever came of it. After the publication of *It Can't Happen Here,* when Lewis had been accused of being a Communist, a young radical Dartmouth student named Budd Schulberg invited him to Hanover to talk to some

SINCLAIR LEWIS

"Is the wanderer like me homeless?"

Marxist undergraduates. They soon found out that Lewis hadn't a political bone in his body, and then they began to bait him, until he shouted, "You young sons of bitches can all go to hell!" and walked out on them.

With *The Prodigal Parents,* Lewis turned his back once and for all on the idealistic labor novel and instead took a petulant revenge on Budd Schulberg's friends. The parents were a mawkish couple named Fred and Hazel Cornplow, and their children were silly left-wing college kids who were taken in by a cartoon-page Commie. Even I—who knew none of this background—could see that it was awful. It was destined to receive some scathing reviews. Lloyd Morris would write that Lewis "has never been less of an artist." Malcolm Cowley would find the book "flat, obvious, and full of horse-play that wouldn't raise a laugh at an Elks' convention."

But I was twenty-three. Sinclair Lewis had won the Nobel Prize. I wanted this job. I had courage only up to a point—to the point of telling the author that he had got his students' vernacular all wrong. We went through the dialogue line by line, and I think now I must have helped Lewis to make his book a little more obvious than it already was.

Lewis's life was in a mess. But I was to have a marvelous summer, oblivious of his suffering. He never took a single drink while I worked for him; I remained in total ignorance of his history. I saw a surface that was gentle, kindly, boyish, and vividly entertaining. He treated me as a young friend, insisting that I call him "Red." My work was fun. Taking his rapid dictation and reading it back to type it was like doing a crossword puzzle: I caught every fourth word with a squiggle of Gregg and had to figure out what went between. "If you want my autograph," he would dictate in a note to a fan, "you must send me a self-addressed envelope with a postage stamp on it"—chuckling at the idea that I would have to address an envelope and put a stamp on it to send the note. He wrote his new work on a typewriter, making many changes in longhand, and I copied the pages fresh. I was his chauffeur. One important task, every other day, was to buy a box of chocolates—no nougats in the fillings, no nuts, Louis Sherry creams preferred—to appease a liver which, to my unknowing, had been mightily revved up by his years of drinking. In the evenings, when he entertained at home, I was his bartender, serving his guests. When he was invited out, he asked his hosts to include me, and I sat in on evenings, thrilling to me, with John Marquand, Owen Johnson, Ellery Sedgwick, Jr., and others.

He was endlessly playful. "He could no more stop telling stories than he could stop his hair growing," Carl Van Doren once said. When we lunched alone, he would start a tale—either true or invented on the spur of the moment—and then, all for me, and of course for his own pleasure, he would jump up from the table and become the people in the story, switching from side to side as he conversed with himself in the telling. His improvisations were uncanny; one forgot his cadaverous face and *saw* John L. Lewis, F. D. R., Huey Long, Father Coughlin. He could reel off astonishing footages of Milton, Blake, Edward Lear. In company he organized games. Once, with John Marquand and others, he passed around pads and pencils and made everyone see how many names of rivers beginning with "M" they could write down. He would assign guests outrageous names from telephone books and tell them to converse in character with the names. He would hand out a set of end rhymes and get people writing sonnets with them against the clock; Schorer records that Lewis's own best time was three minutes and fifty seconds. He hired a small donkey one day when two very tall people were to be at the house; for some reason he wanted to see them riding around with their feet dragging on the ground.

Word games and letter games were his favorites. He rattled off tongue twisters, spoonerisms, oxymorons. I must preface examples of alphabetic Jewish dialogues that he wrote down for me one day with the assertion that anti-Semitism was not among his problems; it horrified him. His incomplete works included a play, *Undiscovered Country,* about anti-Semitism in New York medical schools and hospitals, and a novel on the subject that he sketched out. Here, at any rate, was an exchange between a father and his son Abraham:

> ABCD goldfish?
> LMNO goldfish!
> SARA goldfish.
> OICD goldfish.

And a conversation with a waiter in a restaurant:

> FUNEX?
> SVFX
> FUNEM?
> SVFM
> MNX, please.

Apart from correspondence, my secretarial work consisted of copying draft pages of a play he was writing about the horrors of Communism in an imaginary Balkan kingdom, Kronland. It was my secret knowledge that it was even worse, alas, than *The Prodigal Parents.* Lewis had long been stagestruck. His writing gift was mimetic, his ear a high-fidelity recorder, and he loved nothing better than to stand and recite to an audience—even of one, me—what his inner tapes had caught. He had collaborated with Lloyd Lewis on *Jayhawker,* a play about a roistering Civil War Kansas senator, which had lasted less than three weeks on Broadway in 1934; and he had written

a stage adaptation of *It Can't Happen Here,* which had opened
to mixed notices in simultaneous W.P.A. productions in eighteen cities in 1936. In years after I worked for him, he would
pluckily go on both writing for and acting on the stage.

A pleasure for him—and for me—was that because of this
interest the house would be alive evening after evening with
the chatter of the young actors and actresses of the summer
theater in Stockbridge. "The theater fascinated him," his friend
Marc Connelly would later write, "but I do not think he ever
had any comprehension of its technical demands." During
those evenings, in intermissions between parlor games, Lewis
would endlessly ask primitive technical questions of the young
summer-stockers: How do I get a character on and off stage in
such-and-such circumstance? Does it matter if the speaker is
upstage of the listener? Looking back, I think I can visualize
better than I could at the time, in those gatherings, what
Schorer would speak of as his "uncritical gregariousness and
concomitant loneliness"—the disfigured redheaded Great Man
with a second wrecked marriage whispering to his young secretary that he should make a date with the ingénue of the
company.

A sure sign of his loneliness was to be found in his parade
of guests, for meals and for weekends. He and I almost never
ate dinner alone. One of the most touching manifestations of
his kindness was his concern for my future as a writer. If a
weekend visitor was to be the publisher Harrison Smith or
Thomas Costain, an editor of the *Saturday Evening Post,* he
would carefully instruct me on their fancies and foibles, so that
I could most effectively ingratiate myself with them, against
rainy days to come.

During one of the visits of his warm friend Harrison
Smith, I learned much of the story of Lewis's roller-

coaster relationship with Yale. As an undergraduate, he had written pieces for the two campus magazines, the *Yale Literary Magazine* and the *Yale Courant*—no less than thirty-seven of them; but of course this yokel, who thought nothing of walking down Chapel Street on a warm spring evening in his pajamas, was not chosen as editor. Called upon to make a speech at his fifteenth reunion, after *Main Street* but before *Babbitt,* he said, "When I was in college, you fellows didn't give a damn about me, and I'm here to say that now I don't give a damn about you."

But drinking with Hal Smith in New York one day nine years later, he decided on a whim to drive to his farm in Vermont, and to stop off on the way and give his Nobel medal to the Sterling Library at Yale. The two set off in rough working clothes, and, as Smith told it to me, paused at a number of roadhouses on the Post Road on the way to New Haven to rehearse, over refreshment, the solemn ceremony of donation. Arrived at New Haven, they looked up Selden Rodman, an editor of the radical student magazine the *Harkness Hoot,* who had defended Lewis in one of its issues against a savage attack on him by another undergraduate, Eugene V. Rostow. Rodman took them reeling to the library. The librarian was out of town. A genteel young employee named Rush, confronted by what seemed to him to be two inebriated hobos, one of whom swung some sort of medallion back and forth under his nose like a pendulum, said, with elegant diction, "You wish to see our collection of medals?" Lewis flew into a wild rage and stalked out, swearing never again to have "anything to do with any Yale activity."

Came, however, Brendan Gill, six years later. After Lewis's piece for the *Lit,* "Random Thoughts on Literature as a Business," had been polished to Gill's satisfaction and published, Gill kept on calling on Lewis. One day, Lewis said he had been invited by an obscure Western college to accept an honorary degree. Wasn't it strange that Yale had never proposed such a thing? Gill told William Lyon Phelps about Lewis's question, Phelps told Carl Lohmann, the University Secretary, and Lohmann, who had heard the library story, shot Gill back to Bronxville to find out whether Lewis would accept a degree if it was offered to him. Lewis wrote Phelps:

> I'm very pleased to accept the Litt. D. degree, and I'm so writing Secretary Lohmann today. And triply pleased that it's you who are to present it. I suspect how many foul and secret plots you and that agent of the Yale O. G. P. U., Brendan Gill, have undertaken to accomplish this. . . .

In July of my summer with him came the tenth anniversary of Lewis's first meeting, at a press conference and tea party in the German Foreign Ministry in Berlin, with Dorothy Thompson, then the Berlin correspondent of the *Philadelphia Public Ledger* and the *New York Post*. The day after the press conference was to be her thirty-third birthday, and she invited Lewis to a party. Later she would write him about that evening in her apartment: "I will never forget how you looked, or how I felt, that first night. I felt a terrific indignation. I thought, 'My God, how he suffers.'" Lewis, evidently sensing that he might be given tender loving care by this dashing, energetic, and compassionate woman, proposed marriage to her that very night, and he kept repeating the proposal every time he saw her until, sometime in August, she accepted her role as his marital nurse. He told me once that *Dodsworth* was in part a replay of his pursuit of Thompson all over Europe. He talked to me about her a lot. He seemed to miss her, and each time we were to drive to Barnard, Vermont, to spend a weekend with her, he would have me take his clothes to the cleaners beforehand, and he would have a haircut, and on the road on the way up he would be in high spirits. Within an hour of our arrival, he would be fighting with her.

Lewis flew through life, a helpless missile rocketed along by some furious inner propulsion. "Is the wanderer like me homeless," he wrote during a honeymoon tour of England, "or does he merely have more homes than most people?" In the ten years after he met Thompson in Berlin, he alighted—several different times in a few of the places, but always hurrying on to some inviting elsewhere—in Paris, Moscow, Sicily, Rome, London, New York, the New York suburbs, Vermont, ten towns in Florida, North Carolina, Toronto, Boston, New Jersey, Pittsburgh, Reno, San Francisco, Carmel, Los Angeles, Kansas City, Baltimore, Annapolis, Austria, Bronxville, Bermuda, and, briefly, the little center-cone of the twister where it had all started, Sauk Centre. Thompson was a vagabond, too, and during his peripatetic courtship of her, he had written to her promising that when they were married they would settle down on a farm in Vermont (of a sort the restless Dodsworth had yearned for), where they might at last find a pastoral inertia—a repose of spirit as well as body. Even before they were married, she began shopping for linen for that imaginary haven.

On their first return to the United States, they had bought Twin Farms, to which I was to drive Lewis for visits that summer, a three-hundred-acre place near Barnard, Vermont, with two houses on it, one a farmhouse built in 1796, the other a larger house perhaps converted from a barn. The following year, they remodeled the latter, creating a huge, light-filled living room and a bedroom-study for Lewis. It was—for me—a heavenly place to visit. I had the old farmhouse all to myself.

Repose, sad to say, was not to be given to the Lewises. As Thompson went from success to success and Lewis from bottle to bottle, he apparently began to see his nurse-wife first as a nanny and then as some kind of malevolent tyrant. He complained that he had to share his marital bed with world affairs; he threatened to divorce her and name Hitler as corespondent; he said he felt as if he were married to a senator; and when her name was seriously put forward to run for President in 1936 he said, "Fine. I'll write 'My Day.'" Once as we drove away to return to Stockbridge, he cried out, "If I ever hear any more talk about Conditions and Situations, John, I'll commit either suicide or murder." In the evenings, during our weekends at Barnard, troops of witty young men like Joseph Alsop, Alexander Woollcott, and Vincent Sheean, and their friends, would sit on the floor in an entranced circle around Mrs. Lewis as she held forth after dinner, while Lewis—without the comfort of the brandy they were all sipping—would sit behind the curtain of a newspaper on the other side of the room, occasionally rattling the paper in outrage at something Thompson had said. At breakfast the next morning, he would pick up on one of these somethings, telling her she had had her facts all wrong on Yugoslavia, or John L. Lewis, or Franco. Then a few days later, in one of a series of her columns entitled "Grouse for Breakfast," he would have to read her mockery of his arguments.

I couldn't help being on Lewis's side. I must have been too young to recognize the bitterness of an exhausted gift, and of course I was ignorant of the drinking history. Dorothy Thompson seemed to me an overpowering figure in a Wagnerian opera, a Valkyrie, deciding with careless pointing of her spear who should die on the battlefield. Some things about my boss's home life, if it could be called that, did make me uneasy. Lewis's son by his first wife, Wells, then a Harvard student about to be twenty years old, was sometimes at Twin Farms, and Michael, seven that summer, was always there; Lewis seemed distant from both boys. I liked Wells, a rather shy and studious person, and I couldn't help noticing that his father seemed unable to talk with him. Michael made his father jumpy and irascible. I think Schorer must have got from Dorothy Thompson a report that at about this time Micky said, "I hate my father and when I grow up I'll kill him."

It was a relief to get back to Stockbridge, where Lewis's outward cheerfulness and playfulness were quickly restored.

No matter that Lewis's Muse was spent: I was fascinated by his habits as a writer. It was exciting for a kid who wanted to write to be around a man who lived so intensely by, for, and in his work. He would sometimes get up at two in the morning, brew up coffee, type for three hours, and go back to bed. He left notebooks all around the house, and he urged me to look through them, so that we—or, rather, he, before a dumbstruck sounding board—could discuss possible undertakings. He said he needed to know everything about the characters and the setting of a story before he started writing. Maps of imaginary towns sketched in pencil, floor plans of houses, life histories, word portraits in the most painstaking detail, characterizing anecdotes, breeds of pets, dishes served at table, names of eccentric specimen shrubs that a particular character would be sure to have planted outside the house—there was an astonishing wealth of groundwork in those loose-leaf notebooks. Most of the material would never be mined. Waste didn't seem to bother a man with such a store of visual and aural memory and such speed of reference to it—and with such lack of pity for his own work. It would horrify me, as I endlessly retyped his drafts, to see thousands upon thousands of words—not scattered words and phrases but long passages, whole scenes—ruthlessly slashed out.

He doted on names; he believed people *became* their names. He had a stack of telephone books from all over the world, so he could find an odd but apt name for a character from New Orleans, or, if needed, a Roman, or an Alpine innkeeper. When he had to name a new character, he would make a list of a dozen possibilities and leave the list on the piano in the living room; day after day he would pick up the list and cross off a name or two, until he had made his final choice by elimination. I would sometimes hear him at his desk calling out names, as if summoning lost souls.

I n the autumn, his feet must have begun to itch again; he wanted to be near New York theater people, and he moved back to the city, taking an apartment at the Wyndham, at 42 West Fifty-eighth Street. I moved into quarters with my brother and five other recent college graduates and would turn up for work at the Wyndham at nine in the morning—once to find that Lewis had been up until five with the director Jed Harris and was still up, at his typewriter, in a fever of excitement over new ideas.

It began to be evident that he no longer really needed me. We didn't dine together now, and at lunchtime he would send me out to fetch him a take-out sandwich. (Once we did go out together, in midafternoon, for a snack. We wound up at a Longchamps. As we had sometimes done during the summer, we each had a doughnut and a cup of coffee. In Massachusetts the whole bill had been twenty cents; here, when the check came, I saw the rouge of rage bloom on Lewis's pocked cheeks. The check was for a dollar-fifty-seven. Lewis said nothing, tipped the waiter, rose to leave. Near the door, where on a brass pedestal a large bowl of dainty mints of many colors stood, he reached down and scooped a double handful into his coat pocket. He went out with his head high.) I still served as his bartender during evenings when he had friends in, and it was then that I saw that my time with him was rounding out, for he took particular care to introduce me to people who might be helpful to my future: Irita Van Doren, editor of the *Herald*

Tribune Sunday book section (for whom I did indeed later write reviews, my first signed pieces); John Gunther, whom Lewis urged to give me advice about journalism; Laura Hobson, then the advertising manager of *Time,* who might (and who, in fact, soon did) help me get a job at the magazine; Jed Harris, in case I ever caught stage fever (who, years later, did invite me to write a play for him); and others.

An even more explicit hint of my disposability took a bizarre form. The main point Lewis had made in his piece for Brendan Gill and the centennial issue of the Yale *Lit* was that it was getting difficult for a young person to break into print and earn a decent living by writing; therefore aspiring writers should first make a nest egg in some other line of work, which would then support a full life of letters. Lewis now preached this doctrine to me. He further had a suggestion as to a line of work. The year was 1937. War loomed, he said. When it came, he said, there would surely be a boom in the demand from small boys for lead soldiers. I should study the craft of their manufacture, make a pile, and *then* write my heart out. He was perfectly serious, and he even mesmerized me into going to F. A. O. Schwarz, Macy's, Gimbels, and several smaller stores to look into the lead-soldier market. Try as I might to picture myself as a lead-soldier tycoon, I failed, thanked Lewis for his suggestion, and, having had a lovely summer with a vivid, brilliant, kind, driven, suffering man, I resigned, got from Laura Hobson the name of the person who was then hiring writers for *Time,* remembered with some asperity their having turned me down flat the previous spring, wrote a twenty-four-page essay on how rotten the magazine was, handed it in, and was hired the next day.

Henry R. Luce

Henry Luce underwent profound changes between 1937 and 1948. These were the years of his greatest involvement with China. I was his employee during all but the last three of those years.

When I first went to work for him at *Time,* at thirty-five dollars a week, he seemed a walking wonder of possibilities to a mishkid like me— a missionary offspring, that is. He was a mishkid who had made good in a big way. He was exciting to be around. Emotions—feelings that had to do with a human touch—were enigmatic in him, but abstractions lit up his face, as if in a dazzling *son et lumière* at the Sphinx. His mind darted and jumped. He was astonished and delighted by whatever he had not previously known. He stammered because there were so many enthusiasms trying to make simultaneous escape across his Calvinist tongue. Because I, too, was a China mishkid, he would in those earlier days call me up to the thirty-third floor, now and then, to discuss a China story. This was great. Together we would explore a dozen approaches. Then he would say, "Go and write it"—and it would be for me to choose which of the approaches to use.

By the end of the period, it was another and much more

"Henry Luce's China Dream," *New Republic,* May 2, 1983.

terrible case. A conference on a story would begin, "John, the way I see this thing is . . ." Sometimes his commands or correctives were in memo form, in prose hewn by a chilled axe. It got so bad that T. S. Matthews, as managing editor, on receiving one of Luce's lightning bolts, wrote back:

> No decent human being would answer your memo by accepting it. . . . You have written as if to dogs, not to human beings. And you have made a mistake. If you're really degenerating into a barking boss, you'll soon have behind you only the anxious, stupid, dishonest subservience that kind of boss can command.

As Luce's temperament hardened during those years, so did his views on China. Early we find him urging resistance to China's enemy, Japan; deploring American sales of scrap steel to the Japanese; warmly praising progressive undertakings like the Chinese Industrial Cooperatives founded by the New Zealander Rewi Alley. Next he is an Asia-firster, with growing differences with Roosevelt on the conduct of the war. Then he writes a personal letter to every subscriber to *Time* asking for support of United China Relief. Next he is squarely in the pro-Chiang China Lobby. And finally, in 1948, he is the bitter author of a letter to Senator Arthur Vandenberg:

> The measure of the degradation of American policy in the Pacific is the fact that a few guys like [Representative Walter H.] Judd and me have to go about peddling a vital interest of the United States and a historic article of U.S. foreign policy as if it were some sort of bottled chop suey that we were trying to sneak through the Pure Food Laws.

Now here is an intriguing question. Why did that particular missionary son reach a destination on the China question so very different from that reached by other sons of missionaries—notably, for a couple of examples, John Paton Davies and John Service? Those two mishkids were hounded out of the Foreign Service by Senator Joseph McCarthy for the sin of seeing the China picture, as we know now, far more accurately than Henry Luce was seeing it.

Why the difference?

First of all, there was the matter of Henry Robinson Luce's foremost model and mentor—his father, Henry Winters Luce, called, as his son was to be, Harry. I have been working for about four years on a fictional biography of a missionary in China. I have done a great deal of research, and I must say I have found no other missionary figure quite like Harry Luce the First. He was a wheeler and dealer. He thought big; the minute he saw a small missionary college, he wanted it to be a university. He had a lifelong romance, sometimes stormy, with money. It was his fate to be not a soul-saver but a fund-raiser. Sherwood Eddy, who roomed with Luce and Horace Pitkin at Union Theological Seminary, before they went out, tells that one night the three of them talked so fervently about money that in bed later he dreamed he saw a hand up near the ceiling holding a fistful of cash; he leaped out of bed to reach for it and crashed to the floor. Of the senior Luce's thirty years as a missionary, he spent eleven back in the States raising money for Tengchow College, Cheeloo University, and Yenching University, for the last of which he attracted more than two million dollars. This moneyman instilled a hot ambition in his son. "Character is destiny," he kept telling him. And his constant exhortation to young Henry was "Use your native Lucepower." At about twelve years of age, the son wrote home from Chefoo School, "I would like to be Alexander if I were not Socrates."

Early on, father Harry had made connections that would pay off in son Harry's career. The headmaster of the tiny Scranton private school he went to was Walter H. Buell, later to be headmaster of the Hotchkiss School, to which the younger

Harry would go. The wealthy Scranton businessman who put up the entire support for the father's mission was James A. Linen, whose grandson would later show up as president of Time Inc. Mrs. Cyrus McCormick, widow of the inventor of the harvester, built a house for the father in Weihsien and years later gave the son a thousand-dollar gift on his graduation from Yale, which made it possible for him to take a year of graduate study at Oxford.

Here is an interesting fact, for what it's worth: Harry Luce the elder went out to China before the Boxer uprising of 1900; the fathers of Davies and Service went out after it. Luce *père* escaped to Korea, but his close friend Horace Pitkin was killed in Paotingfu. I touch glancingly on this fact because the Boxer time appears to me to have been the watershed between two quite different breeds of missionaries—the dedicated evangelists before it, the slightly more worldly social-gospel missionaries, who wanted to help improve the quality of the life of the Chinese, after it; this difference may have been reflected in the outlooks of the sons.

At any rate, religion seems to have been more tenacious in Luce than in Service and Davies; he held on to his Presbyterianism, while they seem to have been in varying degrees apostate. "An ample road to salvation was marked out for me in childhood," he once said. He was baptized by one of the craggy giants of the Protestant Church in China, Dr. Calvin Mateer; and that wet touch on his forehead left a kind of scald that stayed hot all his life long. His sister Beth has an early memory of his standing on a stool in the mission compound preaching a sermon to amahs and babies. Among the family papers there is a sermon he wrote, at age six, on II Timothy 1:7: "For God hath not given us the spirit of fear." His faith was not always easy. More than once he said in the presence of colleagues, "O Lord, I believe—help Thou my unbelief." It was understood by all of us that he should be allowed to ride alone in the

HENRY LUCE WITH CHIANG KAI-SHEK

"The way I see this thing is ..."

elevator each day, and he confided to a very few friends that he spent those moments of daily ascension and fall in prayer.

Luce's editorial associate John Jessup wrote some years ago:

> John Courtney Murray made a curious point in reflecting on his Protestant friend's "astonishing and all but unclassifiable" mind. It was that many of the serious thinkers to whom Luce was most attracted—Hocking, Toynbee, Tillich, Heard, and later Pierre Teilhard de Chardin—were all what Murray called "gnostics." By this Murray did not mean that they were followers of the second-century heresy. He meant that they were all semi-mystic followers of personal paths to truth who put more of their puzzled faith in intuition than in revelation or authority. "Poor indeed is the unmystical philosophy," wrote Luce in college, and he never ceased to believe in the possibility of private visions of God. Yet he could not himself be called a gnostic. His own religion was less mystical than historical, rooted in time and place.
>
> It was rooted in Palestine in the first three decades A.D. This historical event, as Luce saw it, was the high point of God's intervention in human affairs that began with the Creation, picked up speed with Abraham, left signs for the eye of faith in every century, and will make its purpose fully clear at the end of the world. Luce's providential view of history remained intact against the arguments of his more learned and less certain friends.

Pressed once about his rigidity on some issue, Luce rather testily blurted out: "I *am* biased in favor of God, the Republican Party, and free enterprise." What is interesting here is the interconnection of those biases. For Henry Luce held to a Presbyterian interpretation of history. In a speech at the centennial of Lake Forest College, in Illinois, in 1957, he said: "[What] I want to emphasize tonight is that God is the ruler of human history. . . . We need not," he said, "exaggerate the dominance of Calvinist influence in the founding of the United States. Enough to say that Presbyterians played an immense part in it—and without the Calvinist influence, the American form of government and the American ethos are inconceivable. . . ." And he went on: "God moves in a mysterious way. Who would have thought that He would have dedicated the New World, the new hope of mankind, to freedom, by the means of such ornery people as us Presbyterians. But the record is there— facts are facts." He also said in that speech:

> Presbyterians are credited with the invention of modern capitalism—and if we accept the credit, as we might as well, we are accountable for the horrible sins of capitalism as well as for the revolutionary advance of human productivity and physical well-being.

Thus he could account for his own fast-growing material well-being as God-sent—though he knew that some thought him in touch with Mammon. He was aware—and hurt—that certain clergymen considered his publications materialistic and unprincipled, and his mother let him know she was worried about his immortal soul because, among other reasons, he presided over what was then the world's largest medium for the advertising of alcoholic beverages.

The younger Luce's connection with money was far closer than his father's. His father raised it; he made it. Of course this distinction sharply marks off Henry R. Luce from Davies and Service, and indeed from other mishkids in general. Luce-power, it turned out, was money power; such power of influence as the other two gained and later lost was manifestly not material. At Hotchkiss, where Luce waited on tables and swept out classrooms as a scholarship student, he thought of becoming a businessman in China—as he put it at the time, in "some big economic movement—railroads, mining, wholesale farming, 5 and 10-cent store, news syndicates." He seemed to think of this opportunity as a kind of mission in itself, because, as he wrote, "before the [Chinese] people as a whole become alive to the 'higher things' they must get their noses off the economic grindstone." Someone once called Luce "the very embodiment of Max Weber's Protestant ethic," one who must have agreed with Victorian divines that God is in league with riches. Be that as it may, by the beginning of the period we are talking about, Luce held shares of Time Inc. stock worth on paper more than twenty million dollars, and, not yet forty years old, he drew dividends from them, as the Depression dwindled away, of something like eight hundred thousand dollars a year. Nineteen-thirties dollars.

The money power was of course ancillary to his growing power as an editor. He became sure of himself. He had not always been. At Hotchkiss and Yale, the boy who had wanted to be an Alexander—you will remember that whoever untied the Gordian knot would rule all of Asia, and books said that Alexander had cut the knot with a single daring blow of his sword—this young dreamer suffered the humiliation of being second in magnetism, popularity, and power to his friend Briton Hadden, who was chosen over Luce to be editor first of the *Hotchkiss Record* and later of the *Yale Daily News*. At school and college, Luce had the hated nickname "Chink." Undergraduate life was a bit heavy. Sardonic Hadden, meeting Luce one day on the campus, called to him, "Watch out, Harry, you'll drop the college." When the two founded Time, Hadden again got the top spot, as editor. At the height of prosperity in the late twenties, Luce wanted to start a magazine on business, to which he wanted to give the name *Power*. Hadden was opposed, but in 1929, at age thirty-one, he considerately died, and Luce at last became top dog, as editor of *Time*, and he was free to found *Fortune;* and on the eve of the period we are considering, he had just started the fabulously successful *Life*.

In this period of change, there was one constant in Luce. At a dinner of *Time* editors, he said: "I regard America as a special dispensation—under Providence. . . . My spiritual pastors shake their heads about this view of mine. They say it tends to idolatry—to idolatry of nation." Luce's particular strain of patriotism was fixed in him early. Speaking to *Time*'s so-called Senior Group of executives on another occasion, he told of going, at age ten, to the Chefoo School, where only about a fifth of the students were American. "We were," he said,

a strong, conspicuous, successful minority [among which, by the way, was Thornton Wilder]. The British code—flogging and toadying—violated every American instinct. No wonder that hardly an hour passed that an American did not have to run up the flag. A master insists that Ohio is pronounced O-hee-ho. What are you going to do? Will you agree? The American can't agree; it would betray every other American. So first your knuckles are rapped, then you get your face slapped by the master then you are publicly caned. By this time you are crying, but still you can't say O-hee-ho.

"In some ways," Luce said in 1950,

that background endowed me with special qualifications to be editor-in-chief of great American publications. . . . In some ways, it disqualified me. I probably gained a too romantic, too idealistic view of America. The Americans I grew up with— all of them—were good people. Missionaries have their faults, but their faults are comparatively trivial. I had no experience of evil in terms of Americans. . . . Put along with that the idea that America was a wonderful country, with opportunity and freedom and justice for all, and you got not only an idealistic, but a romantic view—a profoundly false romantic view.

This insight may have come as hindsight, for it was uttered long after the public reaction to his famous essay "The Amer-

ican Century," published in 1941. Luce was right in saying that
his romantic Americanism had been planted in him early. I
have come across a fascinating preview of "The American
Century." Partly, no doubt, because of his stammer—or, rather,
because when he spoke forensically he did not stammer—he
set great store by oratory in his school and college years. Win-
ning the Deforest Oration prize at Yale in 1920, he pronounced
some amazingly predictive words, which he more or less pla-
giarized from himself in "The American Century." In his college speech, as in the later essay, Luce took the high tone of the
pre-Boxer missionaries who advocated both Christian charity
and gunboats:

> When we say "America" twenty years from now may it be
> that the great name will signify throughout the world at least
> two things: First, that American interests shall be respected,
> American citizens entitled to trade and to live in every corner
> of the globe, American business ideals recognized wherever
> the trader goes; second, that America may be counted upon to
> do her share in every international difficulty, that she will be
> the great friend of the lame, the halt and the blind among
> nations, the comrade of all nations that struggle to rise to
> higher planes of social and political organization, and withal
> the implacable and *immediate* foe of whatever nation shall offer
> to disturb the peace of the world. If this shall be, then the
> America of this century shall have glory and honor to take into
> that City of God far outshining the glory and honor which the
> kings do bring. . . .

Three months after the publication of "The American Century," Luce went to China, and in Chungking he extended his
idolatry of nation to embrace as well the one—or the part of
one—presided over by the Christian Chiang Kai-shek and the
Christian Soong Mei-ling, Chiang's wife. During that visit, he

also encountered and was dazzled, charmed, and challenged by the brilliant young *Time* correspondent there, Theodore H. White; and on his return to the States he took White with him, to make him an editor of the magazine—but more importantly, to adopt him, to take possession of him. As he had done, in a different but no less paternal way, over the years, with me. Four years later, both White and I had, not without pain, torn ourselves away from him.

At this point I should probably mention two people who had a great deal to do with the change in Luce during the years I am talking about. The first, of course, was Clare Boothe, whom he married two years before this period began. Her diamond-hard mind and her religious journey toward Rome, which culminated in her conversion just at the height of White's and my struggles with Luce, certainly bore on his views on China. Her conversion to Catholicism could not have been easy for this faithful Presbyterian missionary's son, but he accepted it with Calvinist fortitude. Clare reinforced his bias in favor of God and against the Godless. In an interview with *McCall's* she said the experience of her conversion had given her increased moral ammunition against the Communists—because of their denial of personal sin.

The other person, who figured much more directly in the White and Hersey outcomes, was Whittaker Chambers. He had joined the *Time* staff in 1939, the year after his renunciation of the Communist Party, and he had become the Foreign News editor. By late 1944, the monotone of paranoia he imposed on *Time*'s foreign news had begun to alarm not only White in China and me in Moscow but also Walter Graebner in London, Charles Wertenbaker in Paris, John Osborne in Rome, and others. "Some recent copies of *Time* have just reached me," I cabled Tom Matthews one week.

In all honor I must report to you that I do not like the tone of many Foreign News stories. I need not itemize: You know what I mean. . . . For this week, and until I cool off, I shall abstain from corresponding with Foreign News.

This was also the juncture at which Teddy White sent back from China a long and considered account of the firing of Stilwell, which he managed to have flown home on Stilwell's plane. When he read a Domei news-agency summary of the cover story Chambers wrote on Stilwell, White blew up, threatened to quit, and flew off to Yenan.

There were so many complaints like these that Luce ordered a survey of a number of correspondents' opinions of Chambers' editing. A query was sent to us in the field. The replies were unanimous. All cabled back essentially what I cabled back: passages used from my dispatches were "torn from the context . . . and put into [the] new context of *Time*'s editorial bias," which, I said, was "grossly unfair" and "actually vicious."

In the very midst of all this, Luce, with his gifts of charm and seduction, cabled me offering to bring me home and train me for the top job on the magazine, the managing editorship—just as he had taken Teddy White home to make him what he could never be, an editor. I declined, asserting that I was a writer and that I would anyway have been a prickly choice, in view of his bias in favor of the Republican Party and the fact that I was a convinced Democrat.

Luce soon gave the correspondents his judgment of their replies to the survey, and there was no doubt where he came out. "The posture of events in January, 1945," he cabled,

seems to have confirmed Editor Chambers about as fully as a news-editor is ever confirmed. . . . I have just been told, in a highly confidential manner, that Stalin is, after all, a Communist. I am also somewhat less confidentially informed that the

Pope is a Christian. Some will say: what does it matter in either case? And what does it matter that Hersey advises me that he, John Hersey, is a Democrat? Well, I cannot say for sure what these pieces of information signify, but one must respect the data in each case. A good Foreign News Editor, while guarding against the prejudices arising from his own convictions, will not ignore the circumstance that the Pope is a Christian and Stalin a Communist and Hersey, God bless him, a Democrat.

Cryptic stuff—but the message was clear. So far as the boss was concerned, Chambers was right, and the men in the field were wrong. Take it or leave it.

In February, Teddy White sent a cable about a new breakdown of negotiations between the Nationalists and Communists; Chambers used not a word of the dispatch. White quarreled along until April. Luce was evidently shaken by Teddy's arguments, because he wrote a memo to his management executive committee, advising them "of the possible serious error of my policy in re China." He went on: "For myself, barring details of execution, I have not the slightest doubt that [*Time*'s] policy has been right. . . . Nevertheless, it is, in some respects, a dangerous policy to pursue and I shall be glad to receive from you advice and counsel thereon." The committee did not ask for a change, and soon Luce sent White an extraordinary message through a third party: "After consultation with Luce," the cable said, "here's what he (and most emphatically he) would like you to do: stay in and near Chungking . . . to report not political China . . . [but] mainly small indigenous colorful yarns." As a sample of the kind of reportage Luce expected of him, the editor sent an excerpt of a London bureau cable of England's two-thousandth day of war: "Yellow crocuses bloomed, daffodils sold for dollar and a half per bunch, Commons passing bill making rear lights compulsory on bicycles. . . ." Till the end of the war, White limited himself to reporting on the fighting. In his book *In Search of History,* he tells movingly of the final break on his return to the States, when Luce put to him, in effect, the question "Will you do whatever I tell you to do as my employee?" Teddy said no, and that was that.

J ust about then I left *Time* and went to China and Japan on contracts with strange bedfellows, *Life* and *The New Yorker.* *The New Yorker* asked me to do a story on the damage in Hiroshima; *Life* made no such suggestion. Several years later, I saw Luce walking toward me on a sidewalk in New York, and he saw me, and it was clear that he intended to cut me dead. I blocked his way and spoke to him, however, and I found that he was still furious at my disloyalty in not having given the Hiroshima story to *Life*. He and I came to quite different reasons for wishing there had never been an atom bomb. In an unpublished book he was working on at the time of his death, he wrote:

If the bomb had not been dropped and if the well-laid plans for the MacArthur invasion had been carried out—then, almost certainly, the following would have occurred on the mainland of China. In September–October of 1945 there would have been a major Chinese offensive, with American-trained Chinese divisions, leading out of the mountain fastness and down to Canton. It would have been successful. Then, during the winter, having regrouped around Canton, the Generalissimo would have marched north and taken the Yangtze Valley as he had done twenty years before. If the Japanese had then surrendered in the spring of 1946, Chiang Kai-shek would have been in a position to move armies up to Peking and Manchuria. He would still have had to face the Mao Tse-tung trouble. . . . But

Chiang would have had a chance—and I think he deserved that chance.

And so Henry Robinson Luce had reached his final destination in a wish: that the sword could have done it. That Alexander, who cut the Gordian knot, could have made the dream come true. For it had all become a dream. He spoke to the Senior Group of Time Inc. once about his revisit in 1945 to Tsingtao, which he said was

the most beautiful of all places on this earth, where the mountains come down to the sea. Kaiser Wilhelm II called it the fairest jewel in his crown. It was the last grab of European imperialism in Asia. . . . All I wanted was to swim on the beaches of the bay. And I did. And I took with me the finest swimmer in the United States Marine Corps, Major General [Lemuel] Shepherd. I tell you very solemnly, if American affairs had been entrusted to Major General Shepherd and me, China would not now be Communist.

James Agee

It must have been on a Tuesday evening. *Time* went to bed late on Monday nights in those years—this was in the fall of 1939—and such was the intensity of the last two or three days of our work weeks that we did all we could to set fire to our weekends, which fell on Tuesdays and Wednesdays. That night Wilder Hobson, a madcap cousin of Thornton Wilder's who had been Dwight Macdonald's roommate at Yale, was giving a party in his apartment for some of the magazine's writers (all of whom were male then) and their wives or girls. I was recently back from a stint for *Time* in Japan and China, and I saw that there was a new guy in the crowd.

He was at the heart of a constellation on the other side of the room, and he seemed to be doing all the talking. There were rockets of laughter going up. Someone told me the man was Jim Agee. There was no particular reason to know the name then. I vaguely remembered Hobson's having told me some zany stories about Agee, with whom he had worked at *Fortune,* over in the Chrysler Building; *Time's* offices had been on a different floor, and I'd never happened to meet Agee. I think I had heard that with the support of Archibald Mac-

Introduction to new edition of *Let Us Now Praise Famous Men,* by James Agee. Boston: Houghton Mifflin, 1989.

Leish, who had also been writing for *Fortune* then, he had had a book of poems published in the Yale Younger Poets series, and that he had a reputation for having written, on assignment, a series of such relentlessly brilliant and quirky articles that Henry Luce and the editors of *Fortune* were obliged to scrap several of them. He was now reviewing books for *Time*.

I drifted over to his claque. I saw a tall set of muscles draped on an armature of long bones. In those days most of us dressed in jackets and ties, even during off hours, but he seemed to be in old work clothes, open-necked and warped by long use to the shapes of his body. He ducked his head now and then, as if to dodge unthinkable thoughts, and his dark hair was wild. He had a prominent vein down the middle of his forehead; blue-gray eyes, which seemed to change color with the tones of his talk; the bulging bags of an all-night writer under them; a deep woundlike dimple in his right cheek when he laughed; a big brave nose; and expressive lips over tobacco-stained and badly snaggled teeth. The second incisor on the left was missing, leaving a gap through which tobacco smoke jetted and curled. Yet he was somehow, all in all, wonderfully, passionately handsome.

No one else got many words in. He talked with both his tongue and his hands. It seemed that for this person words had not only sound and meaning but also physical weight, volume, and shape, and to those qualities he tried, as he spoke, to give their full value with his long fingers and strong palms—molding the clay of abstractions, arranging mental flowers, tightening difficult screws, caressing lusted-after erogenous zones, touching ideal chords on a ghost piano, and even, in moments of awe or vehemence, stretching his arms out and tilting the axis of the whole world. A performance.

The night wore on, bottles were emptied, tongues thickened—but not Agee's, though he drank enough to stun a rhinoceros. Hobson got out his trombone and blatted and booped

along with Louis Armstrong on a record. People teased Agee
to do his famous send-up of Leopold Stokowski conducting his
execrable orchestral arrangement of the Bach D-Minor Toccata
and Fugue. Finally he obliged. He was very drunk, but suddenly he became, with infinite control and with a rage of critical intelligence, not only Stoki but all 108 instruments of the
Philadelphia Orchestra. Standing his hair on end with his fingers, and ours with his hilarity, he conducted and played and
made the sounds of mulberry cellos and farting tubas and
twiddly fiddles—and at the same time set before our eyes the
figure of Bach himself, turning in his grave at one of the many
scandalous vulgarities of the twentieth century.

It is not easy to give a coherent account of James Agee's life,
for it was extraordinarily rich and chaotic. His own fictions
were partly autobiographical, but it is impossible to know at
what points, in the joy and pain of putting things down, he
shaded and heightened and altered his experiences. At the time
of this book's going to press only two full-length biographies
have been published: Genevieve Moreau's *The Restless Journey
of James Agee,* which focuses more on his writings than on the
events of his life, and Laurence Bergreen's *James Agee: A Life,*
which falls into the difficulty of separating the writings from
the life. In what follows I have drawn on these biographies
only to the extent that the material could be reasonably confirmed from other sources. (Published sources are listed in an
appendix.)

James Rufus Agee was born on November 27, 1909, in
Knoxville, Tennessee. His mother, Laura Whitman Tyler
Agee, an ardently devout Episcopalian, came from well-
educated, bookish folks. His father, Hugh James Agee, known
as Jay, a jovial, generous, and outgoing countryman, was a dot-
ing parent to his son and a younger daughter, Emma. When

James was six years old, Jay Agee, returning in his Ford from a visit to his sick father, drove off a road down a steep embankment and was killed. This loss cut a terrible wound in the son, the scar of which burned in his skin his whole life long.

Three years later Agee's mother entered him in St. Andrew's, an Anglo-Catholic school mostly for poor boys, a mile from Sewanee, Tennessee. The students were roughnecks, ranging in age from six to about twenty. Agee wanted to be called by his rustic middle name, Rufus, but the boys nicknamed him Socrates. He was hopelessly sloppy, and he could never do anything on time, so he would be summoned before the student council and sentenced to five or ten whacks with a paddle, which were then administered by one of the older boys. His mother and sister lived in a tiny wooden bungalow near the school, but he had to stay in a dormitory and was only allowed to see his mother once a week.

His miseries were eased by a person who became a lifelong confidant and consoler. ("My love to you always; my oldest and dearest friend," Agee wrote at the end of a letter many years later.) This was a teacher at the school, a kind and intelligent priest named James Harold Flye, who had been finely tuned, at Yale and the General Theological Seminary in New York, to become a worthy substitute father to this boy whom critics like Dwight Macdonald and F. W. Dupee would in the fullness of time shamelessly call a genius. For his part, Father Flye found Rufus "by nature gentle, sympathetic, affectionate, outgoing, and trusting—some fine qualities." At St. Andrew's, under Father Flye's tutelage, the boy fell permanently in love, if not with pure belief, at least with the beautiful language of Christendom. He worshipped the holy words. In *Let Us Now Praise Famous Men,* he wrote:

> I used as a child in the innocence of faith to bring myself
> out of bed through the cold lucid water of the Cumberland

morning and to serve at the altar at earliest lonely Mass, whose words were thrilling brooks of music and whose motions, a grave dance: and there between spread hands the body and the blood of Christ was created among words and lifted before God in a threshing of triplicate bells.

At fifteen he entered Phillips Exeter Academy, and there he was born again—as a writer. The school's English Department was strong, and Agee soon set his cap for the Exeter literary club, the Lantern, and its literary magazine, the *Monthly;* eventually he became president of one and editor of the other. He scraped along with C's and D's in most subjects, but got straight A's in English. The Lantern was host to Booth Tarkington, an Exeter graduate, for a speech, and Agee befriended Freeman Lewis, nephew of Sinclair, whose work he briefly admired. He wrote for the *Monthly* several short stories and romantic poems, the latter Whitman-flavored at first; one poem was clearly inspired by his father's death. He avidly read Dos Passos, Dreiser, Hemingway, Jeffers, Frost. When Frost did a reading at the school, he showed the poet some of his poems, and he also had the temerity to send a verse play to Edna St. Vincent Millay, Hilda Doolittle, Ezra Pound, and others. The responses he got were encouraging. His best work at Exeter, a long narrative poem, "Ann Garner," later found a respectable life in his Yale Younger Poets collection, *Permit Me Voyage.* It was at Exeter that movies first began to print themselves indelibly on his retinas. And here, as at St. Andrew's, he launched another lifelong friendship—this time through the mail, with an Exeter alumnus who had become a literary hot dog at Yale, Dwight Macdonald.

Uninfluenced by Macdonald, when it was time for college Agee trooped with his Exeter friends to Harvard. There he stamped out the patterns of his whole life: became a nocturnal animal by choice; a maverick, rebellious against the conventions of his habitat, too fond of the release of alcohol; a non-stop talker; a bonfire of tobacco; an amorist; and a wizard with perfectly unexpected words. The summer after his freshman year he went bumming across the land as a bindlestiff, decades before Kerouac: working hard with his body in the wheat harvest on the plains and living on pittances—empathizing with the outcasts of the world, and pretending with all his heart that he was one of them. At college he made friends with a gentle, thoughtful fellow-poet, Robert Fitzgerald, a class behind. Agee wrote for and eventually became the president of the undergraduate literary magazine, the *Harvard Advocate*.

In the spring of 1930 a tutor took Agee to Clinton, New York, to visit the family of Dr. Arthur Percy Saunders, a professor of chemistry at Hamilton College, a musician, a painter, and an exemplar, Agee wrote to Father Flye, of "Greek *moderation*"—a trait Agee never acquired. He and his "electric" wife, Louise, had lost a fifteen-year-old son who had shown promise as a poet, and now they took this charming, witty Harvard boy lovingly into the family circle. The next year Agee spent part of the summer in their home, and this time he harvested two decisive consequences. One was an apprenticeship in wordcraft with a house guest, the British poet and critic and gifted glassblower of language I. A. Richards, who was teaching at Harvard. The other was to fall for the Saunderses' second daughter, Olivia, called Via, who was six years older and a lot more conventional than he. Happily for him, she spent the next year in Cambridge.

I n his senior year, Agee's *Advocate* issued a parody of the most successful magazine on the market, *Time.* As Agee put it in a letter to Roy Larsen, a former business manager of the *Advocate* and now the same for *Time,* he and his friends had imagined a *Time* staff "set down in Ancient Greece, Rome,

Egypt, and Palestine, with an uncommonly long nose for news, several amphoras of rye, vivid but confused recollections of the 20th century, a somewhat cockeyed sense of TIME, and no sense whatever of chronology." Written a bit creakily in hokey, neologistic Timestyle, the parody got widespread attention in the papers—and, of course, in the Chrysler Building.

Real time passed, and Agee, facing the prospect of diving into the icy-cold river of the Depression, told his pen pal Dwight Macdonald, by then a leftward-leaning writer for the monthly manual of capitalism, Henry Luce's *Fortune,* that he needed a job. Macdonald spoke for the Harvard boy to Ralph Ingersoll, the magazine's liberal managing editor (who was later the publisher of the leftish newspaper *PM*), and Ingersoll, well aware of the famous *Time* parody, undertook to give its young originator a trial job.

And so Agee went to work, in the summer of 1932, on the fifty-second floor of the Chrysler Building for the magazine that Luce had founded to celebrate wealth and power—at a time when the havoc of the Depression was all too visible in the city's streets: evicted tenants, beggars, desperate vendors of whatever they could find to sell. What a strange haven for this prickly young man, in whom a vague social anger was beginning to bloom like a pale cereus unfolding in the dark. Robert Fitzgerald later commented that for *Fortune* to hire Agee was "like Germany enlisting France." Yet there was a nurturing atmosphere on the magazine, a sense of a seedbed. Besides Macdonald, vivid Wilder Hobson wrote for it, and the star of the staff was Archibald MacLeish, whose *Conquistador* had won a Pulitzer Prize. Even Hart Crane had done a short stint there.

The efficient MacLeish wrote his pieces and at five o'clock put on his hat and left. But for Agee no word in journalism had been so appropriately chosen as "deadline": it originally meant a line drawn around a prison, which no inmate could

JAMES AGEE

"The cruel radiance of what is"

cross without being shot. He stayed up nights writing a miniature script in pencil, with a record-player at full blast. To
Father Flye he wrote, "Something attracts me very much about
playing Beethoven's Ninth Symphony . . . with all New York
about 600 feet below you, and with that *swell* ode, taking in
the whole earth, and with everyone on earth supposedly singing it." Later, in a spooky passage in *Let Us Now Praise Famous
Men,* he instructed the reader in how to *become* the music of
Beethoven or Schubert. (In spare time that fall, by the way, he
wrote a now lost short story entitled "Let Us Now Praise Famous Men.") In the winter he married Via Saunders, moved
with her into a pleasant two-room apartment in Greenwich
Village, read writers who became his teachers—Joyce and Céline and Malraux—and went to a million movies.

After rather bumpy experiences with articles on sheep,
strawberries, and baldness, Agee was asked to write a piece on
one of Franklin D. Roosevelt's more successful undertakings,
the Tennessee Valley Authority. This took him to his natal
ground, and he rose to the challenge with the first outcry of
his mature voice. His opening lines:

> The Tennessee River system begins on the worn magnifi-
> cent crests of the southern Appalachians, among the earth's
> older mountains, and the Tennessee River shapes its valley into
> the form of a boomerang, bowing to its sweep through seven
> states. Near Knoxville the streams still fresh from the moun-
> tains are linked and thence the master stream spreads the val-
> ley most richly southward, swims past Chattanooga and bends
> down into Alabama to roar like blown smoke through the
> flood-gates of Wilson Dam, to slide becalmed along the crop-
> cleansed fields of Shiloh, to march due north across the high
> diminished plains of Tennessee and through Kentucky spread-
> ing marshes toward the valley's end where, finally, at the toes
> of Paducah, in one wide glassy golden swarm the water stoops
> forward and continuously dies into the Ohio.

Luce called Agee in and told him that the T.V.A. story was one of the finest pieces *Fortune* had ever run, and that it was time for Agee to learn how to write about business; word went around that he had volunteered to send Agee to the Harvard Business School—but Agee, thank you, had had enough of Harvard. Later Luce heard disturbing reports that Agee didn't follow very closely the generally understood Time Inc. dress code. All too true. At a time when white-collar workers who had jobs at all prided themselves on keeping their collars white, Agee usually wore dark shirts, often plaid, so that their being soiled would not be visible; he wore each of them long enough to trail pungently after him a very particular scent of his Ageeness. Luce apparently sent Agee a memo to "watch it." Luce then assigned Agee an article on the price of steel rails, tore his draft apart, and reassigned the piece to another writer. Agee began to mutter to his friends about shooting the boss. According to Fitzgerald, "Jim imagined himself laying the barrel of the pistol at chest level on the Founder's desk and making a great bang."

He became depressed, both by *Fortune* and by friction with Via. He wrote to Fitzgerald about his job, "It varies with me from a sort of hard, masochistic liking . . . to direct nausea at the sight of the symbol $ and this % and this *biggest* and this some blank billion. . . . But in the long run I suspect the fault, dear *Fortune,* is in me: that I hate any job on earth, as a job and a hindrance and semi suicide." Indeed, he soon wrote to Father Flye about a much more literal attraction to death. His problem, he said, was "how to become what I wish I could when I can't," and this kept him "balancing over suicide as you might lean out over the edge of a high building, as far as you could and keep from falling out with no special or constant desire not to fall."

In 1934 Agee wrote the text to accompany a portfolio of photographs of that year's drought taken by Margaret Bourke-

White, whose later work, with its emotionalism and overdramatization, he came to despise. The next year he was given the orchid to write about, and the prose of draft passages he sent to Father Flye was distilled rage: "The orchid gets its name from the Greek *orchis,* which means testicle; and there are those who condemn that title as understating the case, since to them the flower resembles nothing printable so much as a psychopathic nightmare in Technicolor." The piece was toned down before it appeared. Agee put in for six months' leave and went to Florida, where he read Joyce and Freud, struggled with Via, and drafted a reminiscence of Knoxville—an early, tender bud of *A Death in the Family.*

Then, suddenly, in June 1936, a month after his return, all that had been dark turned light. Eric Hodgins, who had replaced Ingersoll as managing editor, assigned him to do a story on sharecroppers in the Deep South. Furthermore, the editors granted his request for Walker Evans, not Bourke-White, to be the photographer to work with him. He rushed to Fitzgerald to tell him of his luck. "He was stunned," Fitzgerald later wrote, "exalted, scared clean through, and felt like impregnating every woman on the fifty-second floor." That night Agee wrote to Father Flye and told of his assignment: "Best break I ever had on *Fortune.* Feel terrific personal responsibility toward story; considerable doubts of my ability to bring it off; considerable more of *Fortune'*s ultimate willingness to use it as it seems (in theory) to me."

Walker Evans was at the peak of his powers. The son of an advertising executive, he had grown up in Kenilworth, a middle-class suburb of Chicago, attended two prep schools, Loomis and Andover, and entered Williams College. He dropped out after his freshman year, and in the midtwenties went to Paris, hoping to write; he audited at the Sorbonne, read Flaubert and Baudelaire, and gazed at James Joyce from across the room in Sylvia Beach's bookstore, but found he couldn't for the life of him haul words up out of the deep well of his reserve. In 1928, back in New York, by then a walking oxymoron—a bohemian fashion plate—and out of money, he decided to try to make a living by taking pictures, and he bought a pocket camera. His approach to the craft was careful and studied. He was repelled by what he then considered (he later changed his mind) the artiness of Alfred Stieglitz and the commercialism of Edward Steichen, and he thought he might be able to give precision and clarity to a humbler mode—that shared by newspaper pictures, newsreels, postcards, real-estate ads. With the help of people such as Muriel Draper, Lincoln Kirstein, Hart Crane, and Ben Shahn, he developed a style distinctly his own, based on a strict standard: he must let his eye and the camera's lens discover reality, not fabricate it.

Agee, who had met Evans a few years earlier, was entranced by this self-effacing scrupulousness. He admired enormously the photographs of the rural poor Evans did for the New Deal's Resettlement Administration, and he yearned now to achieve their merciless, unsentimental exactness in his prose. He shared Evans' dislike of government bureaucrats and Luce bureaucrats, and he also felt comfortable with Evans' slightly vinegary temperament, his irony and candor.

The two men went to Alabama, where they put their "overcomplicated youthful intelligences," as Agee would have it, to the painfully difficult task of trying to find a family of white tenant farmers who could be represented as typical. Agee had written to Father Flye that he foresaw a month of work, but they wandered about for longer than that searching for their models. Evans later said, "You couldn't just go up to somebody's house and say, 'I want to come in and live here.'" Agee's extreme sensitivity made him respect the suspicion and fear that the local folk felt toward people of a different social class—"a fear," he would write, "that was saying, 'o lord god please for once, just for once, don't let this man laugh at me up his sleeve, or do any meanness to me.'"

Finally, one afternoon, as Evans was taking some pictures of a farmer lounging by the courthouse in Greensville, he got talking with him—a man named Frank Tingle (who wound up in the book as one of Agee's famous men, Fred Ricketts). Agee, who had been scouting around in the courthouse, came out and joined them. Then two friends of Tingle's, Bud Fields (Bud Woods of the book) and Floyd Burroughs (George Gudger), happened along. After a while Fields invited Evans and Agee to his house—and there, at last, both knew they had found what they were looking for. They won the trust of all three families, eventually telling them exactly what they were up to, and the families wholeheartedly accepted them. Evans later said, "I think it was really largely because they liked Agee, who had a great gift of making people not only like him but love him."

The two spent a fortnight as daily visitors to the families, taking pictures and making notes. Then they went off to Birmingham, Evans to develop some photographs and Agee to unwind his mind. Agee decided he had to think alone, and he drove off for a long day of self-searching and sexual fantasy. He felt himself sucked as if by a whirlpool back to the three shacks. Burroughs asked him in and, as a thunderstorm came on, invited him to spend the night. Yearning to accept but too shy to, he drove away and soon skidded off the road and bogged the car immovably in the roadside's wet clay. He slogged back to the Burroughses' and was warmly taken in, to spend many nights. He had found his roundabout way to the masterpiece of his life.

M any years later, speaking for a documentary film made
by Ross Spears, entitled *Agee,* Elizabeth Tingle (Margaret Ricketts in the book) recalled the visitors:

> At the start it was a little hard for us to understand them,
> but I'll tell you, there wasn't any harm said to one, or anybody
> made fun of them or anything. You could understand them,
> but they just sounded funny. I asked Mr. Jimmy, I said, "What
> kind of sound does your voice got?" He said, "That is the
> northern kind of talk. All of them up there's like that." But
> you know, when they left here, they got to where they was
> talking our kind of talk.

Self-conscious about the intrusiveness of their mission, Agee
began to think of himself and Evans, with heavy irony, as
"spies." Ellie Mae Burroughs (Annie Mae Gudger), in retro-
spect, put a different gloss on that word:

> The big people, you know, the big bugs around Moundville,
> they would tell us that they were spies from Russia, and that
> they was trying to get all they could out of the United States.
> . . . Afraid they might tell us some way to get by, tell us some
> way to make a better living, so we wouldn't have to dig it out
> with them, you see. It was the landlords mostly. . . . I don't
> know what spies does, dear, but anyway we knowed that they
> wasn't going to hurt us, and they didn't.

Agee, intoxicated by the blessedness in spirit of the poor,
dizzy with the intensity of his feelings of admiration, love, humility, anger, and guilt, wrote and wrote in the dark cabin at
night. Finally it was time to go back to the other world, which

had so quickly begun to seem unreal to him. Elizabeth Tingle recounted:

> They said they was leaving and wouldn't be back, and Mama's children cried. Every one of us cried; they were so good to us, you know. They told us not to cry. "We'll be letting you hear from us," they said, which they did do. But it kind of hurt Jim, you know, that crying. And Ruth told them, she said, "You're going to leave and ain't never gonna come back." She was real little then.

When the two men returned to the *Fortune* office, they found that Dwight Macdonald and Wilder Hobson were, for different reasons, about to quit. *Fortune's* businessmen readers had been criticizing the liberal tone of many of the magazine's pieces, and Luce had decided that *Fortune* must set a more fittingly Republican course. Eric Hodgins had laid down strict guidelines for future articles. Agee struggled with his piece. He wrote to Father Flye, "Impossible in any form and length *Fortune* can use; and I am now so stultified trying to do that, that I'm afraid I've lost ability to make it right in my own way." He submitted a draft that was ten times too long and that was, according to Evans, "pretty thunderous"—miles outside the new guidelines. The editor tried chopping it but soon gave up on it as hopeless for their purposes.

A friend of Agee's, Edward Aswell, an editor at Harper & Brothers, soon persuaded that firm to offer Agee and Evans a contract and a modest advance for a book on the tenant families. But *Fortune* told Agee that his text was the property of the magazine; he could forget the thievery of using it for a book of his own. It would do Agee no good to object that property *is* theft; he was stymied.

His life then seemed to fall apart. Unable to afford to quit *Fortune* altogether, he made a free-lance arrangement with the magazine. His first assignment, again with Evans, was to write about the lot of a tourist on a cruise to Havana aboard the luxury liner *Oriente*. (Via went along.) Agee submitted his piece—Fitzgerald characterized it as "a masterpiece of ferocity"—in July, 1937. Somewhat earlier, Alma Mailman, a modest, shy, unspoiled violinist who had played in a quartet with Via's father, had moved to New York, and Agee had become involved with her. In a film scenario that Agee wrote twenty years later for his friend the photographer Helen Levitt, tentatively entitled "Bigger Than We Are," Agee dramatized the breakup of a marriage. (Levitt asked Agee, after reading it, if some of the sections of the story were true. "For God's sake," Agee said, "give me credit for a little imagination.") Not bothering, in one draft of the scenario, to change the names of the actual players, he visualized a three-act drama: In the first, a character named Jim meets a woman named Alma through the sister of his wife, V, and a triangle of innocents is formed— "babies playing with firearms." In the second act, Jim and Alma sneak off from V on a trip to the South. The couple in the scenario drive all the way to New Orleans, where they listen to jazz and eat oysters "as big as tennis shoes." On the way North again, they stop in Alabama, where Jim has done journalistic work on some tenant families, and when they drop in to dine with one of these families, Jim introduces Alma as his wife. In the third act, in a style "of brutal and heightened naturalism," we see Jim "torn apart between a desire to preserve the marriage and his desire for the girl." In the end, the marriage is destroyed and all three principals are on the verge of nervous breakdowns.

In August the real-life Via did leave Agee. By the end of the year the break was complete, and the couple divorced. Soon Luce relinquished the rights to the sharecropper story, Evans found a house for Agee in Frenchtown, New Jersey, and Agee signed with Aswell. He and Alma moved to the country at the beginning of 1938. His plan was to live for a year on his five-hundred-dollar advance and finish the book in that time.

It didn't turn out to be quite that simple. "The first thing that happened," Alma said years later, "was Walker Evans coming with a crate of Scotch whisky." Jim and Alma acted as if they were on an everlasting honeymoon, though they weren't yet married. Life was a playful game. Jim bought Alma a baby goat, and its constant bleating (among other things) kept Jim from working. One day Alma tied a ribbon in his hair—"a dainty blue bow," as she tells the story, "dead center on top of his head." Jim went to work writing. Hours later some church ladies rang the doorbell, and Jim chatted courteously with them, the ribbon "bobbing about on his head." Through the winter and spring of 1938, he struggled with the book. He read passages to Alma, who loved them because she loved him. He wrote to Father Flye that he was "disintegrating and 'growing up,' whatever that means, simultaneously."

He turned restless, took trips to New York, and finally put aside the sharecropper book in favor of a return to the Knoxville reminiscence. He submitted a passage of the latter, set in the summer of 1915, to Dwight Macdonald, who, with Mary McCarthy, William Phillips, Philip Rahv, and Delmore Schwartz, was now editing the *Partisan Review;* they accepted the piece. Edward Aswell shocked Jim by suddenly setting a deadline of August 1st for delivery of the Alabama book. Agee wrote to Father Flye that his work was "in bad shape." His subject, he wrote, "cannot be seriously looked at without intensifying itself toward a centre which is beyond what I, or anyone else, is capable of writing of: the whole problem and nature of existence." Aswell mercifully extended the deadline to midwinter. Jim's eyes began a worrisome trembling; he developed a boil in one ear. In a mad act of compassion, he and Alma took a hobo into their home. In December they were married, paid their rent, and found they had twelve dollars and fifty-two cents. Jim decided to return to New York, where Wilder Hobson offered him a rent-free house in Brooklyn, and where he would earn money from free-lance articles for *Fortune*. They left the hobo in Frenchtown, but they took with them the uninhibited exuberance of their days and nights. When Hobson visited them once, he saw a graffito written on the front steps by kids: THE MAN WHO LIVES HERE IS A LOONEY.

Fortune assigned Agee an article about Brooklyn for an issue that the magazine was preparing on New York City. He wrote two drafts; *Fortune* rejected both. He puttered away the spring in a low mood. He encouraged Evans to like Alma; indeed, he perversely wanted him not just to like her but to love her. In May, 1939, he received from Macdonald a *Partisan Review* list of "Some Questions Which Face American Writers Today." He was outraged by the "bad and . . . betraying" questions, and his angry answers to them amounted to oblique meditations on art which he eventually decided to include in his book.

Summer came, and so that Jim could resume work on the book, he and Alma rented a decrepit stone house, Monk's Farm, in Stockton, New Jersey, for twenty-five dollars a month—a place somewhat, but not much, above sharecroppers' standards. It had an outhouse; water came from a well; they used kerosene lamps. He read his drafts aloud to a series of guests, to great praise. But the mood of the nation had been inexorably shifting, like a continental plate; his topic was no longer earthshaking. The Depression had waned. Hitler had seized Austria and the Czech Sudetenland, and now he was threatening Poland. A war loomed.

Father Flye visited, and one day Jim felt he was ready to deliver the book to Aswell. He and the priest set off in Agee's flivver. On the way to New York, Jim suddenly decided that one part of the book needed rewriting, and they turned around and went back. Toward the end of August he finally handed in his manuscript, entitled *Cotton Tenants: Three Families*. A few days later the Nazi armies swept into Poland. The last thing on the public mind was the plight of the sharecropper. Agee was flat broke. Aswell took forever to respond, and when he finally did, he said that the firm's senior editors wanted extensive revisions. At first Agee agreed to make them; then he refused. At that, Harpers decided to drop the book.

Agee hit bottom. Three years' work and the deepest engagement of heart and mind of his whole life had been wasted. He had already borrowed money from Evans and had no prospect of earnings. He had nothing to do except to go on scribbling on the pages of his manuscript. He changed the title to *Let Us Now Praise Famous Men*. He drank. He wrote to Father Flye that he felt "cold, sick, vindictive, powerless and guilty."

Then, as had so often happened, a friend threw him a life preserver. Robert Fitzgerald was reviewing books for *Time,* and he persuaded T. S. Matthews, the editor of the back of the book and a prince among Luce hirelings, to take Agee on. A sensitive and literate craftsman, Matthews had tucked under his wing a remarkable brood of writers. Besides Fitzgerald, they included Wilder Hobson, the novelist and essayist Louis Kronenberger, and two leftists, the novelist Robert Cantwell and a gifted book reviewer named Calvin Fixx. (A son of Fixx's, James, would turn out, decades later, to be the unfortunate avatar of the fad of jogging, who died while jogging.) Agee's officemate was the apostate Communist Whittaker Chambers, later to be the famous accuser of Alger Hiss. These were writers with such distinctive voices, even in stagy, anonymous Timestyle, that I could tell at once, reading each issue, who among them had written what.

In this company, in a room on the twenty-ninth floor of the new Time & Life Building in Rockefeller Center, with a wide panning view of the Hudson and the Palisades beyond, living a life much less oppressive than the one he had had at *Fortune,* reading books he wanted to read, writing reviews sympathetically edited by Matthews, and finding that he was fascinated by the quirky, half-mad Chambers, whose eyes were hooded with paranoia and whose teeth were even more horrendously cigarette-stained and root-sprung than his own—in this heady setting, Jim bounced back and before long had earned his editor's respect, and to an extent his own self-respect. It was at about this time that I met him at Hobson's party, and soon I, like everyone else on the staff, reverberated to the beautiful arias of James Agee in the book section and knew that he was the best writer *Time* had ever had.

About a year later, Eunice Jessup, the wife of a friend of Agee's at *Fortune* and a talent scout for Houghton Mifflin, the Boston publishers, took the manuscript of Agee's book to Paul Brooks, an editor there. He and others at the firm recognized a work of great oddity and power, with passages worthy of comparison to some of Hawthorne and Melville and Thoreau. The obscenities would be a problem, but Brooks proposed the solution of dropping whatever words were "illegal in Massachusetts," and Agee accepted that sensible suggestion. Agee urged Brooks to produce the book on newsprint, to make it cheap enough for tenant farmers to buy. Brooks pointed out that "in fifty years newsprint will crumble away to dust." Agee replied, "That's what I mean." But of course he was talked out of the notion.

Success terrified Agee, and his personal life again fell into disarray. He met an Austrian emigrée, Mia Fritsch, who had taken a job as a researcher for *Fortune,* and before long, as Alma was coming to term with Agee's first child, Jim and Mia began an affair. Sophisticated, articulate, and calm, Mia was his equal intellectually, and she was tolerant of his failings. Alma gave birth to a son, Joel, and Bergreen writes that Agee, suffering a familiar agony of guilt and vacillation, soon confessed to

Alma his infidelity. There followed, Alma later recalled, "a dreadful year. . . . I guess maybe he wanted both. . . . He might hit his head against a stone building after leaving a party or a situation which would upset him"—agonizing, Alma felt, over the pain he was inflicting on others. Alma remembered "two or three attempts on my part to run away and being pulled back." She went to his office one day to say she was going to take Joel to Mexico. Agee threw his leg over the windowsill and threatened to jump. She called his bluff and walked away to the elevator, but then panicked and went back. The room was empty. She found him hiding behind the door. After that, Agee went on seeing Mia, and finally, when Joel was a year old, Alma did in fact pack off to Mexico.

Agee grieved at the separation; the hot scars in his skin multiplied. He wrote to Fitzgerald, "I'm in a bad period: incertitude and disintegration on almost every count." In the spring and summer, though, with Mia's help, he got his spirits back, revising his book yet again and then correcting proofs.

In August, 1941, five years after the trip to Alabama, *Let Us Now Praise Famous Men* was published.

"The very blood and semen of journalism . . . is a broad and successful form of lying," James Agee wrote in this classic work of metajournalism. "Remove that form of lying and you no longer have journalism." At the beginning of his book he expressed his revulsion against what he himself had seemed to be abetting *Fortune* in doing:

> It seems to me curious, not to say obscene and thoroughly terrifying, that it could occur to an association of human beings drawn together through need and chance and for profit into a company, an organ of journalism, to pry intimately into the lives of an undefended and appallingly damaged group of

human beings, an ignorant and helpless rural family, for the purpose of parading the nakedness, disadvantage and humiliation of these lives before another group of human beings, in the name of science, of "honest journalism" (whatever that paradox may mean).

While other writers for the company that he here excoriated—Dwight Macdonald, Archibald MacLeish, Robert Fitzgerald, Louis Kronenberger, Whittaker Chambers, Theodore H. White, Charles Wertenbaker, and I, among many others—quit or were fired in droves, Jim Agee stayed on and on. His full-time stint for the magazine that sent him to Alabama had lasted three weary (and deceitful?) years. Then came *Time*. When Luce and his partner, Briton Hadden, founded that magazine, they decided to put a fictitious name, Peter Mathews, on the masthead, so that if a large corporation bridled at something they published and threatened to yank its advertising, they could blame the offending piece on "a young writer named Peter Mathews" and angrily "fire" him, taking the name off the masthead. An irony tied to this bald intention of journalistic mendacity is that while other names rapidly came and went, those of Peter Mathews and James Agee hung together on the masthead year after year. Agee's was there for nine years.

What kept it there? Did he have, all that time, "a sort of hard, masochistic liking" for the job? Was he in a sense moonlighting for the sake of more important movements of his mind off the job? Or was it just that he was a victim of the passive, vacillating drift of his temperament, which caused many crucial events of his life to seem to happen to him, often thanks to the merciful last-minute nudging of friends?

What needs to be pointed out first is that we would not have the treasure of *Let Us Now Praise Famous Men* if Jim Agee had not been working as a journalist for Henry Luce. The job had in it a special challenge for Agee—to try to set truth free in what he saw as the headquarters of lying. His kind of truth, Robert Fitzgerald wrote, was quite simply "correspondence between what is said and what is the case." As a poet fights the rigid meters of his chosen prosodies to allow the living truth of speech rhythms to shine through, so Agee fought "the primal cliché and complacency of journalism," embedded in its traditional demands for the who, what, where, when, and why, to enable himself to set *reality* before the reader, as nearly as James Agee could photograph it through the lenses of his eyes and record it through the microphones of his ears and clarify it through the delicate filter of his consciousness. He strove to record "the cruel radiance of what is."

To accomplish this in the writing of *Let Us Now Praise Famous Men,* he knew he would have to transcend traditional journalism, but he realized he could not, for his purposes, fall back on any of the known stratagems of poetry or of word painting—of literary "art." He described this difficulty in an unsuccessful application for a Guggenheim Fellowship as he was starting work on the book. The text, he wrote,

> is to be as exhaustive a reproduction and analysis of personal experience, including the phases and problems of memory and recall and revisitation and the problems of writing and of communication, as I am capable of, with constant bearing on two points: to tell everything possible as accurately as possible: and to invent nothing. It involves therefore as total a suspicion of "creative" and "artistic" as of "reportorial" attitudes and methods, and it is likely therefore to involve the development of some more or less new forms of writing and observation.

Develop them he did. There had never been, and there never will be, anything quite like this book. For one thing, tones of light and dark in the visible world had always seemed to his delicate sensibility almost audible, and in the book he strove through the sounds and meanings of words to mimic— no, more than mimic, achieve—photography, worthy of being set beside that of his collaborator, Walker Evans. Ever since Exeter he had adored pictures, both moving and still. He heard a kind of verbal music in the Civil War photographs of Mathew Brady, and the grainy, pale light in the photography of Erich von Stroheim's *Greed* had made him vibrate like a tuning fork.

It would not be easy to live up to Evans's photographs. These were not "candid"; they did not "expose"; they were not glimpses of lurid Americana stolen from tricky angles, as in many of Bourke-White's pictures. In setting up a group photograph, Evans would let his subjects assemble and arrange themselves in any way they wished, and he would take his picture only when they were at ease and fully conscious of the camera eye staring straight at them, at home in their setting and in command of themselves. He bestowed on the objects in the families' homes a similar tact and respect, as if things too had the right to defend themselves against the lens. The resulting photographs did not propagandize squalor; they gave full scope to the timeless dignity, beauty, and pain of rounded lives. Nor would they turn out to be mere illustrations of Agee's prose; they were, in the end, a powerful collaboration with it. A reader of Agee's words finds it necessary to go back and back, time and again, to the photographs, in order to understand all the meanings of the work.

To live up to such images, Agee would have to try in his writing to make words *become* people and things. The task of a serious writer, he wrote, is to "continually [bring] words as near as he can to an illusion of embodiment." But he saw difficulties. Freud and Marx and semanticists such as I. A. Richards had complicated the very idea of "truth." Meaning itself had shades of meaning, objective and subjective. When the reality of a thing was rendered in words, it took the shape of its truth in two minds—those of the writer and of the reader. On the writer's part, eyes and ears and the other senses might be objective enough, but the filter of consciousness was something else. Each writer's "truth" about each separate "thing" would be different. Agee struggled in *Let Us Now Praise Famous Men* to set up a counterpoint between stark verbal photographs and—as if to provide glasses to help the reader see the pictures more clearly—long passages of filtration of their substance through his deeply kind, generous, quirky, guilt-ridden, hypersensitive consciousness. The result is prose partly documentary, partly autobiographical and confessional on very high and sometimes difficult planes—those, at times, of St. Augustine, of Pascal, and in a more worldly sense, of Joyce.

His was the consciousness of a moralist—one in whom anger against wrong and injustice burned hotly, but also one in whom conviction was forever being shaken by doubt. Robert Fitzgerald, a devout believer, said that "the religious sense of life is at the heart of all of Agee's work." Agee had indeed taken from the altar at St. Andrew's School a soaring sense of wonder and mystery, and he had absorbed from the Good Book the intensity of the anger of Jeremiah and of Isaiah and of Christ tipping over the counters of the money changers; but he had also seen, and hated, in the church and its adherents, piousness, bigotry, hypocrisy, and seeds of the guilt that endlessly tortured him. Father Flye, on first reading Jim's book, wrote to him, "I find in it a sympathy, a love, a care for human beings which make me think of our Lord; I call it in a true sense deeply religious." But Agee replied: "What you write of the book needless to say is good to hear to the point of shaming me—for it is a sinful book at least in all degrees of 'falling short of the mark' and I think in more corrupt ways as well."

His political consciousness was that of a revolutionary, but one who saw that all revolutionaries are fallible human beings, often wicked, cruel, power-mad. Among the many items that crowd the front matter of the book (to which this introduction now adds its further impediment), there stands the Marxist battle cry, "Workers of the world, unite and fight. You have nothing to lose but your chains, and a world to win." But a footnote at once puts that shout into a strange, distorting echo chamber. Fitzgerald, discussing Agee's politics, told how he endlessly examined all sides of every question and found that "all sides turned out to be unsatisfactory in the end, " adding, "And they did, of course. He was right." This moralist was not, as that footnote makes clear, "the property of any political party, faith, or faction." He was purely driven—and wanted the reader to be commanded—by the instruction in the lines from *King Lear* on the page facing the words from *The Communist Manifesto:* "Take physick, pomp; / Expose thyself to feel what wretches feel."

The moralist set forth his aim in the book as grimly as an ancient prophet:

> I am not at all trying to lay out a thesis, far less to substantiate or to solve. I do not consider myself qualified. I know only that murder is being done, against nearly every individual in the planet, and that there are dimensions and correlations of cure which not only are not being used but appear to be scarcely considered or suspected. I know there is cure, even now available, if only it were available, in science and in the fear and joy of God. This is only a brief personal statement of these convictions: and my self-disgust is less in my ignorance, and far less in my "failure" to "defend" or "support" the statement, than in my inability to state it even so far as I see it, and in my inability to blow out the brains with it of you who take what it is talking of lightly, or not seriously enough.

It was at once clear that there would be those who would not respond with pleasure to this hectoring tone. The first big review of the book, by Ralph Thompson in the *New York Times,* was scathing. Agee, he wrote, was "arrogant, mannered, precious, gross," and his book was "the choicest recent example of how to write self-inspired, self-conscious, and self-indulgent prose." Agee's friends were somewhat kinder, but their reviews did not attract readers to the book. Harvey Breit wrote in the *New Republic* that "Mr. Agee does a good deal to antagonize the reader" but that this was "a rich, many-eyed book." Selden Rodman wrote in the *Saturday Review* that its excesses might make a reader "throw down the volume in rage, and curse the author for a confused adolescent, an Ezra Pound in Wolfe's clothing, a shocking snob, or a belligerent mystic posing with a purple pencil on the Left Bank of *Fortune,*" but he praised "the unparalleled intensity of much of the writing." At *Time,* Matthews assigned the book to Fitzgerald but then rejected his "stiff and reverent" review and reassigned it to John Jessup, who hailed it as "the most distinguished failure of the season."

It certainly was a flop in the bookstores. By the end of the year it had sold only a few more than six hundred copies. And before the end of the year Japan had attacked Pearl Harbor, and the American mind had gone off to war.

A year later—too late—the book finally got its due. Lionel Trilling wrote an evaluation of it in *Kenyon Review:*

> I feel sure that this is a great book. . . . Agee has a sensibility so precise, so unremitting, that it is sometimes appalling; and though nothing can be more tiresome than protracted sensibility, Agee's never wearies us: I think this is because it is brilliantly normal and because it is a moral rather than a physical sensibility. . . . The book is full of marvelous writing which gives a kind of hot pleasure that words can do so much.

But Trilling took notice of what he saw as the one weakness in the book, "a failure of moral realism":

It lies in Agee's inability to see these people as anything but good. Not that he falsifies what is apparent: for example he can note with perfect directness their hatred of Negroes; and not that he is ever pious or sentimental, like Steinbeck and Hemingway. But he writes of his people as if there were no human unregenerateness in them, no flicker of malice or meanness, no darkness or wildness of feeling, only a sure and simple virtue, the growth, we must suppose, of their hard, un-lovely poverty. He shuts out, that is, what is part of the moral job to take in. What creates this falsification is guilt—the ob-server's guilt at his own relative freedom. Agee is perfectly con-scious of this guilt and it is in order to take it into account that he gives us so many passages of autobiography and self-examination; he wants the reader to be aware of what is pecu-liar and distorting in the recording instrument, himself. . . .

And yet, even when this failure has been noted, Agee's text still is, it seems to me, the most realistic and the most impor-tant moral effort of our American generation.

Agee accepted the initial failure of *Let Us Now Praise Famous Men* as if he had expected it. He went on with the rest of his brief life, into which he managed to cram three distinct new careers.

Not long after the publication of the book, Robert Fitzger-ald came back to *Time* from a leave he had taken to work on his own writing, and this gave Agee a chance to persuade Mat-thews to shift him from books to cinema. With the thud of his book already silenced in his mind, and excused, with *Time's* help, from serving in a war he despised, he now lived in a heaven of darkened houses. He regarded movies as *the* Amer-ican art form, flickering with all that was best and worst in the culture. In late 1942 Margaret Marshall, the editor of *The Nation's* critical columns, invited Agee to do moonlighting re-views for that magazine, and *Time* gave him permission. Soon

Agee was writing stunning criticism for *The Nation,* many examples of which outlived the films they examined. Film-buff
Agee readers cohered into a cult.

In 1948 *Let Us Now Praise Famous Men* fizzled out of print,
having sold only 1,025 copies. Agee resigned from both *Time*
and *The Nation* and embraced a new craft—that of novelist.
He had already started work on two novels at once, both of
them autobiographical and both overhung with a foxfire of
death. One, to be entitled *The Morning Watch,* would tell of a
boy's vigil at a school like St. Andrew's in contemplation of the
crucifixion of Jesus; the book was an attempt to deal with his
"own shapeless personal religious sense." A taut text of only a
hundred and twenty pages, it was published in 1951 to faint
praise and a very short shelf life. The other, which would be
A Death in the Family, was a reliving of the pain of the loss of
his father. He would wrestle with the rich and eloquent writing of this novel for the rest of his life.

The third of the careers that followed his "failed" masterpiece was as a writer of film scripts. As early as 1937 and 1939
he had done two exercises in screenwriting: a scenario entitled
"Notes for a Moving Picture; The House" and another based
on a harrowing scene in Malraux's *Man's Fate.* Neither was
filmed. One of Agee's heroes in the movie world was John
Huston. He praised Huston's films, especially *The Battle of San
Pietro* and *The Treasure of the Sierra Madre,* and shortly after
Jim left *Time* Huston helped him get a contract with a fledg-
ling producer, Huntington Hartford, to write a script based on
Stephen Crane's story "The Blue Hotel." It was brilliant but
unfilmable. Agee wrote a long profile of Huston for *Life,* and
Huston hired him to write a screenplay adapting the C. S. For-
ester adventure novel *The African Queen.* The success of that
film brought Agee other offers, and he subsequently wrote,
among other things, scripts for *The Bride Comes to Yellow Sky,*
from another Crane story; a television series on Lincoln for
"Omnibus"; *Noa Noa,* on Gauguin; and *The Night of the*

Hunter, an adaptation of a popular novel, for Charles Laughton
to direct.

Through the years of these various lives, Jim's behavior and
his body were both abrading badly. Mia bore him four children; the first of them died in an incubator, forty hours old.
Jim was repeatedly and carelessly and grossly unfaithful to her,
and grew more and more violent in his frustrations and guilt
and feelings of failure, but Mia cleaved to him, buoyed
him, and after his heart began to fray, nursed him. He could
detect—and he hated—the frittering away of his gifts. Angina
seemed a kind of punishment. In low times all through his life,
self-loathing and suicide had hung at the edge of his mind. In
the end, as it turned out, he jumped to his death by indirection;
he was defenestrated from the upper stories of life, as if in slow
motion, by alcohol, nicotine, insomnia, overwork, misused sex,
searing guilt, and—above all, we can guess—by his anger and
want and despair at finding that with all his wild talent he had
never been able to write the whole of the universe down on the
head of a pin. On May 16, 1955, James Rufus Agee died of a
broken heart in a New York taxicab. He was only forty-five
years old.

A t his death, Agee was in worldly reckoning just what he
had thought he was—a failure. Nothing of his—not his
book of poems, *Permit Me Voyage,* not *The Morning Watch,* not
Let Us Now Praise Famous Men—was in print, nothing at all
save some scraps in anthologies. Except by a handful of friends
and a few New York cognoscenti who knew his worth, he was
soon forgotten.

Within ten years, this same James Agee was praised as a
famous man.

One of Agee's friends, David McDowell, who had attended
St. Andrew's after him, had met him through Father Flye, and
had grown faithfully close to him, formed a publishing firm,

McDowell, Obolensky, and two years after Agee's death he published *A Death in the Family.* The novel won the Pulitzer Prize and sold enormously well. Within three years McDowell had published two volumes of *Agee on Film,* Agee's criticism in one and five film scripts in the other; Houghton Mifflin had reissued *Let Us Now Praise Famous Men,* which eventually sold almost sixty thousand copies; and *All the Way Home,* Tad Mosel's adaptation for the stage of *A Death in the Family,* had been a Broadway hit and won a Pulitzer. And within three years after that, George Braziller had published *Letters of James Agee to Father Flye,* and David Susskind had produced a film version of *All the Way Home.*

The new edition of *Let Us Now Praise Famous Men* arrived on a scene very different from the wartime one in which it had first been exposed. In 1960 America's social consciousness seemed to be standing up and stretching after a long nap. The civil-rights movement had gained impetus from the Supreme Court school desegregation decision a few years before, then from Rosa Parks' refusal to move to the back of a bus and Martin Luther King, Jr.'s eloquence and radiant acts of civil disobedience. John Kennedy was elected President the year the book reappeared, and there followed, in a decade of growing turmoil, the agonies and violence and aspirations of Southern sit-ins, the Mississippi voter-registration summer, the Vietnam War, the draft, campus unrest, LSD, rock and roll, the rise of the feminist movement, race riots in Northern cities, appalling assassinations, and an upheaval in social and cultural values that left the country changed forever.

Those were the years when *Let Us Now Praise Famous Men* became a kind of Bible, especially for bright young people who, like James Agee, had the privilege of attending good schools and colleges. Those children were delicately tuned to Agee's irony and idealism and guilt, and his wondrous susceptibility to unpeeled emotions. His excesses and inconsistencies were their norms. When he wrote that "a Harvard education is by no means an unqualified advantage," students from Bowdoin to Berkeley cheered. Young men incarcerated in colleges, as they saw it, because of the Vietnam draft thought Agee spoke for them when he wrote, "'Education' as it stands is tied in with every bondage"—and agreeing with him further, that education "is the chief cause of these bondages," they were moved to capture college buildings and trash their campuses. Half deafened by rock and roll, they loved his praise of loud music, not noticing that he wrote only of amplifying Beethoven and Schubert. They were delighted by his wondering whether tenant farmers, who were "among the only 'honest' and 'beautiful' users of language," should be forced to become literate by semiliterate teachers—apparently not noticing that he also quoted Kafka, Blake, Céline. They could laugh at his epigraph for his section on "Money," which, intending irony, quoted the patrician Franklin Roosevelt as saying: "You are farmers; I am a farmer myself," for they didn't remember—probably weren't even aware—that this gentleman farmer Roosevelt had in fact greatly improved the lot of the tenant farmer. Above all—a redeeming trait in that wounded generation—they shared the symptoms of the "failure of moral realism" that Trilling had seen in Agee's book: the elements of both courage and guilt in his compassion for the downtrodden.

In the hot summer of 1964, I went—I too as a journalist—to Holmes County, Mississippi, and I lived for a time in a small house with a poor and very brave black farmer and his wife and their many children. All around us were the Northern white college kids who had risked their lives—and those of their black hosts—by invading the state that summer to help with voter registration. An astonishing number of them had brought Agee along with them. They gave his book to the young blacks and the Student Nonviolent Coordinating Committee. White and black alike, those young people, whose partnership that summer left its mark on a changing South, were shocked and motivated by the naked fraternity of Jim Agee's desperate impulse to humble himself before the black couple he met on a back road in Alabama, his urge to throw himself down and kiss their feet. The students who had read Agee's book "failed" that summer and went back North, but not many years later a black mayor was elected in the town nearest to where I stayed.

The appeal to American readers of *Let Us Now Praise Famous Men* has reached far beyond the troubled sixties. There lies deep in the Judeo-Christian American psyche a powerful nostalgia for lost innocence and spent decency, and it is perhaps this nostalgia that has continued to open readers' minds to Agee's enormous humanity and pity and sorrow. He certainly did, as Trilling pointed out, idealize his three tenant families. Love idealizes, and one of the attractive things about Jim Agee's writing is that with all his remarkably skeptical intelligence, and despite his many declared doubts and weaknesses, he was capable of copious, unsentimental, generous, searing love.

But there is another reason for the lasting appeal of *Let Us Now Praise Famous Men*—one that raises the complex and troubling substance of the book to a feverish, ecstatic pitch. This lies in the quirkiness and uneven flow and the many surprises and dazzling beauty of the prose Agee devised in an effort to solve his journalistic riddle. This prose has the effect finally of enlarging the figures of the tale, until they become mythic, like Ahab, like Hester Prynne, like the children in *The Sound and the Fury*.

A journalist, in any effort to render truth, has three responsibilities: to his reader, to his conscience, and to his human subjects. What did Agee's tenant families think of how he fulfilled his responsibility to them? Had he, with his "failure of moral realism," failed them? Years later, Ellie Mae Burroughs admitted that when the book came out the families had mixed feelings about it. Some members were proud of being "famous," but there was also talk of the shame of being photographed "half dressed," and talk—as there so often is when even the faintest scent of money hangs on the air—of suing the authors. But Mrs. Burroughs told that she had said then, "Well, I don't know what you're going to sue them for, 'cause I wouldn't want to hurt 'em if I could, because they was too good to me."

Mrs. Burroughs said:

We wasn't the onliest ones that had it hard, you know. Everybody did at that time. . . . We didn't believe that times would ever get any better with us; [Jim] was trying to encourage me that they would. He told me that I might not live to see it, but my children would have a better living than we was having then. But I couldn't believe it. But I'll have to say he was right, not that we're rich now, but one thing I can say is that they got their own homes, and they got a better living. They have anything they want near 'bout. He was right. I did live to see it.

With an authority no one could deny, Mrs. Burroughs gave *Let Us Now Praise Famous Men* its ultimate book review:

I don't guess it's been over ten years ago that I seen the book if it's been that long. My daughter got one of 'em; I don't know where in the world she got it, but she got it and told me she had it, and she wanted me to look at it and give it to me. And I took it home and I read it plumb through. And when I read it plumb through I give it back to her and I said, "Well everything in there's true." What they wrote in there was true.

John F. Kennedy

Lieutenant John F. Kennedy, the ex-Ambassador's son and lately a PT skipper in the Solomons, came through town the other day and told me the story of his survival in the South Pacific. I asked Kennedy if I might write the story down. He asked me if I wouldn't talk first with some of his crew, so I went up to the Motor Torpedo Boat Training Center at Melville, Rhode Island, and there, under the curving iron of a Quonset hut, three enlisted men named Johnston, McMahon, and McGuire filled in the gaps.

It seems that Kennedy's PT, the 109, was out one night with a squadron patrolling Blackett Strait, in mid-Solomons. Blackett Strait is a patch of water bounded on the northeast by the volcano called Kolombangara, on the west by the island of Vella Lavella, on the south by the island of Gizo and a string of coral-fringed islets, and on the east by the bulk of New Georgia. The boats were working about forty miles away from their base on the island of Rendova, on the south side of New Georgia. They had entered Blackett Strait, as was their habit, through Ferguson Passage, between the coral islets and New Georgia.

The night was a starless black and Japanese destroyers were

"Survival," *The New Yorker,* June 17, 1944 (Hersey's thirtieth birthday).

around. It was about two-thirty. The 109, with three officers and ten enlisted men aboard, was leading three boats on a sweep for a target. An officer named George Ross was up on the bow, magnifying the void with binoculars. Kennedy was at the wheel, and he saw Ross turn and point into the darkness. The man in the forward machine-gun turret shouted, "Ship at two o'clock!" Kennedy saw a shape and spun the wheel to turn for an attack, but the 109 answered sluggishly. She was running slowly on only one of her three engines, so as to make a minimum wake and avoid detection from the air. The shape became a Japanese destroyer, cutting through the night at forty knots and heading straight for the 109. The thirteen men on the PT hardly had time to brace themselves. Those who saw the Japanese ship coming were paralyzed by fear in a curious way: they could move their hands but not their feet. Kennedy whirled the wheel to the left, but again the 109 did not respond. Ross went through the gallant but futile motions of slamming a shell into the breach of the 37-millimeter anti-tank gun which had been temporarily mounted that very day, wheels and all, on the foredeck. The urge to bolt and dive over the side was terribly strong, but still no one was able to move; all hands froze to their battle stations. Then the Japanese crashed into the 109 and cut her right in two. The sharp enemy forefoot struck the PT on the starboard side about fifteen feet from the bow and crunched diagonally across with a racking noise. The PT's wooden hull hardly even delayed the destroyer. Kennedy was thrown hard to the left in the cockpit, and he thought, This is how it feels to be killed. In a moment, he found himself on his back on the deck, looking up at the destroyer as it passed through his boat. There was another loud noise and a huge flash of yellow-red light, and the destroyer glowed. Its peculiar, raked, inverted-Y stack stood out in the brilliant light and, later, in Kennedy's memory.

There was only one man belowdecks at the moment of collision. That was McMahon, engineer. He had no idea what was up. He was just reaching forward to engage the starboard engine in gear when a ship came into his engine room. He was lifted from the narrow passage between two of the engines and thrown painfully against the starboard bulkhead aft of the boat's auxiliary generator. He landed in a sitting position. A tremendous burst of flame came back at him from the dayroom, where some of the gas tanks were. He put his hands over his face, drew his legs up tight, and waited to die. But he felt water hit him after the fire, and he was sucked far downward as his half of the PT sank. He began to struggle upward through the water. He had held his breath since the impact, so his lungs were tight and they hurt. He looked up through the water. Over his head he saw a yellow glow—gasoline burning on the water. He broke the surface and was in fire again. He splashed hard to keep a little island of water around him.

Johnston, another engineer, had been asleep on deck when the collision came. It lifted him and dropped him overboard. He saw the flame and the destroyer for a moment. Then a huge propeller pounded by near him and the awful turbulence of the destroyer's wake took him down, turned him over and over, held him down, shook him, and drubbed on his ribs. He hung on and came up in water that was like a river rapids. The next day, his body turned black-and-blue from the beating.

Kennedy's half of the PT stayed afloat. The bulkheads were sealed, so the undamaged watertight compartments up forward kept the half hull floating. The destroyer rushed off into the dark. There was an awful quiet: only the sound of gasoline burning.

Kennedy shouted, "Who's aboard?"

Feeble answers came from three of the enlisted men, McGuire, Mauer, and Albert; and from one of the officers, Thom.

Kennedy saw the fire only ten feet from the boat. He

thought it might reach her and explode the remaining gas tanks, so he shouted, "Over the side!"

The five men slid into the water. But the wake of the destroyer swept the fire away from the PT, so after a few minutes, Kennedy and the others crawled back aboard. Kennedy shouted for survivors in the water. One by one they answered: Ross, the third officer; Harris, McMahon, Johnston, Zinsser, Starkey, enlisted men. Two did not answer: Kirksey and Marney, enlisted men. Since the last bombing at base, Kirksey had been sure he would die. He had huddled at his battle station by the fantail gun, with his kapok life jacket tied tight up to his cheeks. No one knows what happened to him or to Marney.

Harris shouted from the darkness, "Mr. Kennedy! Mr. Kennedy! McMahon is badly hurt." Kennedy took his shoes, his shirt, and his sidearms off, told Mauer to blink a light so that the men in the water would know where the half hull was, then dived in and swam toward the voice. The survivors were widely scattered. McMahon and Harris were a hundred yards away.

When Kennedy reached McMahon, he asked, "How are you, Mac?"

McMahon said, "I'm all right. I'm kind of burnt."

Kennedy shouted out, "How are the others?"

Harris said softly, "I hurt my leg."

Kennedy, who had been on the Harvard swimming team five years before, took McMahon in tow and headed for the PT. A gentle breeze kept blowing the boat away from the swimmers. It took forty-five minutes to make what had been an easy hundred yards. On the way in, Harris said, "I can't go any farther." Kennedy, of the Boston Kennedys, said to Harris, of the same hometown, "For a guy from Boston, you're certainly putting up a great exhibition out here, Harris." Harris made it all right and didn't complain anymore. Then Kennedy swam from man to man, to see how they were doing. All who had survived the crash were able to stay afloat, since they were wearing life preservers—kapok jackets shaped like overstuffed vests, aviators' yellow Mae Wests, or air-filled belts like small inner tubes. But those who couldn't swim had to be towed back to the wreckage by those who could. One of the men screamed for help. When Ross reached him, he found that the screaming man had two life jackets on. Johnston was treading water in a film of gasoline which did not catch fire. The fumes filled his lungs and he fainted. Thom towed him in. The others got in under their own power. It was now after 5 A.M., but still dark. It had taken nearly three hours to get everyone aboard.

The men stretched out on the tilted deck of the PT. Johnston, McMahon, and Ross collapsed into sleep. The men talked about how wonderful it was to be alive and speculated on when the other PTs would come back to rescue them. Mauer kept blinking the light to point their way. But the other boats had no idea of coming back. They had seen a collision, a sheet of flame, and a slow burning on the water. When the skipper of one of the boats saw the sight, he put his hands over his face and sobbed, "My God! My God!" He and the others turned away. Back at the base, after a couple of days, the squadron held services for the souls of the thirteen men, and one of the officers wrote his mother, "George Ross lost his life for a cause that he believed in stronger than any one of us, because he was an idealist in the purest sense. Jack Kennedy, the Ambassador's son, was on the same boat and also lost his life. The man that said the cream of a nation is lost in war can never be accused of making an overstatement of a very cruel fact. . . ."

When day broke, the men on the remains of the 109 stirred and looked around. To the northeast, three miles off, they saw the monumental cone of Kolombangara; there, the men knew, ten thousand Japanese swarmed. To the

LIEUTENANT KENNEDY IN THE SOLOMONS

"Only the good die young."

west, five miles away, they saw Vella Lavella; more Japs. To the south, only a mile or so away, they actually could see a Japanese camp on Gizo. Kennedy ordered his men to keep as low as possible, so that no moving silhouettes would show against the sky. The listing hulk was gurgling and gradually settling. Kennedy said, "What do you want to do if the Japs come out? Fight or surrender?" One said, "Fight with what?" So they took an inventory of their armament. The .37-millimeter gun had flopped over the side and was hanging there by a chain. They had one tommy gun, six 45-caliber automatics, and one .38. Not much.

"Well," Kennedy said, "what do you want to do?"

One said, "Anything you say, Mr. Kennedy. You're the boss."

Kennedy said, "There's nothing in the book about a situation like this. Seems to me we're not a military organization anymore. Let's just talk this over."

They talked it over, and pretty soon they argued, and Kennedy could see that they would never survive in anarchy. So he took command again.

It was vital that McMahon and Johnston should have room to lie down. McMahon's face, neck, hands, wrists, and feet were horribly burned. Johnston was pale and he coughed continually. There was scarcely space for everyone, so Kennedy ordered the other men into the water to make room, and went in himself. All morning they clung to the hulk and talked about how incredible it was that no one had come to rescue them. All morning they watched for the plane which they thought would be looking for them. They cursed war in general and PTs in particular. At about ten o'clock, the hull heaved a moist sigh and turned turtle. McMahon and Johnston had to hang on as best they could. It was clear that the remains of the 109 would soon sink. When the sun had passed the meridian, Kennedy said, "We will swim to that small island," pointing to one of a group three miles to the southeast. "We have less chance of making it than some of these other islands here, but there'll be less chance of Japs, too." Those who could not swim well grouped themselves around a long two-by-six timber with which carpenters had braced the 37-millimeter cannon on deck and which had been knocked overboard by the force of the collision. They tied several pairs of shoes to the timber, as well as the ship's lantern, wrapped in a life jacket to keep it afloat. Thom took charge of this unwieldy group. Kennedy took McMahon in tow again. He cut loose one end of a long strap on McMahon's Mae West and took the end in his teeth. He swam breast stroke, pulling the helpless McMahon along on his back. It took over five hours to reach the island. Water lapped into Kennedy's mouth through his clenched teeth, and he swallowed a lot. The salt water cut into McMahon's awful burns, but he did not complain. Every few minutes, when Kennedy stopped to rest, taking the strap out of his mouth and holding it in his hand, McMahon would simply say, "How far do we have to go?"

Kennedy would reply, "We're going good." Then he would ask, "How do you feel, Mac?"

McMahon always answered, "I'm O.K., Mr. Kennedy. How about you?"

In spite of his burden, Kennedy beat the other men to the reef that surrounded the island. He left McMahon on the reef and told him to keep low, so as not to be spotted by Japs. Kennedy went ahead and explored the island. It was only a hundred yards in diameter; coconuts on the trees but none on the ground; no visible Japs. Just as the others reached the island, one of them spotted a Japanese barge chugging along close to shore. They all lay low. The barge went on. Johnston, who was very pale and weak and who was still coughing a lot, said, "They wouldn't come here. What'd they be walking around here for? It's too small." Kennedy lay in some bushes, exhausted by his effort, his stomach heavy with the water he had swallowed. He had been in the sea, except for short intervals on the hulk, for fifteen and a half hours. Now he started thinking. Every night for several nights the PTs had cut through Ferguson Passage on their way to action. Ferguson Passage was just beyond the next little island. Maybe . . .

He stood up. He put on one of the pairs of shoes. He fastened one of the rubber life belts around his waist. He hung the .38 around his neck on a lanyard. He took his pants off. He picked up the ship's lantern, a heavy battery affair ten inches by ten inches, still wrapped in the kapok jacket. He said, "If I find a boat, I'll flash the lantern twice. The password will be 'Roger,' the answer will be 'Wilco.'" He walked toward the water. After fifteen paces he was dizzy, but in the water he felt all right.

It was early evening. It took half an hour to swim to the reef around the next island. Just as he planted his feet on the reef, which lay about four feet under the surface, he saw the shape of a very big fish in the clear water. He flashed the light at it and splashed hard. The fish went away. Kennedy remembered what one of his men had said a few days before, "These barracuda will come up under a swimming man and eat his testicles." He had many occasions to think of that remark in the next few hours.

Now it was dark. Kennedy blundered along the uneven reef in water up to his waist. Sometimes he would reach forward with his leg and cut one of his shins or ankles on sharp coral. Other times he would step forward onto emptiness. He made his way like a slow-motion drunk, hugging the lantern. At about nine o'clock, he came to the end of the reef, alongside Ferguson Passage. He took his shoes off and tied them to the life jacket, then struck out into open water. He swam about an hour, until he felt he was far enough out to intercept the PTs. Treading water, he listened for the muffled roar of motors, getting chilled, waiting, holding the lamp. Once, he looked west and saw flares and the false gaiety of an action. The lights were far beyond the little islands, even beyond Gizo, ten miles away. Kennedy realized that the PT boats had chosen, for the first night in many, to go around Gizo instead of through Ferguson Passage. There was no hope. He started back. He made the same painful promenade of the reef and struck out for the tiny island where his friends were. But this swim was different. He was very tired and now the current was running fast, carrying him to the right. He saw that he could not make the island, so he flashed the light once and shouted "Roger! Roger!" to identify himself.

On the beach, the men were hopefully vigilant. They saw the light and heard the shouts. They were very happy, because they thought that Kennedy had found a PT. They walked out onto the reef, sometimes up to their waists in water, and waited. It was very painful for those who had no shoes. The men shouted, but not much, because they were afraid of Japanese.

One said, "There's another flash."

A few minutes later, a second said, "There's a light over there."

A third said, "We're seeing things in this dark."

They waited a long time, but they saw nothing except phosphorescence and heard nothing but the sound of waves. They went back, very discouraged.

One said despairingly, "We're going to die."

Johnston said, "Aw, shut up. You can't die. Only the good die young."

Kennedy had drifted right by the little island. He thought he had never known such deep trouble, but something he did shows that unconsciously he had not given up hope. He dropped his shoes, but he held onto the heavy lantern, his symbol of contact with his fellows. He stopped trying to swim. He seemed to stop caring. His body drifted through the wet hours, and he was very cold. His mind was a jumble. A few hours before, he had wanted desperately to get to the base at Rendova. Now he only wanted to get back to the little island he had left that night, but he didn't try to get there; he just wanted to. His mind seemed to float away from his body. Darkness and time took the place of a mind in his skull. For a long time he slept, or was crazy, or floated in a chill trance.

The currents of the Solomon Islands are queer. The tide shoves and sucks through the islands and makes the currents curl in odd patterns. It was a fateful pattern into which Jack Kennedy drifted. He drifted in it all night. His mind was blank, but his fist was tightly clenched on the kapok around the lantern. The current moved in a huge circle—west past Gizo, then north and east past Kolombangara, then south into Ferguson Passage. Early in the morning, the sky turned from black to gray, and so did Kennedy's mind. Light came to both at about six. Kennedy looked around and saw that he was exactly where he had been the night before when he saw the flares beyond Gizo. For a second time, he started home. He thought for a while that he had lost his mind and that he only imagined that he was repeating his attempt to reach the island. But the chill of the water was real enough, the lantern was real, his progress was measurable. He made the reef, crossed the lagoon, and got to the first island. He lay on the beach awhile. He found that his lantern did not work anymore, so he left it and started back to the next island, where his men were. This time the trip along the reef was awful. He had discarded his shoes, and every step on the coral was painful. This time the swim across the gap where the current had caught him the night before seemed endless. But the current had changed; he made the island. He crawled up on the beach. He was vomiting when his men came up to him. He said, "Ross, you try it tonight." Then he passed out.

Ross, seeing Kennedy so sick, did not look forward to the

execution of the order. He distracted himself by complaining about his hunger. There were a few coconuts on the trees, but the men were too weak to climb up for them. One of the men thought of seafood, stirred his tired body, and found a snail on the beach. He said, "If we were desperate, we could eat these." Ross said, "Desperate, hell. Give me that. I'll eat that." He took it in his hand and looked at it. The snail put its head out and looked at him. Ross was startled, but he shelled the snail and ate it, making faces because it was bitter.

In the afternoon, Ross swam across to the next island. He took a pistol to signal with, and he spent the night watching Ferguson Passage from the reef around the island. Nothing came through. Kennedy slept badly that night; he was cold and sick.

The next morning, everyone felt wretched. Planes which the men were unable to identify flew overhead and there were dogfights. That meant Japs as well as friends, so the men dragged themselves into the bushes and lay low. Some prayed. Johnston said, "You guys make me sore. You didn't spend ten cents in church in ten years, then all of a sudden you're in trouble and you see the light." Kennedy felt a little better now. When Ross came back, Kennedy decided that the group should move to another, larger island to the southeast, where there seemed to be more coconut trees and where the party would be nearer Ferguson Passage. Again, Kennedy took McMahon in tow with the strap in his teeth, and the nine others grouped themselves around the timber.

This swim took three hours. The nine around the timber were caught by the current and barely made the far tip of the island. Kennedy found walking the quarter-mile across to them much harder than the three-hour swim. The cuts on his bare feet had festered and looked like small balloons. The men were suffering most from thirst, and they broke open some coconuts lying on the ground and avidly drank the milk. Kennedy and McMahon, the first to drink, were sickened, and Thom told the others to drink sparingly. In the middle of the night, it rained and someone suggested moving into the underbrush and licking water off the leaves. Ross and McMahon kept contact at first by touching feet as they licked. Somehow they got separated, and, being uncertain whether there were any Japs on the island, they became frightened. McMahon, trying to make his way back to the beach, bumped into someone and froze. It turned out to be Johnston, licking leaves on his own. In the morning, the group saw that all the leaves were covered with droppings. Bitterly, they named the place Bird Island.

On this fourth day, the men were low. Even Johnston was low. He had changed his mind about praying. McGuire had a rosary around his neck, and Johnston said, "McGuire, give that necklace a working over." McGuire said quietly, "Yes, I'll take care of all you fellows." Kennedy was still unwilling to admit that things were hopeless. He asked Ross if he would swim with him to an island called Nauru to the southeast and even nearer Ferguson Passage. They were very weak indeed by now, but after an hour's swim they made it.

They walked painfully across Nauru to the Ferguson Passage side, where they saw a Japanese barge aground on the reef. There were two men by the barge—possibly Japs. They apparently spotted Kennedy and Ross, for they got into a dugout canoe and hurriedly paddled to the other side of the island. Kennedy and Ross moved up the beach. They came upon an unopened rope-bound box and, back in the trees, a little shelter containing a keg of water, a Japanese gas mask, and a crude wooden fetish shaped like a fish. There were Japanese hardtack and candy in the box and the two had a wary feast. Down by the water they found a one-man canoe. They hid from imagined Japs all day. When night fell, Kennedy left Ross and took the canoe, with some hardtack and a can of water from the keg, out into Ferguson Passage. But no PTs came, so he paddled to Bird Island. The men there told him that the two men he had spotted by the barge that morning were natives, who had paddled to Bird Island. The natives had said that there were Japs on Nauru, and the men had given Kennedy and Ross up for lost. Then the natives had gone away. Kennedy gave out small rations of crackers and water, and the men went to sleep. During the night, one man, who kept himself awake until the rest were asleep, drank all the water in the can Kennedy had brought back. In the morning the others figured out which man was the guilty one. They swore at him and found it hard to forgive him.

Before dawn, Kennedy started out in the canoe to rejoin Ross on Nauru, but when day broke a wind arose and the canoe was swamped. Some natives appeared from nowhere in a canoe, rescued Kennedy, and took him to Nauru. There they showed him where a two-man canoe was cached. Kennedy picked up a coconut with a smooth shell and scratched a message on it with a jackknife: "ELEVEN ALIVE NATIVE KNOWS POSIT AND REEFS NAURU ISLAND KENNEDY." Then he said to the natives, "Rendova, Rendova."

One of the natives seemed to understand. They took the coconut and paddled off.

Ross and Kennedy lay in a sickly daze all day. Toward evening it rained and they crawled under a bush. When it got dark, conscience took hold of Kennedy and he persuaded Ross to go out into Ferguson Passage with him in the two-man canoe. Ross argued against it. Kennedy insisted. The two started out in the canoe. They had shaped paddles from the boards of the Japanese box, and they took a coconut shell to bail with. As they got out into the Passage, the wind rose again and the water became choppy. The canoe began to fill. Ross bailed and Kennedy kept the bow into the wind. The waves grew until they were five or six feet high. Kennedy shouted, "Better turn around and go back!" As soon as the canoe was broadside to the waves, the water poured in and the dugout was swamped. The two clung to it, Kennedy at the bow, Ross at the stern. The tide carried them southward toward the open sea, so they kicked and tugged the canoe, aiming northwest. They struggled that way for two hours, not knowing whether they would hit the small island or drift into the endless open.

The weather got worse; rain poured down and they couldn't see more than ten feet. Kennedy shouted, "Sorry I got you out here, Barney!" Ross shouted back, "This time would be a great time to say I told you so, but I won't!"

Soon the two could see a white line ahead and could hear a frightening roar—waves crashing on a reef. They had got out of the tidal current and were approaching the island all right, but now they realized that the wind and the waves were carrying them toward the reef. But it was too late to do anything, now that their canoe was swamped, except hang on and wait.

When they were near the reef, a wave broke Kennedy's hold, ripped him away from the canoe, turned him head over heels, and spun him in a violent rush. His ears roared and his eyes pinwheeled, and for the third time since the collision he thought he was dying. Somehow he was not thrown against the coral but floated into a kind of eddy. Suddenly, he felt the reef under his feet. Steadying himself so that he would not be swept off it, he shouted, "Barney!" There was no reply. Kennedy thought of how he had insisted on going out in the canoe, and he screamed, "Barney!" This time Ross answered. He, too, had been thrown onto the reef. He had not been as lucky as Kennedy; his right arm and shoulder had been cruelly lacer-

ated by the coral, and his feet, which were already infected
from earlier wounds, were cut some more.

The procession of Kennedy and Ross from reef to beach was
a crazy one. Ross's feet hurt so much that Kennedy would hold
one paddle on the bottom while Ross put a foot on it, then the
other paddle forward for another step, then the first paddle
forward again, until they reached sand. They fell on the beach
and slept.

Kennedy and Ross were wakened early in the morning by
a noise. They looked up and saw four husky natives. One
walked up to them and said, in an excellent English accent, "I
have a letter for you, sir." Kennedy tore the note open. It said,
"On His Majesty's Service. To the Senior Officer, Nauru Island.
I have just learned of your presence on Nauru Is. I am in
command of a New Zealand infantry patrol operating in con-
junction with U.S. Army troops on New Georgia. I strongly
advise that you come with these natives to me. Meanwhile I
shall be in radio communication with your authorities at Rendova, and we can finalize plans to collect balance of your party.
Lt. Wincote. P. S. Will warn aviation of your crossing Ferguson
Passage."

Everyone shook hands and the four natives took Ross and
Kennedy in their war canoe across to Bird Island to tell the
others the good news. There the natives broke out a spirit stove
and cooked a feast of yams and C ration. Then they built a
lean-to for McMahon, whose burns had begun to rot and stink,
and for Ross, whose arm had swelled to the size of a thigh
because of the coral cuts. The natives put Kennedy in the bottom of their canoe and covered him with sacking and palm
fronds, in case Japanese planes should buzz them. The long
trip was fun for the natives. They stopped once to try to grab
a turtle, and laughed at the sport they were having. Thirty

Japanese planes went over low toward Rendova, and the natives waved and shouted gaily. They rowed with a strange rhythm, pounding paddles on the gunwales between strokes. At last, they reached a censored place. Lieutenant Wincote came to the water's edge and said formally, "How do you do. Leftenant Wincote."

Kennedy said, "Hello. I'm Kennedy."

Wincote said, "Come up to my tent and have a cup of tea."

I n the middle of the night, after several radio conversations between Wincote's outfit and the PT base, Kennedy sat in the war canoe waiting at an arranged rendezvous for a PT. The moon went down at eleven-twenty. Shortly afterward, Kennedy heard the signal he was waiting for—four shots. Kennedy fired four answering shots.

A voice shouted to him, "Hey, Jack!"

Kennedy said, "Where the hell you been?"

The voice said, "We got some food for you."

Kennedy said bitterly, "No, thanks, I just had a coconut."

A moment later, a PT came alongside. Kennedy jumped onto it and hugged the men aboard—his friends. In the American tradition, Kennedy held under his arm a couple of souvenirs: one of the improvised paddles and the Japanese gas mask.

With the help of the natives, the PT made its way to Bird Island. A skiff went in and picked up the men. In the deep of the night, the PT and its happy cargo roared back toward base. The squadron medic had sent some brandy along to revive the weakened men. Johnston felt the need of a little revival. In fact, he needed quite a bit of revival. After taking care of that, he retired topside and sat with his arms around a couple of roly-poly, mission-trained natives. And in the fresh breeze on the way home they sang together a hymn all three happened to know:

"Jesus loves me, this I know,
For the Bible tells me so;
Little ones to him belong,
They are weak, but He is strong.
Yes, Jesus loves me; yes, Jesus loves me ..."

Private John Daniel Ramey

Until a few days ago, Private John Daniel Ramey was a jughead. That, at any rate, is what the permanent cadre of the Army school for illiterates near Harrisburg, Pennsylvania, calls the students, and up to very recently Ramey was one of them. The school, officially known as the Special Training Unit of the 3384th Service Unit, is a remarkable place at which an absolute illiterate can, in about three months' time, pick up the equivalent of a fifth-grade or sixth-grade facility in reading, writing, and arithmetic. The Pennsylvania S.T.U. now turns out brand-new literates at the rate of two hundred a week, and since its activation, on July 12, 1943, the school has graduated a hundred and five classes, or something over thirteen thousand men.

The Pennsylvania unit is not the only Army school for illiterates. It could not possibly handle the traffic alone. Most of us have come to take literacy for granted, and yet there are still five million illiterates in the United States, one person in every thirty. In due course the able-bodied men among the illiterates have been drafted. There are, in all, fourteen Special Training Units like the one in Pennsylvania to take care of them. So far, these schools have taught more than two hundred and fifty thousand men to read and write. That is the equivalent of

---

"The Brilliant Jughead," *The New Yorker,* July 28, 1945.

seventeen American divisions; thirteen divisions won the Battle of the Bulge, six took Okinawa. In a sense, at least, by a kind of displacement, the men whom the Army's schools have salvaged from illiteracy have made possible some great victories. But far more important than that, these schools have given a very large number of Americans a marvelous new skill. The Special Training Units have opened blind eyes; they have given men, quite suddenly, the thrilling, frightening trick of knowledge.

To the soldiers of the permanent cadres that run these units, the excitement implicit in their work is understandably dimmed by everyday living with men much less educated than they themselves are. The members of the cadre at the Pennsylvania school cannot be blamed, really, for the mild intellectual snobbery that makes them call the students jugheads. But in many cases the epithet is unjustly applied. It certainly is in that of Private Ramey. There is some debate around the post about the origin and the exact definition of the term "jughead." The word antecedes the school, but there is at least one sergeant in the cadre who thinks he invented it. An officer of the post, a Southerner, recollects it from his boyhood. "A jughead," he says, "is a human mule. I grew up trying to push jugheaded mules around on the farm." A definition attributed to the commanding officer, Lieutenant Colonel Wellington B. Searls, requires some acquaintance with the habits of fowl, for he compares a jughead to "a duck in a thunderstorm." During electrical storms, a duck, in dull panic, hunches his wing shoulders forward, withdraws most of his head under the forward part of one wing, and tucks his bill under the other, so that he seems not to have any head at all. One of the students of the school, who, like many of his fellows, is a Virginian from the hills, put the matter to me this way the other day. "What," he asked, "has a jug got in it when you pour all the liquor out of it into your neck?"

A few of the students are heartbreakingly slow, but not

many. The school has been able to graduate ninety-three per cent of the men assigned to it, and only two per cent have been discharged under Section Eight, which defines men who are hopelessly unqualified for military life. The rest of the discharges have been medical or disciplinary. When draftees come up for induction, they are given a literacy test consisting of what seems to most men very simple questions. There are thirty-five questions. Anyone who cannot answer at least nine correctly is classed as illiterate. Illiterates are then given two further tests, which screen out most of the unsalvageables. Men who pass these screening tests are assigned to Special Training Units.

Private Ramey, who was assigned to the Pennsylvania school toward the end of March, 1945, could hardly be called a typical jughead. There is, in fact, no typical illiterate, any more than there is a typical college graduate. Ramey is above whatever average there is. He finished the course, which usually takes twelve weeks, in ten. By jughead standards, Ramey is brilliant. He says that he was often embarrassed, when he was a civilian, by not being able to read and write, but the surprising thing about his life before the war is how much he, an illiterate, was able to do for himself: at one time he owned a house, ran a small coal mine employing twenty-eight men, and had two automobiles, the better of which was a Mercury with, as he says, "one of them cloth tops on it," bought brand-new. The fact that he is above average makes him especially grateful for the opportunities, the amazements, opened up for him by being introduced, for the first time in his life, to the written word.

Ramey is thirty years and eight months old. He is a small, quiet man. He has blue eyes, black hair, and a deeply ruddy complexion, and two of his front teeth are crowned with gold. He has a rather intense face and a look of solid, if untutored, worth; his Army record has, in capital letters in the space of "Character," this assessment: "VERY GOOD." His voice is quiet and he almost never swears. His best friend at the school, a redhead named Harold Edward Rutherford, says he likes Ramey because "he don't talk like some of the men, he always talks nice to you; when you're worrying about something, he always talks good to you—you always have company with him." Mrs. Elizabeth Harpel, who was Ramey's teacher all the way through the school, came to have quite a bit of respect for him. "He doesn't jump around like some of them," she told me on the last day of his course. "He's quite a study, that young man. I looked at him today and he seemed to speak to me through his eyes; he has very strange eyes; did you notice his eyes? They get so big—and he's a rather intelligent-looking man. His skin has a strange shine to it; did you notice his skin? It makes me think maybe he has liver trouble. But he would never mention it unless you asked him. Some of them complain—oh, their eyes hurt and they tell me all their troubles and if they have a toothache I know it. But not him. I think he's rather deep."

Ramey was born and grew up, the third of five children, on a farm near Norton, in Wise County, Virginia. He says he didn't learn to read and write because it was too far to walk to school. His parents did not tutor him, because his father, Tom Ramey, was a drummer for the Broadwater Feed Company, Wholesalers, and was seldom at home, and his mother "was kind of sickly—she never did feel up to schooling us kids; I had a good home, as far as that goes." John was fifteen before he left the farm, and by then, he says, "why, I reckon I just like any other boy; I thought I was too big to go to school—something like that. I wanted to do a job of work, I wanted to make my own living—in fact, I never did realize till it was too late what a education could mean." Off and on through the years, he thought of taking time out to get some learning, but life went too fast and things seemed to run along O.K.; he just never did.

In his first few jobs, being an illiterate did not seem to make any difference. After he left home, he worked at a filling station, and that simply meant cranking a pump and making change. When he was seventeen, he went to a government employment agency and signed up for a job with General Motors, in Detroit. Out there he became a gasket cutter. "All we had to do," he says, "was to lay the material on, mash a button, and then pick it off—it was automatic electric." He returned to Virginia shortly after reaching his majority and worked in a C.C.C. camp near Richmond; he drove a half-ton surveyors' truck. He settled in Clintwood, Dickenson County, Virginia, in 1937, and there met his wife. She is the daughter of a preacher named McFall, who follows the faith of the Freewill, or soft-shell, Baptists. Ramey remembers very well the first time he met Irma Joyce McFall. It was in church. "Her father 'bout to kill her for letting me go home with her," he recalls. "I'd been going to church several times there, but I never paid any attention to her till one time she got right in front of me and, well, I got to paying attention to her." His paying attention to Joyce rather than her father's sermons continued week after week, and was intensified, and John and Joyce were married a year later, on her birthday, Christmas Eve. The marriage has worked out very well.

Mrs. Ramey is three months younger than her husband, four inches taller, and thirteen pounds lighter. She has long black hair and is quite pretty. The marriage rewarded Ramey with two daughters, Gaynell and Danta, and somewhat compensated for his illiteracy. Joyce's father is an educated man, and she herself went through the eighth grade. She taught John addition, subtraction, and the multiplication tables, but she never tried to teach him to read and write. Mrs. Ramey inherits

HERSEY AND RAMEY

"They can take away my Gun also my Uniform but they
wont ever take away how to read and write."

from her father, soft-shell though he may be, a tenacious purity of spirit. "She's always been a Christian woman," Ramey says. "She'll visit with people and listen to the radio; otherwise, going to a show, anything like that, she won't have a thing to do with it. I slip off sometimes and go to a show. I never did think there was so much harm in going to a show, if you just went to a show and saw a show and didn't take to it like you would something to eat. She would say, 'It don't help anybody, going to a show.' I always say anything that won't help anybody won't hurt anybody."

During his courtship, Ramey became an entrepreneur. He took over a "wagon mine." Wagon mining is common practice in parts of Virginia and Pennsylvania; when a small, isolated seam of coal lies on the surface of the earth and seems not to be worth exploiting on a large scale, the mining firm that owns the right turns the seam over to a man with a truck—in the old days, a wagon. Ramey opened up a seam near Banner, Virginia, and took out lump coal. He paid the Bannerville Coal Company fifteen cents a ton royalty and sold the coal to householders for $2.85 a ton. What with wages to twenty-eight men and upkeep of equipment—"so much dead work and dead money"—he cleared only about fifty dollars a week. Nevertheless, he saved enough money to build a small house. He chose a site half a mile from Clintwood, looking down the whole length of a seven-mile valley. He built the house himself, to his own plan. It has a living room, a dining room, a kitchen, and a bedroom on the ground floor. There is a bedroom upstairs, too, even though, he says, "I didn't get my walls as high as I was going to on the sides; I meant to make them ten feet, but then I thought that was a little high and my lumber was kind of short that I wanted to start the frame with." The whole family sleeps in the downstairs bedroom. The house is wood outside and beaverboard inside, and has both electricity and plumbing. For his water supply, he built a concrete reservoir, which holds sixteen hundred gallons, around a spring trickling from a vein of coal on the hill above the house. In the kitchen there is an electric stove, which cost $209 new, and a refrigerator, which Ramey bought second-hand for $80 from a friend who was moving to Detroit. Over the years, he has put more than $4,000 into the house, and he is proud to be able to say, "I never borrowed a penny of money from the bank or anything in my life."

About eighteen months after his marriage, Ramey "got shet of" the coal mine and went to work for the Haysi Motor Company, the Chevrolet agency in Haysi, Virginia, as a metal worker and spray painter. That has been his line of civilian work ever since. It was at this point that illiteracy began to bother Ramey. Although his wife's and father-in-law's literacy made things easier for him, their learning made him, by the same measure, conscious of his lack. In Detroit, it had not particularly bothered him, when the work sheets were posted each evening with the assignments for the next day, to ask a friend to read them for him. But now all sorts of embarrassments cropped up. He would buy some paint and put the cans on a shelf and next day would have to ask someone to find him the right color for a certain spray job. He would slip off to a show and stand right in front of the billboard out front and have to ask someone what was playing. "I like to never got a driver's permit," he says. "I had an awful time there. I think I made six or seven trials." The Clintwood cop, Dewey Buck Hannon, would patiently take him the rounds of the driving test and then would put the Virginia motor-vehicle codebook before him for the literacy test; and Ramey would say, "Dewey Buck, you know I can't read." Finally, with Dewey Buck's encouragement, he found a solution. He had Joyce sit down with him and read the codebook over and over. She must have read it a hundred times before he had memorized every word. Then he passed his test. But out on the roads he would have to stop at a fork that was cluttered up with road signs and ask his way. People always pointed to the signs first; he would have to explain. The miracle was that with all the rubs and humiliations, Ramey never lost his temper and almost never got a contemptuous answer. He says, "I always tried to be kind in everything, always tried to ask everything in a kind way. I try to express myself before I ask a question."

The climax of Ramey's frustration, and in a way the turning point of his life, came in January of this year. He had worked since July, 1943, as a camouflage spray painter at the Portsmouth Navy Yard. He was earning $1.38 an hour, which, with overtime, came to $114.87 a week. The men, and especially his foreman, liked him. One day the foreman came to him and offered to make him a group leader, at $1.52 an hour. He was taken to the yard headquarters and an application form was put before him. When he said he could not write, a yard official told him he would need at least a fifth-grade education to be able to handle the pencilwork as leader. "I got so mad at myself," Ramey says, "that I could have kicked myself out." In fact, he did just that. He went home to Clintwood, terribly discouraged. Since he was no longer doing essential work, the local draft board took him.

Ramey entered the Army on March 19th. At the induction center in Roanoke, he signed his name, John D. Ramey, on a form. This much he had learned to do. But when he was told to spell his name out in full, he did not know the letters for Danul, as he had always pronounced his middle name, much less Daniel, as he had been christened. Nevertheless, he scribbled something. Later he was given the literacy test; his score was zero. But in the screening tests his innate intelligence showed itself. He was accepted. About the time the inductees were lining up outside to be marched away, he heard his name called. He was taken back into the building to an officer at a desk—"a tall man with a little old bald head," he recalls. The officer's words embarrassed Ramey more than anything else in his life ever had. "At your age," the man sneered, "can't even write your own name!"

This was the sort of raw material that arrived at the Special Training Unit late in March this year, ready—in this case more than ready—to learn to read and write. For the first few days Ramey bunked in white barracks, listened to lectures by platoon sergeants about Army spirit, marched up and down, and took tests. On April 5th he moved to green barracks and was assigned to Unit A, the beginners' class. Not all the men at the S.T.U. go into A. Those who have had a little schooling start out in more advanced groups. Ramey started from scratch.

Ramey was lucky in the teacher he drew. Originally the teachers at the school were all Army men, mostly noncommissioned officers. Later, civilians were taken in, both men and women, at a salary of about two thousand dollars a year. Ramey's teacher, Mrs. Harpel, has had wide experience, both in teaching and in life, and is a wise and charming lady. She is a widow of indefinite age. When pressed to place it within a decade, she says she believes she is "anywhere between sixty and seventy." When congratulated on her wonderful appearance (she looks fifty), she replies, "They all say that. It's because I'm interested." From her youngest days, her mother urged her to become a teacher. "My mother," she says, "had a hard time. She was born in Ireland, but she grew up in England on a farm—they were poor. But she was so eager to learn that a woman of the nobility took an interest in her. This woman taught a class in—I believe it was in some part of the Church. My mother was so anxious to learn that she soon was teaching the other children, helping this woman, and for that she got a little heirloom in the family and I wish I had it now; it's the dearest little black-walnut case, has a little drawer for spools and things, and there's a cushion on top. My oldest sister has

it, don't you know. You can see why my mother wanted me to
be a teacher." It was only natural that after Mrs. Harpel got
through a Sisters' school and high school in Detroit, she went
to the Detroit Training School, a school for teachers. After
that, she went to Wayne University for a year. Her teaching
experiences include everything from a two-room, two-teacher
primary school in Detroit to an adult-education course in civics
in Cleveland. She has taken a course in short-story writing
at the University of Chicago and worked in a hardware store,
and she even took up the study of law and passed the Ohio
bar exams because "the stories in the book of cases were so
exciting."

The classes at the S.T.U. are small; they range from six or
eight in the beginning to twenty toward the end. Ramey found
himself, on his first day, with a group of seven other total illiterates, sitting in a small classroom fitted out with long, backless
benches, narrow tables, and a blackboard across the front wall.
Mrs. Harpel had been waiting for them. After a brief intro-
ductory speech, in which she at once established herself as a
nice, motherly grab bag full of anecdotes, she started in with
the alphabet. She wrote the letters on the board, told the soldiers the names of the letters, and then gave their sounds. Since
one of the tenets of the school is that reading and writing
should be integrated all the way, she had the men write the
letters after her, then went around to check on the various
shapes they had drawn. Since another S.T.U. rule is, in the
jargon of the teachers' manuals, to "make use of the concepts
which as adults the trainees can be assumed to have brought
into the classroom already developed in good measure," she
often used the letters as heavily stressed initials of words with
which they had lately become very familiar: "This is 'S.' The
sound is '*sss*.' 'S' is for '*ss*ergeant.'" From day to day, she went
quite fast, not stopping to make sure that every letter was
learned by every man; she hoped to achieve that gradually, by

repetition. If one man could not answer a question, she went quickly to another, operating on the manual's theory that pausing over one man's forgetfulness only produces a disabling emotional tension in him, and on her own that life is too short to hurt anybody's feelings. Very soon she began giving the men simple words, teaching them to think of the sound of the initial consonant, plus the vowel, plus the following sound that completed the word. She chose words that are spelled the way they sound, like "dad," "tag," "job," "top," and "net." She told stories to go with some words and drew pictures to illustrate others. Toward the end of the three weeks the men spent in Unit A, she began giving more complicated words, with two consonants at the beginning. She taught the reading of these words by what the school calls "phonic analysis." She taught "brake" as "b-rake." By the end of the three weeks she had given Ramey and his classmates about three hundred simple words, most of which would be useful in the "phonic analysis" of the more complicated words they were soon to learn.

Meanwhile, Ramey was exposed to other facets of Army life. His classes began at seven-thirty-five each morning and, with a ten-minute break every hour, lasted until lunchtime. Chow was heavy, monotonous, and good. In the afternoon, the men drilled. The evenings were free. Most of the time Ramey just sat in the barracks and talked or sang with his friend Red Rutherford, whom he had met at the induction center. One night, when they had nearly finished Unit A, they sang a song called "Precious Memory," which made Ramey homesick:

> Precious memory, how it lingers,
> How it ever fills my flitting soul!
> In the stillness of my homelife . . .

Ramey decided then and there to write a letter to his wife. He was far from equipped to do so, but Mrs. Harpel had given

him confidence and he decided to try. Here is the first letter of
his whole life:

Arpil 15 1945
Pul John Ramey
Co B STU
33914278

Joyce I got last 5⁰⁰ Dile you sene me lat night. Joyce I am Fine
and hope you R the cam. Yousse gott $22.00 Mond and the
take $7.20 off an me and $7.50 Fore Bond Joyce lat oline lase
me $12.30 and old the love in my hort. Yall shold whit love
fom

Pul John Ramey
Co B STU
33914278

The handwriting was jagged. The letters were formed laboriously and often had breaks between them. The thought
was practical. Joyce undoubtedly knew that he meant he had
received five dollars from her the night before, that he was fine
and hoped she was the same, that she would get twenty-two
dollars a month (for her allotment) and they were taking $7.20
"off'n" him (for insurance) and $7.50 for bonds, and that this
left him only $12.30 (his arithmetic, despite her tutelage, was
off by one dollar), and that he sent all the love in his heart. The
final reproach, "You all should write," was a proud invitation
from a writing man to correspond. In later letters the serial
number after his signature was replaced by amorous crosses
and circles, the secret of which he learned not from Mrs. Harpel but from another student.

On April 18th, Ramey entered Unit 1, after having passed
an informal test given by Mrs. Harpel. In Unit 1, he be-

gan, for the first time, to read a book—*Technical Manual 21–500,* which jugheads know as "Private Pete." On the first page, at the top, is printed, "This is Chapter 1." Below, under a full-length drawing of an impossibly handsome soldier, are the words "A Soldier—Private Pete." The second page has a picture of men on parade with rifles slung, and under it is the sentence "The soldiers march." Within a surprisingly few days, Mrs. Harpel had her class, now twelve men, on Chapter 2. There, aided by pictures to illustrate nearly every sentence, they read, "A soldier keeps his things in order in the barracks. There is a place for everything. He keeps everything in the right place. Every soldier has a place for his things in the barracks. Pete's locker is near his bed. The soldier blows the bugle in the morning. The bugle call wakes the soldiers. Soldiers must get up when they hear the bugle call. Soldiers wash in the morning. They also take showers. Soldiers shave in the morning. Private Pete gets dressed. He puts on his socks. He puts on his shoes. He puts on his shirt. He puts on his trousers. He puts on his tie. He puts on his cap. Here is Private Pete in his uniform." And the final picture shows him fully clothed and surrounded by a dazzling light much like the one which enveloped the Wizard of Oz.

Mrs. Harpel's technique in Unit 1, and throughout the course, was about the same. Before each lesson in "Private Pete," she would survey the day's text and note down the unfamiliar and difficult words. These she would give the men by phonic analysis. Gradually, the words got more complicated. "She kept raising the words," Ramey says. To keep the earlier words fresh in their minds, she constantly reviewed, both by combining old words with new ones and by flashing cards with the old words stenciled on them. All the time she drew on her years of experience to illustrate the words. One of the things the school stresses is "word concept," which means that a man should understand a word when he sees it and

not just read the sound without thought for the meaning.
The Army judiciously mixes modern ideas—word concept,
filmstrips, flash cards, and phonic analysis—with the tried
and true method of the little red schoolhouse. Mrs. Harpel's
storytelling helped build "word concept." Unlike most of the
teachers, who draw on the movies, radio, and big-league
baseball for examples, "traveling," as the manuals say, "from
the known to the unknown," Mrs. Harpel kept telling
Ramey's class homely parables and episodes from her own
life.

Mrs. Harpel's classes never dragged. One day she began by
saying, "Good morning, boys—or men, I should say. I know
you still like to be called boys."

She read the roll. Then she asked, "Well, how do you feel
this morning?"

A chorus rose: "Oh, we feel great . . . rugged . . . O.K. . . ."

She said, "Let us put our pencils down. Sit up like soldiers.
We are going to review our sounds and combinations of sounds
this morning." She wrote the letter "E" on the board. "May I
have an example of the short sound, please?"

"'Exercise'!" said Ramey.

"'Fret,'" Mrs. Harpel said. "Let's take 'fret.' A baby frets.
What is the difference between 'to fret' and 'to worry'? A person must think to worry. Babies don't think much, do they? I
saw a baby just a month old last night, a healthful codger, but
it was fretting. I went up and talked to it calmly and that little
rascal just listened to me. We can't tell what they're thinking,
can we? I wonder how we spell 'split'?"

"S-l-i-t!" one of the men said.

"That's right," Mrs. Harpel said, not wishing to hurt anyone's feelings. "That's right, s-p-l-i-t. Now, here's a word." And
she wrote "sin" on the blackboard. "That's a little word we do
not like, but sometimes we must say it anyway. Look! We can
make it nice just by putting a letter in right here." She trans-

formed "SIN" into "SPIN." "What does that mean, Davis?" she asked.

Davis said, "Well, it's like spinning wool."

"That's right! They used to spin wool by hand. Do they now, Lam?"

Lam said, "I never have been to a cotton mill. I been down around Chatham, where they raise a little cotton, but I never did get in a mill."

"Is that Virginia?" Mrs. Harpel asked. "Seems to me a lot of my boys are from Virginia. Stand up, you Virginians."

Seven of the twelve men stood.

"My, what a fine lot of men. How tall are you, Lam?"

"Five foot ten, Ma'am."

"How tall are you, Rutherford?"

"Five foot eleven."

"How tall are you, Ramey?"

"Five foot six and a quarter inches."

"Well, you didn't happen to grow. How tall are you, Pearsall?"

"I don't know, Ma'am."

"You ought to know that. You go over and stand against the measuring post," she said, pointing at one of the uprights of the rear wall, a two-by-four that had about thirty pencil marks on it, where other men had already been measured. "Who will volunteer to measure Pearsall?" Mrs. Harpel asked.

Smith, who was not a Virginian, put his hand up. He marked Pearsall's height on the beam, then measured it with a ruler. "Five foot ten, exact," he announced.

Mrs. Harpel said, "How in the world did we get this far when we started with the word 'spin'? That's the way the mind works; it gets from one thing to another. I'm going to give you a long word. It's the study of the mind. I'm going to write it down." She wrote "PSYCHOLOGY." She had several of the men pronounce it.

"Now," she said, "here's another little word. 'Ore.' What is the difference between ore and iron, Ramey? Stand up. Let's see how tall you are."

"It's like mining," Ramey said. "Ore's got to be taken from under the ground and it's brought out and as it comes to the mill it's washed and the dirt is washed from the ore stone, and the stone is run into the furnaces. The ore comes out of the stone, out of the shale, and the shale goes out; it's a waste. The ore is poured into forms and makes pig iron. The form is a small steel frame; it's got a sand pack on the inside of it, has some kind of chemical into it that'll make it bind and stick together, otherwise to hold the pig iron in the forms till it cools off."

Mrs. Harpel said, "Oh, that's very interesting! I want you to teach me a little more, Ramey."

"Well," he said, "it gets smaller when it cools. Any kind of metal expands when it's hot. You take sheet steel for a ship— you have to allow for expansion where you're welding; if you don't she'll buckle."

"Will you tell me how they weld this sheet metal?"

"Which one you want, acetylene or electric?"

Mrs. Harpel dodged that one nicely. "What did you do before you came here, Ramey?" she asked.

"Spray-painted," he said. "Camouflage in a shipyard."

"We were talking about ore. That's a big jump to welding, isn't it? Well, that's how the human mind moves from place to place." She pointed a finger at "PSYCHOLOGY."

Then she said, "I'm going to tell you a story I know about ore. I went to an auction store one day and I saw a lamp and this lamp was all metal from the base right to the top, so it must have come from ore. A woman, she was standing next to me, she said, 'That's a valuable thing, that's a Chinese incense burner; it's not supposed to be a lamp.' It was taller than I am. I got interested because I like antiques. I said to this woman, who was a stranger to me, by the way, 'How much do you think it's worth?' She called this clerk over and the clerk said, 'Ten dollars.' I was so anxious to get such a rare thing—what does 'rare' mean?—that I said I'd take it. Well, I got interested and I got some books and I studied up on it. The work is called cloisonné. Some of you might get interested in cloisonné some-day. Say 'cloisonné.' . . . Here is how they make it. They take little wires and fasten them on the incense burner in the form of pictures; they draw people and faces with the wires, and the book says they fuse the wires on the metal. On my incense burner there are little saints with halos. Halos must be hard to draw with wire because they have to be a perfect circle. Some-thing irregular would be easier. What is something irregular?"

"A flower," one of the men said. "Even in nature you get flowers so they grow irregular."

"Well, they get everything just right with these little wires, even the eyes. What would happen if they got the pupils of the eyes wrong? Lam, what would happen?"

Lam said, "The saints might be cross-eyed."

"That's right! Well, they fill in between the wires with this beautiful enamel. The faces are white, the clothes are Chinese red and turquoise blue. Saints usually have blue eyes; that's the color of the beautiful sky. The whole incense burner is copper. Sometimes I think it's brass, because in places it looks like a brass penny." She hesitated. "Do you *really* want me to talk about my lamp, men?" she asked.

The men shouted together, "Yes!"

"Well, these human figures on it are climbing ladders . . ." And she told many more details about her incense burner. Finally a bell rang, marking the end of the first period. "Oh, dear," Mrs. Harpel said. "Men! Don't forget 'ore.' O-r-e. Look at it! Don't forget it! Class excused."

I doubt that the men who were there will ever forget the shape of that small word.

Ramey was not the most brilliant pupil Mrs. Harpel had had, but before he passed into Unit 2, she had begun to take special notice of him. There were several reasons. For one thing, he had had wider experience than some of the men, and could tell an illustrative story himself if he had to. For another, he was more serious-minded than some, and each evening he read the work for the next day, so that he would have the jump, for self-esteem was apparently important to him. He says that he will always remember the word "determination" and the night he came across it. "Straight I say that word, I don't have to spell it out—I can see it," he told me. Long words like that, especially if they are meaningful, are easier for the men than the everyday small change of literacy—"am," "they," "are," "but"—and Ramey still has to think harder about those small words than he does about "determination." Ramey stuck to his work better than some, and, perhaps on the theory that what won't hurt anybody won't help anybody, did not even go to the enlisted men's dances on Wednesday nights. He was also assisted in his progress by a relatively good memory. He has an excellent memory for names. When he is asked about his two gold teeth, which he acquired in Detroit twelve years ago, he promptly says, "I remember the old doc who put them in— Whittaker, Dr. Whittaker, George A. Whittaker. I remember him well. I broke one of my teeth out and the other one was rotten; it got a little speck in it and I never did think much about filling teeth—I thought I'd just have it ground and crowned. Doc Whittaker, he didn't have much mercy on mankind at all, it didn't seem like. He wouldn't let you shut your mouth or swush your mouth out; he'd just want to get through. Never will forget him. George A. Whittaker."

Ramey moved into Unit 2, still under Mrs. Harpel, on May 2nd. At the end of each unit, the men take an examination. In the test before going to Unit 2, Ramey scored thirty-two out of a possible thirty-five points. "Private Pete" appears in Unit 2, which is mostly concerned with military drill. "Integration" is one of the catchwords of the Special Training Unit; reading is integrated with writing, and the students never do one without the other; arithmetic, which students begin in Unit 2, is integrated with both, for the problems are written out, and the students must read the problems, solve them, and write the answers in words and numbers; and the reading matter provided them is all integrated with Army life. So, in Unit 2, Ramey read all about drill, and learned something, too, about military courtesy. On page 59 of "Private Pete," he read, "The captain came to our drill field on Saturday. Our sergeant gave the command, '1. SQUAD, 2. HALT!' Then we stood at attention while the sergeant saluted the captain. We did not move or talk." Ramey and his companions were still drilling every afternoon. One of the greatest handicaps for most illiterates is lack of confidence. The drill at S.T.U. eventually gives them confidence, for after graduation, when they move on to another camp for ordinary basic training, they find they are smarter soldiers than some men who have been to college. The school gives the men a new and exciting sense that perhaps they are not so dumb after all. In class they compete with fellow-illiterates; everybody is in the same boat. One man in the Pennsylvania S.T.U. recently said, "I thought I was the dumbest man in Virginia until I came here and saw all my friends and neighbors." The camp life also gives the men a group spirit. Ramey wrote me a letter a while ago in which he said, "Drill make you keep your mind on what you are doing it make you think it keep you on the alert. I like to drill whith other men."

After he had been in Unit 2 a week, Ramey wrote his second letter to Joyce. His progress was certainly measurable. This time the letters were much better formed and much bolder, and the breaks between letters were less frequent. He wrote:

May 9, 1945

My love I will write yow a fuile line to late you yeare forme
me Joyce have yow got your Mone and the Boond Joyce i have
35 day to stare yere then i will Be coming home sune i maeste
you all vere muche Till the baby bihaves and Be good BaBy
ontal i come home, Joyce how are they gating a lorne out home
i gate a lettre frome home May 4 and toled me how they wirre
at home Joyce you ort to see me in my uniforme it looke good
on me i hope you will sune Joyce write me sune your love
John Ramey.

xxxxxxxx

xxxxxxxx

oooooooo

oooooooo

The next day, Ramey wrote his father-in-law a short postcard, and two days later he wrote his wife another letter. Both
were in the same vein, the same hand, the same grammar, and
at times the same words as the earlier letter, except on the
postcard Ramey said, "Kinle write me a fiver good Pop." Evidently the $13.30 Ramey got from the Army after deductions
was not enough. Ramey had his father-in-law much in mind
during his stay at the school. The two had been on excellent
terms ever since Mr. McFall's flare-up about John's walking
home with Joyce that first night. Ramey now has great admiration for his father-in-law. "Better man never did breathe, to
my notion," Ramey says. "Now, some other people may have
their minds made up different; otherwise he's liked by everybody in that country. He preaches more funerals than any man
I ever guess I saw. He's always preaching a funeral—every
week, sometimes a couple. They send for him from every-
where; everybody knows him from a hundred miles square,
everyone picks him for their funerals. It's because he always do
come out pretty plain, says what he feels, hit or miss, hurt or

feel good." On the day Ramey graduated, with a score of thirty-one out of a possible thirty-five, from Unit 2 to Unit 3, he wrote his father-in-law, with a skimpy but nevertheless respectful number of kisses and hugs at the bottom of the page, as follows:

May 23, 1945

Dare Pop I am geting long fine and hope you are geting long fine at home Pop I have time to write you a fule lines to lite you here fom me I like to get litter forme home you write me sune and lite me no how you all are at home now I get might lonesome up here Pop I hope you are haveing good meatings do that now how are you geting long whith your mine now are you mining it now you sed you had not been mining it Pop do not forget to Pare for me Pop I pare for you I will stay your friend love to all of them left at home, John Ramey

xxxx
oooo

Units 3 and 4 seemed to go fairly fast. Ramey had reached his "plateau," the point at which his rapid accumulation of words stopped and he leveled off to a brief period of forgetfulness and despair, in Unit 2; once he was past that, he was in good shape. Most men reach their plateau in Unit 3. In Unit 3, Ramey and "Private Pete" took up the question of money, which Private Ramey had been discussing in longhand since his first letter. He read about how Private Pete drew his pay and about the sensible things he did with it. There is a high moral tone about *Technical Manual 21–500,* and at times even Mrs. Harpel gets tired of such a goody-goody soldier as Private Pete, who never sees the inside of a guardhouse. In Unit 3 arithmetic, Ramey took up division. In Unit 4, he read about world affairs, about citizenship and freedom and the reasons for the war, about the qualities of a good soldier, about living with other people under the Golden Rule, about the United Nations and global war, about George Washington and Tom Paine.

While he was in Unit 3, Ramey went to Harrisburg with Red Rutherford one day. Red wanted to walk up and down the streets and find a girl or two, but Ramey wanted to drop in at the U.S.O. There was something he had heard about that he wanted to try. He went to a table, picked up a magazine, and sat down, like any other man, to read it. He was so excited that he can't remember what magazine it was; he thinks it may have been *Look,* or perhaps *Collier's.* Later, on the street, he bought a newspaper. He has done that several times since, but he doesn't like papers. "I don't know whether it's the words or the way it's printed up or what those countries are always doing in there," he says. "Don't know what it is. Seem like I can't hardly stand to read it."

During Unit 4, Ramey began "remedial work," which is actually no more than a review. The Army wisely gives the men a second teacher for remedial work; this serves as a check on any weaknesses of the first teacher, and is an attempt to make certain that all gaps are filled. Ramey's teacher for remedial was Dorothy Over, the pretty young wife of a soldier who fought across Europe with the Third Armored Division. Her background for this job was teaching home economics in a junior high school in Harrisburg. Mrs. Harpel carried on with new material in the mornings and Mrs. Over's remedial class took the place of two hours' drill in the afternoons. Mrs. Over says, "The only way to make people remember is repeat, repeat, repeat, and then sometimes repeat." Roughly, that describes remedial. One day, Mrs. Over started class by asking, "Can you tell me the words we had yesterday?"

"Bet I can tell you every one of them," Ramey said. "'Loyal'—you had that yesterday."

Mrs. Over didn't wait for him to finish. She picked up a

piece of chalk and wrote on the blackboard, saying the words as she wrote them: "'Alert,' 'determination,' 'surprise,' 'praise,' 'loyal'—here it is, Ramey, that's for you—'faith,' 'teamwork,' 'know,' 'defend,' 'training,' 'production,' 'property,' 'route,' 'rugged,' 'protect,' 'strong.'"

For fifty minutes she drilled the class on those sixteen words. She had each man read them. She analyzed them. She erased them and had the men write them. She repeated, repeated, repeated, until the men had learned.

At last, on June 14th, Ramey came to his final examination. This he passed as he had his previous tests, with honor. Then he was indoctrinated for graduation exercises. The Pennsylvania Special Training Unit is very thoughtful about the morale of its men. Each Wednesday night a fresh class of literate men is marched to the gymnasium, seated in a triangular formation in the presence of guests, many of them proud families, and given a graduation address by Colonel Searls, the commanding officer. A West Point commencement has no more gravity and dignity. It would be easy for Colonel Searls to grind out the same speech week after week, but he takes pride in his graduations and makes a new speech every time. One week he used the analogy of seeds planted in the ground, from which fine flowers and huge trees would grow if proper care was taken; another week he used the laying of a keel, from which a Liberty ship or a battleship might rise if proper workmanship went into it; another week he used the digging of foundations. On each occasion he seems to make the men feel that they are educated, ambitious, and equal to other men in the land. After Colonel Searls' address, the men step forward, salute, receive a diploma, shake hands, salute again, and move on. Ramey's diploma says, "This is to certify that Private John Daniel Ramey has graduated from the Special Training Unit, 3384th Service Unit." It is signed by Colonel Searls and by the master sergeant, W. Nace. At the bottom is a gold seal, embossed with incontrovertible words: "u.s. army—official."

The noncoms of the cadre are all in favor of morale, but they think that you can have too much of a good thing. Accordingly, their instructions for the graduation exercises are concerned not with the dignity but with the abasement of man. The process of saluting, receiving the diploma, handshaking, and saluting again is hard for some of the men to remember. An indoctrinating sergeant roared at a platoon of Ramey's class, "Any you jugheads can't keep that straight, you're going to come over here after graduation, take a toothbrush, a butt can, and a cake of soap, and brush down that entire barracks staircase! You hear that, you fatheads?" Another cadre sergeant explained to me later, "He said that just so they won't think they're a bunch of Princeton men or something."

On that last day, the morning before his graduation, I asked Ramey for a sample of his handwriting. What he wrote might disappoint a pedagogue; certain habits of nearly three decades of humble grammar could not possibly have been erased in ten weeks, and some of his spellings and punctuation needed further drill. Nevertheless, Ramey had come a wonderfully long way from his first letter, just two months before. And from another viewpoint—that of human hope and the satisfaction still to be had from a life already half spent in the uneasy shadows of illiteracy—the sample was good, very good. Here is what he wrote:

14 June 1945

the United States of America
John D. Ramey

I come in the Army the date of 19 day of March as a civilian. I had no education but now this is the first time that I have

had in my life to get a education and I am glad to be in the
Army to get a little education. I can tell what the Army have
did for me. As a civilian I could not read anything and it made
it hard for me to get a beter job. After the war I can get a job
as lead man at the Place I Work befor. I want to learn some
more. I would not take all the Furloughs in the Army for
What I learned at STU. I tell you when they let me out of this
Army they can take away my Gun also my Uniform but they
wont ever take away how to read and write.

Father Walter P. Morse

The first time I saw Father Walter P. Morse, he was walking up the path of his mission compound in the town of Ichang, reading my calling card over and over, out loud. I had gone there to talk with him, and his gateman had run out into the streets to find him. He made quite a sight as he came swinging up the path. He is of medium height, and his natural roundness of figure was reinforced, I supposed, by a number of layers of clothing, for the late afternoon was chilly. The outermost layer of his outfit was a humble black cotton Chinese coolie gown. A white woolen skullcap rode the top of his head with a jauntiness that was as much in contrast to his coolie coat in mood as the cap was in color. His beard was at least nine inches long, full, virile, cut off square, and all glossy from washings and combings which, I later decided, were the business of a fastidious, rather than a vain, man. He had a mustache, too, which was evenly clipped to within a quarter of an inch of his upper lip. He was reading my card through horn-rimmed glasses balanced on the end of his nose. As he came closer and looked up, I saw a face of benignity, gentleness, humor, and calmness, with round cheeks, a large nose, and tremendous blue eyes; a face flushed a bit by his haste and, in

"The Happy, Happy Beggar," *The New Yorker*, May 11, 1946.

any case, somewhat reddened by a life spent mostly in the open air. "Hello! Hello!" he said, as if we were old friends long parted, though in fact he had never seen me before. I had just arrived, for a longish stay, in Ichang—which is at the dead center of China, near the mouth of the Yangtze Gorges, the point of extreme penetration of Japanese forces during the war—and I had inquired of a few people whether there were any foreigners in town. I had been told then about Father Walter, whom everyone seemed to know, and I had been directed to the Episcopal Mission compound. "Come in to my place," he said. "I'm sorry it's such a poor hovel." And he read the card out loud again. "Well, well, well," he said. "It's nice to have a visitor."

He turned off the main path, which led up to some pretentious-looking buildings at the top of the compound hill, onto a side path. At the junction, there was a sign, neatly lettered in Chinese and English. The English legend said, "To Father Walter P. Morse's Residence." The building thus indicated, though not a hovel, was only a tiny house. Long ago it had been painted white. Beside the path were a number of bamboo trees. The front door was locked, so Father Walter led me around to the back door. On the way we passed a very short and very cheerful-looking Chinese workman. Seeing me, he said to Father Walter, in Chinese, "A guest!" Father Walter answered, "A guest!" We went inside, through a tiny back hallway—evidently used as a combination entrance, washroom, laundry, kitchen, pantry, and storeroom—to the room which served as Father Walter's living and sleeping quarters. This contained a round table, a straight-backed davenport, a couple of chairs, a charcoal brazier, two small end tables, an old upright piano, an iron bedstead, a small piece of furniture that had apparently been a child's dressing table and that now had a few books on it, and a square table, against one wall, for a desk. Over the piano there were two pictures of Christ and one

of the Virgin Mary. On the wall above the desk a large square
of Chinese reed matting had been hung, and to the matting
were pinned, in pyramidal symmetry, a Chinese calendar, a
photograph of the Boston Common, and pictures of pheasants,
quail, thrushes, and wrens cut from magazines and pasted on
squares of corrugated cardboard. There was a crucifix on the
desk. The room looked very plain and yet it had an air of
comfort and warmth. "Well, well, well," Father Walter said.
He motioned me to the davenport and sat in one of the chairs.
As he settled himself, he lifted his beard away from his chest,
then patted it down again. "Tell me about yourself," he said.
Then, quickly, he added, "I'm sorry I have nothing to set before you."

We talked about one thing and another, and gradually, dif-
fidently, he told me about his work. He had a way of rolling
his eyes up and half-closing them in midsentence, so that only
slits of white showed at moments of emphasis or punctuation.
Dusk fell as we talked, and Father Walter lit a candle. In the
dim light his bearded face was deep-lined, broad, and powerful—too round for an El Greco, too healthy for a Hogarth,
but somewhere between the two. He talked of the Chinese, of
the war, of mankind. From the very first, I had the impression
that he was a man of extraordinary tranquillity. As I came to
know him better, that evening and later on, I was obliged to
decide that although he was a strange man in some respects,
he was the happiest adult I had ever known. I thought, too, he
realized how lucky he was. Once he said, after a long silence
and apropos of nothing that had preceded, almost as if talking
to himself, "Oh, yes, I'm a happy, happy man." I have wondered many times since I left Ichang about the basis of Father
Walter's happiness; I have gone back over what I know about
him, and I'm still not sure what his secret is.

Walter Morse was born fifty-four years ago in Milwaukee. His father was a coal dealer, a prosperous and worldly man. His mother was a strong, active, religious woman, and for her Walter developed an attachment which has evidently affected his whole life. "Mother was church," he told me once. "She and I went to services together. My father wasn't much of anything in a religious way; he wasn't baptized until just before he died." Mrs. Morse was a generator of good works, and she had the energy always to be "keeping something going." From her example, Walter got his compulsion to help others. His father had ambitions for him which did not suit him, but he tried hard to grow up in his father's likeness, because that was what his mother seemed to want. He attended high school in Milwaukee and was graduated from Racine College, in Racine, Wisconsin. He worked for three miserable years in a bank in Milwaukee. Then, for the first time, he broke away from home; he went to New York and took a job in a brokerage firm, Orvis Brothers. He began by running the stock board in the customers' room and later became a clerk. Far from getting a few pegs up on a fortune, he just managed to scrimp along. "I learned poverty in Wall Street," he told me. The first year, he earned five dollars a week, the second he earned six. All through his time on the edge of the moneypots of lower and the fleshpots of upper Manhattan, he remained a devout, abstemious, rigid young man.

In 1917, when he was twenty-five, he decided to become a religious. He underwent, he says, no emotional crisis that led him to take monastic orders, unless, perhaps, it was the separation from his mother. "It was just like an amateur becoming a professional," he says. He made up his mind to be a Cowley Father—a member, that is, of the Society of Mission Priests of St. John the Evangelist. The order, which is devoted to missionary work, was founded under the Church of England in 1865, in a suburb of Oxford called Cowley. An Episcopal branch of the Society was formed in the United States seventy-three years ago, with headquarters in Boston. Cowley Fathers are rare: there are only twenty-five in America and only about a hundred the world over. Joining the order was quite a step for a man of twenty-five, for he was obliged to take irrevocable vows of poverty, chastity, and obedience. This meant that he could never again call anything his own except the clothes on his back, that he could never indulge in venery, and that for the rest of his life he must adhere to the laws of the Society and the precepts of the Bible. There is no such thing as resigning from the Society of St. John the Evangelist: once a Cowley Father, always one, until death. Walter's parents were not especially upset when he announced his intention of taking orders; his father, he says, "had always been afraid I would go that way." The Society requires a novitiate period and does not accept members as full Fathers until they have reached their thirtieth year. When the United States entered the First World War, Walter was given leave of absence from the Society and for a year he served in the Army. He was a noncombatant and did not go overseas. After the war he attended Nashotah Seminary, near Milwaukee, and when he was thirty he became a Father.

Soon afterward, Father Walter was sent to his first missionary post, which was in Korea. He spent ten years there. "I thrive on solitude," he told me one Sunday afternoon when I asked if he wasn't lonely in Ichang. "In Korea there were times when I was by myself for days and there were stretches when I didn't hear a voice speak English for six months on end." In Korea, Father Walter learned to read and talk Chinese. Then he spent five years in Japan. In 1937, when the war in China began, he went to Shanghai to help organize shelter, food, and protection for Chinese who had been made homeless by the

HERSEY AND FATHER MORSE

"After all, you know, I'm a professional beggar."

fighting there. Refugee aid got fairly well organized in Shanghai, so, when the Japs showed signs of starting a drive inland,
Father Walter made his way out through their lines and went
by boat up the Yangtze ahead of the invaders to the city of
Wuhu, about two hundred and fifty miles from Shanghai. He
stayed there while the Japanese stormed the city, and then he
rounded up as many as he could of the homeless and provided
relief for them. Then he broke through the Japanese lines
again and moved upriver to Hankow, where once more he
received the Japanese and succored the population.

When, later, he slipped out of Hankow, he found that traveling farther inland by boat on the Yangtze was impossible, so,
with a timorous Chinese guide, he started to walk a hundred
and twenty-five miles overland to the cotton center of Shasi.
All the way, the Chinese guide warned Father Walter of perils
ahead, but such a jolly apparition as Father Walter seemed to
soften the hearts of the Chinese thieves and murderers who
were roaming the panic-stricken countryside. At a ferry station
on a lake, the guide learned that frequently travelers using the
ferry were robbed and killed; he refused at first to go aboard
the ferry. But Father Walter calmed him, and the pair crossed
the water unmolested. As they got near Shasi, they approached
a town notorious for its bandits. The guide again protested,
but Father Walter, magnificent in his beard, ambled into town
and the bandits received him as an honored guest. "Do you
want to look at my things?" Father Walter asked the head
bandit. "I have some very nice things." He had, as a matter of
fact, only a bundle of clothes, a little cutlery, some toilet articles, and a watch and a pen. He had no money; people gave
him food along the way. "Oh, we wouldn't touch *your* things,"
the head bandit said. The next day the bandits sent Father
Walter and the quaking guide on their way, on horseback.
"You'd never find people so helpful in Korea or Japan," Father
Walter told me.

Father Walter went by boat from Shasi to Ichang, and there he settled down in the Episcopal Mission compound to wait for the Japanese. The Episcopal Mission was in the strong and worthy hands of another American, a Deaconess Riebe. Father Walter instructed her in all the tricks of handling relief work during the investment of a city, for by now he was a veteran. In this instance, as it turned out, he had plenty of time to prepare; it took the Japanese nearly a year to get into Ichang. In the interval, Father Walter and Deaconess Riebe laid in a big stock of rice. Finally, the Japanese attacked. The assault lasted five days, during which the city was reduced from a Yangtze transshipment port of a hundred and ten thousand people to a burned-out collection of shattered houses and a population of no more than fifteen thousand, five thousand of whom sought asylum in the five-acre Episcopal Mission compound. It was summer, and they slept on the ground. Father Walter and Deaconess Riebe cooked for them and fed them. In the compound, there was, fortunately, an excellent well that supplied enough water for all. And after the battle was over, the Chinese were able to sneak out of the compound and pick up odds and ends of food and pieces of matting to build some sort of shelter.

Father Walter and Deaconess Riebe entertained their five thousand guests for the next two years. For all of that time, one of the pair was always on duty at the gate of the compound. As Father Walter stood guard, he read Dickens; he had found a complete set in the Custom House library, and he read every word of it at least once. Whenever Japanese soldiers tried to come through the gate, he rebuked them with dignity and just the right amount of heat. They always went away. Sometimes, though, they would climb the wall at some distance from the gate. Father Walter, who despite his girth was in excellent physical shape, always ran down the trespassers, took them by the collar and persuaded them, with Christian firmness and in their own language, which he had learned during his stay in their fatherland, to climb out of the compound right where they had come over the wall. The day after Pearl Harbor, the Japanese rounded up all the other foreigners in town—about thirty of them, mostly British working for trading firms, and Belgian and French Catholic missionaries—and interned them on the grounds of an old Lutheran mission in town. Father Walter and Deaconess Riebe, however, told the Japanese commandant that they intended to stay on in their compound to take care of the refugees. The commandant acquiesced.

Five months later, the Japanese said that an exchange of Japanese and American civilian prisoners was being arranged and that they were prepared to send Father Walter and Deaconess Riebe out of China; leaving was "voluntary." Father Walter and Deaconess Riebe thanked the Japanese but said they thought they'd stay on in Ichang, where they were needed. A few days afterward, the Japanese came back and said that the exchange was now a "military measure" and that the two were to prepare at once to go down the river and get aboard the *Gripsholm,* the repatriation ship. Father Walter hated to go, but in a way the order to depart was a relief. Life had developed a sameness; he was getting well into his second round of the complete works of Dickens.

Father Walter left Ichang in May, 1942. He had then spent, altogether, nearly five years in China doing refugee relief work. He had come to like the Chinese better than any other people he had ever known, better even than his own. A poor man, he had lived at close quarters with poor Chinese, and he had learned what the Chinese needed most. It was medical care. War was, he knew, ephemeral. Disease was most certainly not. In his five years in China, he had seen thousands of horrible tropical ulcers (the kind that is so common in China, years old, inches in diameter, so deep that bone shows at the core); he had seen the sores of scabies and syphilis, scalps whitened with fungus infections, noses and cheeks half eaten with leprosy. In the compound at Ichang, he had felt foreheads scorched by typhoid, typhus, cholera, dysentery, diphtheria, malaria, small-pox, scarlet fever, undulant fever, pneumonia, and fevers for which he did not even know the names. On the way home on the *Gripsholm,* Father Walter, now fifty years old, conceived a noble and rather fantastic idea.

Upon arriving in the States, Father Walter went to Boston. For a few months, dressed in the cassock of his order, he lectured before women's clubs, library associations, town meetings, and school assemblies. Each group paid him a small fee. He hoarded this money. This thriftiness was compatible with his vow of poverty because the money, in his eyes, did not belong to him. He was delighted with America. He thought that the war had made most Americans better people. "It always used to be very hard going around looking so strange," he said to me one day. "But during the war the whole attitude was changed. It was actually pleasant. People really tried to be nice." When he had saved more than a thousand dollars, he asked his acquaintances what they thought was the best hospital in Boston. They recommended the Massachusetts General. Like most hospitals during the war, it was desperately short of help and was issuing appeals for volunteers. He went around and offered his services as an orderly. Father Walter did not particularly like the atmosphere at the hospital. "That's just about the snootiest place, I should think, in the country," he remarked. The personnel interviewer who talked to him said, "We'll let you know." Some time later the hospital sent word, in a roundabout way, that it was terribly sorry but Father Walter's appearance—the beard and cassock—was "too uncouth." He went to the Boston City Hospital, a predominantly

Irish Roman Catholic institution, and there he found the
people more to his liking. He talked awhile with a nurse in the
Voluntary Employment Bureau. She took him to Dr. James W.
Manary, the head of the whole hospital. Dr. Manary laughed
about the Massachusetts General. Then Father Walter told Dr.
Manary what he wanted to do. He said he would like to be an
orderly, so that in time he could learn all there was to know
about every ailment that a layman could relieve without doing
a patient any injury. Then he would return to China and heal
whomever he could among the poor. Dr. Manary said that he
would not think of letting Father Walter waste his time as an
orderly. Father Walter would be given the freedom of the hospital to study. Dr. Manary told him to drop in any day and
every day, visit any department he wished, ask any doctor any
question he wanted, use any book he needed, and learn whatever else he could by acting as an assistant to a nurse. For six
months, Father Walter went to Boston City Hospital every day
except Sunday. He learned a lot.

In the summer of 1943, the State Department announced
that a few missionaries would be allowed to enter Free China.
Father Walter asked permission to go and hurried to New
York to equip himself. First, he studied the catalogues of all
the big drug concerns in the city to find out which specialized
in what medicines. Then he began calling at their offices. He
would simply go in cold, present himself to the receptionist,
tell her what he was after, and ask to see the president of the
company. In most cases the receptionist, out of either amaze-
ment or sympathy, called the president and Father Walter was
ushered in. "After the presidents took one look at me," he told
me, "I didn't have to do much explaining. I look so strange
they knew something was in the wind. I would just say, 'I'm
going out to China to heal people. I want some of those nice
medicines of yours. I want you to give them to me free.'" Almost all the presidents—or vice-presidents, in some cases—

came through handsomely. He went to Lederle, Winthrop, Squibb, Upjohn, Lilly, Merck, American Pharmaceutical, Parke, Davis, and Schieffelin, and if a company did not give him what he asked for outright, it gave him part and sold him the rest at wholesale prices. He continued until he had used up his thousand dollars. Lederle and Winthrop were especially generous. Dr. F. J. Stockman, a vice-president of Winthrop, slipped Father Walter a five-dollar bill at the end of their interview. "I was so touched," Father Walter recalled. "He was the nicest person." At American Pharmaceutical, Benjamin J. Wallach, the advertising manager, said to him, "You just relax, Mister. You let us make up a little list of things we think you'll need in China, and we'll send the stuff around to you." "And they did," Father Walter said. "They sent me aspirin, cascara, bicarbonate of soda, zinc oxide, boric-acid ointment—a great big five-pound jar of it—oh, all sorts of nice things, just the kind of things I would have overlooked."

Father Walter is quite proud, in a not sinful way, of getting these big, impersonal firms to give him what he needed. "After all, you know," he says, "I'm a professional beggar." He did his soliciting absolutely on his own. The Episcopal hierarchy seemed, in fact, to feel that Father Walter's endeavors were a bit embarrassing and low-toned. One clergyman intimated to him that if he must go begging, it would be more dignified to ask for money and buy medicine with it "in the normal way." "Some persons," Father Walter remarked to me, "have a motto: 'Let's be respectable or die.' I'd rather die."

Before he knew it, Father Walter had in his first-aid kit fifteen hundred pounds of drugs, powders, plasters, bandages, instruments, pills, potions, and salves. His next job—and a hard one—was getting them and himself out to the heart of China, free. He wheedled passage and a seventy-five-pound baggage allowance on a British freighter, the *Diomed*, a Blue Funnel ship, Captain Hey master, which was sailing soon for Bombay. Father Walter took a chance on the British skipper's generosity and showed up at the dock with a truck carrying all fifteen hundred pounds of his medicines. Sure enough, Captain Hey took it aboard. The ship sailed on September 15th. In mid-Atlantic, the *Diomed* received a wireless to change its route and go to Durban, in the Union of South Africa. There the ship began to unload. Captain Hey said to Father Walter, "I've no guarantee, but I think that if you stand by for a few weeks, we'll be going on to Bombay, and I'd be glad to ship you and your medicaments." There was no alternative, so Father Walter stood by. But he did not waste his time. He began to practice his profession of begging in Durban. The drug houses there responded most generously. They gave him an assortment of things that it had been almost impossible to get in the States—such as mercurochrome, and gentian violet, acriflavin (for skin diseases), and other aniline-dye drugs—and a treated elastic adhesive tape called Elastoplast, which proved to be one of the most valuable things in the whole collection. The firms in Durban gave him, in all, five hundred pounds of material. The ship began at last to load for Bombay, and Father Walter said to Captain Hey, "Now I have a ton of things. May I bring all that aboard?" "All you want," said Captain Hey. During the *Diomed*'s layover in Durban, the local customs officials stored Father Walter's packages without making the usual charges. Furthermore, when the time came to put them back aboard, the chief customs inspector pitched in and helped Father Walter mark and repack his goods in such a way that nothing would break and he would know which package each thing was in.

The ship got to Bombay. "In India," Father Walter told me, "I met the same courtesy I had met in the United States and South Africa." There he encountered a Parsee named Captain

N. J. Vazifdar, a representative of the Indian Red Cross. Father Walter explained his problem to Captain Vazifdar: he wanted now to get to Calcutta free, with his ton of "hand baggage." Captain Vazifdar said that he could give Father Walter a pass on the railroad and would do so; as for baggage charges, the Indian Red Cross office in Calcutta would gladly pay them if he could get the railroad company to carry the medicines there on credit. Father Walter talked the railroad into accepting this rather tenuous arrangement and got to Calcutta. There he was very much surprised when the Indian Red Cross said that Captain Vazifdar must have been suffering from heatstroke; the Indian Red Cross certainly could not transport the impedimenta of unauthorized persons all over the place. In great distress, Father Walter wrote Captain Vazifdar a letter and sat down to wait. Six weeks later he received from his Parsee friend his own check for two hundred and thirty rupees, and the railroad was paid off.

Now came the hardest part of all—getting from Calcutta over the Hump to China. For the next six weeks, Father Walter trudged to office after office collecting rebuffs. He began with the United States Army, and although he had pleasant conversations with scores of enlisted men, and occasionally was hospitably received by a lieutenant or a captain, he never succeeded in penetrating the Army's defense-in-depth. "I wasn't allowed to see the General," he told me. "I still wonder, sometimes, what sort of a person I would have found him. Probably a very kind man. But busy." Next he tried the Chinese Army, with no greater success. "What was going on then," Father Walter said, unconsciously lowering his voice, "was this great squeeze of contraband flying over the Hump. No one could make any profit out of carrying my poor pills." At the American Red Cross, someone finally made a helpful suggestion: Father Walter should go to see a Mr. Hsu, of the Chinese National Health Administration. He managed to talk with Mr. Hsu and a representative of the Chinese National Aviation Corporation, which was flying planes over the Hump. They said they would be glad to see that he and the medicines got to Kunming. Then Father Walter broke the first rule for a wartime traveler: never get separated from your gear. He flew to Kunming, and there he got a letter from Mr. Hsu. The deal was off; permission, it seemed, had not been granted to transport the medicines; extremely sorry. This cost Father Walter eight months of nightmare. He was, to begin with, far from his precious hoard. Next, he received a letter from the Calcutta customs saying that the ton of parcels was piling up a very handsome demurrage charge. He did not dare to try to go back to Calcutta, for fear he would never get into China again. He started writing letters himself—to soldiers and civilians in both Chungking and Calcutta—and every day he paid influential people of Kunming a few fruitless calls. At last he met a major in the Army Air Forces who said that if he could get his stuff to Dibrugarh, in Assam, the Army would take it over the top. Father Walter wrote Mr. Hsu, who, evidently feeling that he was about to lose face, at once popped the ton over the Hump to Kunming and even persuaded the Calcutta customs to forget the storage charges. When the packages arrived at Kunming, not a bottle had been broken, not a pill had been lost. "That," Father Walter remarked, "says a lot for India and China."

It was now October, 1944. Father Walter had been on the road from New York for more than a year. He was in China, but he was still a long way from Ichang. The Japanese were mounting what appeared to be a heavy attack against southwest China and the American Army was preparing for the evacuation of its forces from the threatened area. "I'd been hoicked up out of China once by the Japs," Father Walter told me, "but I'd come so far this time that I couldn't turn back." Once his luck with the American Army changed, it stayed good. A word to an Army chaplain named McNamara, in

Kunming, brought a whole detachment of G.I.s to see Father Walter. They packed his parcels into crates, put them on a truck, drove them all the way to Chungking, and stored them in a dry room at the Army hospital there. Father Walter himself rode another truck to Kweiyang. The Japanese drive on that city was at that moment collapsing, just thirty miles away. If he had had his drugs, Father Walter thinks he might have stayed in Kweiyang, because he saw "a great need" there. The situation being what it was, he went on by truck to Chungking.

To get free passage downriver, toward Ichang, required three more weeks of supplication. "See a different person, try another channel—my, it was wearing!" he recalled. He finally talked the Ming Sen Company, operators of river steamers, into carrying him as far as Patung, fifty miles up along the Gorges from the Japanese front lines, which were still at Ichang. Patung was an advanced Chinese Army supply base, and in the nine months he had to wait there he practiced with his medicines on the Chinese soldiers. As soon as the war ended and traffic began to run all the way down the river, he begged, and was given, transportation to Ichang for himself and baggage.

Father Walter got back to Ichang in September, 1945, just two years after he had left New York. When he reached the city, the grass was growing tall in Second Horse Street, which before the war had been the main shopping avenue. Only four or five thousand of the inhabitants had returned to town from the mountains and from upriver. Among them there were many with the sores and fevers Father Walter wanted to attend to. He went right to work. Since then the population of the city, both healthy and halt, has steadily swelled, and few hours of his life have been idle.

He wakes up now, literally by cockcrow, at about four-thirty in the morning. He has each day a certain number of devotions to get through, including a reading of Mass. These he does early, and afterward he sterilizes his instruments, breaks out new bandages, and fills his medicine kit with what he thinks he will need that day. At eight o'clock he walks to his home-made clinic—the bombed-out, roofless anteroom of what was once a mission house in the town. He tucks a clean white apron under his beard and sits down on a wooden stool in the open air, walled in by whitewashed ruins, with a couple of piles of bricks as seats for waiting patients to whom standing is painful, and with his medicine kit, a large tin Gold Flake cigarette container holding what he affectionately calls "my various condiments" open beside him on a table made of rubble.

The patients come in by the dozen off the street, through a beautiful white arch that supports nothing. Father Walter didn't have to hang out a shingle; the news of his work spread quickly through the town. An old water carrier whom he cured of an ulcer has appointed himself his assistant (at a moderate salary), and he crouches beside the Gold Flake box, handing Father Walter bandages and instruments and boiled water or whatever he asks for. The Chinese idea of entertainment is not always ours; the patients crowd around Father Walter and watch with earthy delight as he cleans out a monstrous purple-and-green ulcer on a coolie's leg and covers it with Elastoplast, or probes a deep infection in a small boy's thigh and stuffs it with sulfa powder, or puts copper sulphate under the lids of an old woman's trachomatous eye, or smears the sores of a boatman's scabies with sulphur ointment (which, because of the incidence of the disease, is called, in Chinese, the "universal medicine"). There is no horror in these sights for them; there is only pleasure in watching Father Walter's gentle work and listening to his quaint remarks. His Chinese is the literary language that he learned in Korea, a tongue quite unlike the vernacular. "It is like talking on a different plane," Father Walter says, "as if you used nothing but Platonic ideas." The faces of the waiting patients are fascinating to watch: they are full of the primitive awe of aborigines in the presence of a tribal witch doctor, but, unlike aborigines, they do not fear the medicine man; obviously, they love him. They laugh with him and they believe in him enough so that their belief, as well as his unguents and powders, repairs them. Perhaps in those faces is the clue to Father Walter's secret. There is no doubt that he finds a lot of satisfaction in the work. "Some of the cures have been really remarkable," he told me. He does not mix religion with his healing. "People were too shaken up by the war to bother their heads with doctrine," he says. Yet his example unquestionably serves as a kind of preachment.

His "customers," as he calls the patients, are all indigent. Once in a while a man in a fur-lined gown and a round silk hat comes to him, but Father Walter will not treat people of that type. "You can buy your medicines on the street," he tells them. "My things are only for the very poor." Those who have cash can, as a matter of fact, buy their stuff right across the street, because an opportunistic Chinese merchant, seeing the crowds that Father Walter drew to his clinic in the gateway, set up, directly opposite, an establishment called the Great Asiatic Drug Company. "I hear that they do a very poor business," Father Walter told me with satisfaction. He finds the drugstore a convenience, however. Occasionally he barters with the proprietor—when he needed some ichthyol ointment, he swapped some atabrin for a jar of it—and he takes his syphilitic cases there for neoarsphenamine treatments, which he does not feel qualified to administer and for which he pays with sulfathiazole.

Father Walter has time to treat about sixty patients a day. If he had more time, more patients would come; the customers seem to regulate their attendance in accordance with his capacity to handle them. "The Chinese especially like a quack," he says. "People come to me who wouldn't think of going to a hospital." An Army doctor in Chungking told him that he had a better supply of drugs than any civilian hospital in China, so there may be some soundness in their instinct.

At about one o'clock, Father Walter leaves his gateway clinic and goes on foot to visit patients who are too sick to come to him. Among these are cases of typhoid, typhus, dysentery, malaria, cholera, and meningitis. He has cured many people of meningitis, which had always been a notorious killer around Ichang, by using sulfadiazine. Some time around three, he gets home to his white cottage. After washing, he prepares and eats his only meal of the day. His diet is healthful but narrow—potatoes, carrots, beans, Chinese cabbage, and pork, in various stews and permutations, and fruits in their season. He never eats rice. Once in a while he buys himself some small cakes or sweets. He lives on six hundred Chinese dollars a day, currently thirty-five American cents. Out of the five hundred and forty gold dollars he receives each year from the Episcopal Mission Board, he pays all his expenses and the salaries of his gateman at the clinic and his factotum at the cottage. This man, whose name is Yang, is an old, thick-tongued farmer. "I've never understood a word he has said," Father Walter told me. Neither, of course, does Yang understand Father Walter's Platonic ideas. But they get along fine.

To judge by Father Walter's circumference, he subsists well enough on his fare. He welcomes deviations, however. Recently he had his first cup of coffee in a year. One evening I took him to a restaurant to give him some Chinese food, and as he ate he unconsciously uttered soft, monosyllabic exclamations of delight. Another time I took him a half-dozen cans of Army C-rations and vegetable juice a friend had let me have. He at once arranged them in a row on his table and read the labels out loud: "'Meat and vegetable stew,' hmm. . . . 'Meat and beans,' aah. . . . Let me see—'A refreshing and nourishing combination of vegetable juices from eight kinds of selected garden-fresh vegetables, blended in proper proportions to develop a delicious, pleasing flavor'—oh, my goodness! ..."

In what remains of daylight after his meal, Father Walter washes the apron he wears when he is at the clinic, boils water for the next day's session, and cleans his cottage. Then he reads for a while. His medical library consists of two books, and in these he browses now and then: *Manson's Tropical Diseases* and a United States Army manual of dermatology. As often as he can, he reads what he calls "shop." At present it is Volume II of Frederic W. Farrar's *Lives of the Fathers*—the biographies of Saints Augustine, Basil, Jerome, Chrysostom, and Gregory of Nyssa. When he tires of reading, he may play the piano. He is quite an expert. Mostly he plays Chopin études and the preludes and fugues from Bach's "Well-Tempered Clavichord." He has a tuning key with which he keeps the piano, lent him by the mission, in good pitch.

On pleasant evenings, he just sits in the window of his room and looks out. His yard is a peaceful sight, despite the fact, for which he apologizes to visitors, that "the backhouse is in the foreground." Not far from the cottage there is a garden framed by trees of many sorts—camphor, bamboo, peach, apricot, orange, oak, sycamore, acacia, and long-needled pine. Birds like the ones in the pictures over his desk come there, and sometimes parrots and many small birds whose feathers and songs are both brilliant. Monkeys play around the garden once in a while. Watching them, Father Walter says, is much better than reading newspapers. "News I almost never get until it's two or three months old," he told me. "By that time it doesn't make any difference—things have either succeeded or failed."

On Sundays he sees only those customers who need him badly. At eight o'clock in the morning he reads Mass in Chinese, at the chapel in the mission compound, for the thirty-odd Christians who have returned to Ichang out of the three hundred who were there before the war. He has, to assist him, a male and a female catechist, both Chinese. The rest of Sunday he writes letters, reads shop, practices the piano, contemplates the garden, and sometimes takes inventory of his medicines. He has already used up about a quarter of his ton. He has never taken a pill himself. He gets lots of exercise simply by walking around, sleeps well (he goes to bed at eight every night), and enjoys excellent health. Even on the Sabbath, his bearing is not the least sanctimonious. Altogether, he scarcely lives up to the common concept of the missionary as a holier-than-thou prig. He has lost the rigidity of his younger days; he is mellow and easy now. He also gives an impression, despite his prim and careful speech, of an exceedingly solid virility.

Father Walter seems, in fact, to be a match for the entire Twenty-sixth Chinese Army, the headquarters of which is encamped in the mission compound. He is trying hard to get the Army out of the compound. "They're just naughty," he says gently, and then thunders, "The *brigands!*" He has written several times to Chungking, and he has warned the soldiers that the Generalissimo and the American Embassy will someday take action against them. "But Chungking is so far away," he says sadly. "They don't seem to care. If these Twenty-sixth Army people had been as active five years ago as they are today in resisting *me,* the Japs would never have got this far." The soldiers have their own medical detachment in the compound, but whenever any of them gets sick, he goes to Father Walter. The other day, Father Walter went to the Army's prison stockade, which seems to be well populated all the time, and treated the sick through the barbed wire. No one stopped him.

Some of the soldiers have given him a bit of trouble. Not long after Father Walter returned to Ichang, one of them, claiming to be the commanding officer's representative, asked to inspect his supply of medicines, on the pretext that he had to make a report. Father Walter said, "That's personal property. That's more valuable to me than money. You wouldn't ask to see my money, would you?" The "representative," having lost face, retired. Later, some of the medicines disappeared. So did Father Walter's pen and watch. He knows who has the watch. He was treating the "representative" and another soldier in his room one day, and while he was busy with the second one, the watch, which was lying on his desk, disappeared. The "representative" gave himself away the next day, before Father Walter had even said anything, by blurting out, "I hear you have lost your watch." A week later, Father Walter saw the soldier on the street. The soldier turned his head away and pretended not to see him. The next time they passed, Father Walter went up to him and said, "You weren't cured of your trouble. You'd better come back." This was the simple truth. The soldier came back for further treatment, and since then the two of them have become good friends. Father Walter has never asked for his watch. "That man knows that I know what he's done to me," he told me, "and he knows that I don't hold it against him."

The soldier often drops in on Father Walter. On a recent Sunday he paid a formal call with his wife and talked sadly of conditions in China. "All that you say may be true," Father Walter replied, "but I still say that the Chinese heart is good. However bad a Chinese man may be on the outside, his heart is good."

"I think so, too," the soldier said.

"Oh, yes, the Chinese has the heart of a child," Father Walter said. He looked the soldier in the eye. "He's willing to be forgiven. That's the last word in humility."

The soldier blinked and said, "If you understand that, you understand us Chinese. We can't afford to be honest; we're too poor."

The conversation turned to the damage the Japanese had

done to the mission property. The soldier said, "Why don't you put in claims against the Japanese?"

"That's gone and past," Father Walter said. "They didn't know what they were doing."

The soldier suddenly said, "If everyone in the world were like you, Father Walter, there would be no trouble anywhere."

Father Walter was very light-hearted when he told me this story. He laughed off the soldier's tribute. "I don't know that that's true," he said. All the same, I think he has a sneaking feeling that it is.

Robert Capa

Capa, the photographer who is credited by his colleagues and competitors with having taken some of the greatest pictures of the Second World War, does not exist. Capa is an invention. There is a thing in the shape of a man—short, swarthy, and carrying itself as if braced for something, with spaniel's eyes, a carefully cynical upper lip, and a look of having won a bet; and this thing walks along and calls itself Capa and is famous. Yet it has no actuality. It is an invention.

Capa was invented in 1935. In that year, in Paris, a certain Andrei Friedmann was a photographer in one way: he owned a camera. Mostly he carried this instrument—a Leica, with one lens and one button to push—to and from a pawnshop. The camera spent three weeks in pledge at the shop to each week it spent in Friedmann's hands. To facilitate the camera's commutation, the obscure photographer rented an office adjacent to the pawnbroker's; this took what little money he had but simplified the hocking and unhocking. These transactions became monotonous. One evening Friedmann and his sweetheart, a girl named Gerda, had an idea.

Andrei and Gerda decided to form an association of three people. Gerda, who worked in a picture agency, was to serve

———
"The Man Who Invented Himself," '47, September, 1947.

as secretary and sales representative; Andrei was to be a dark-room hired hand; and these two were to be employed by a rich, famous, and talented (and imaginary) American photographer named Robert Capa, then allegedly visiting France. The "three" went to work. Friedmann took the pictures, Gerda sold them, and credit was given the nonexistent Capa. Since this Capa was supposed to be so rich, Gerda refused to let his pictures go to any French newspaper for less than a hundred and fifty francs apiece—three times the prevailing rate.

The strikes and civil disturbances associated with the growing Front Populaire afforded the unreal American and his darkroom man opportunities to make amazing pictures, and for a few months there was a kind of Capa craze. Money poured in. The association was happy, for Capa loved Gerda, Gerda loved Andrei, Andrei loved Capa, and Capa loved Capa. (The fourth of these attachments, incidentally, has persisted as one of the most wholesome and fruitful romances of the twentieth century.) Whenever Capa failed to get an important picture, Gerda made excuses to the editors. "That bastard has run off to the Côte d'Azur again," she would say, "with an actress." Once, when things grew dull, Gerda wrote to an American photographic agency that Capa was a rich, famous, and talented *French* photographer, and soon, in return for his pictures, checks began arriving from the United States.

Late that spring, at a meeting of the League of Nations in Geneva, the freshly beaten Negus of Abyssinia was permitted to speak to the world for the last time. While he was speaking, a dozen Italian correspondents in a balcony at some distance from the speaker began to make loud and insulting noises. A scuffle took place. Most of the photographers were satisfied with pictures taken from far away. When the Italians were finally and roughly ejected by some Swiss policemen, the great American photographer Capa was naturally on hand at the doorway to get the only close-ups of the day. What the great American photographer did not know was that, at the moment of ejection, M. Lucien Vogel, editor of the French illustrated periodical *Vue*, was standing there watching the whole thing. *Vue* was Capa's principal outlet. Three days later, when the close-ups reached M. Vogel's desk, the editor picked up his phone and called Gerda.

Gerda said, "Mr. Capa says the Geneva pictures will cost three hundred francs."

"This is all very interesting about Robert Capa," Vogel said, "but please advise the ridiculous boy Friedmann who goes around shooting pictures in a dirty leather jacket to report to my office at nine tomorrow morning."

That was the end of a certain amount of Capa. But not all. The Spanish Civil War broke out. Vogel hired a special plane in which to fly down from France, and he took the ridiculous boy and Gerda with him. At Barcelona the plane crashed, and Vogel broke his collarbone; the boy and Gerda broke nothing. First the photographer and Gerda, who were now married, went to the mountains of Catalonia, and then to Andalusia, where, in August, the first real battles of the war took place. During one of them—as Capa tells the story—he was in a trench with a company of Republican volunteers, fanatical fighters, who shouted, "*Viva la República!*," jumped up over their parapet, and charged toward a professionally emplaced Fascist machine gun. Capa stayed behind; many were killed; the rest came back. The survivors took some potshots with their rifles in the general direction of the machine gun, and because it did not answer they decided they had knocked it out. They cheered, jumped, and charged again, with exactly the same results.

Other survivors repeated this gallant but costly procedure several times, until finally, as they charged, Capa says, he timidly raised his camera to the top of the parapet, and without looking, but at the instant of the first machine-gun burst, pressed the button. He sent the film to Paris undeveloped. Two months later he was notified that Capa was now in truth a famous, talented, and nearly rich photographer; for the random snapshot had turned out to be a picture of a man apparently in the act of falling dead as he ran, and it had been published, over the name Capa, in newspapers all over the world. From then on Friedmann *was* Capa.

Gerda and Capa covered Madrid through the winter, and in the spring they went to the Asturias and stayed with the encircled Basque Republicans until the army was nearly pushed into the sea. Gerda was killed in the battle of Brunete. Capa went to China.

In China, that summer of 1938, Capa found bureaucrats, restrictions, and very little fighting. He met two remarkable American military men—Stilwell and Evans Carlson. The latter led Capa on foot for eleven days until they reached a town called Taierchwan, where they observed the only significant Chinese victory of the entire war.

In time Capa learned that Capa, because of his pictures of this victory, had become a famous *international* war photographer.

He returned to Europe and to Spain, where he stayed until the end of the civil war, in January, 1939. For a short time after that, there were no wars at all. When Hitler's war broke out, Capa discovered that his corporeal reality, Andrei Friedmann, had been born on the wrong side, in Hungary. For this reason, the French government took his cameras away from him. He went to America and bought new cameras. America got into the war and took the new ones away from him. But still he managed, by various means, to be sent out as a war correspondent with the American forces. By this feat he invented the first and only enemy-alien Allied war correspondent; and this invention took the superb pictures and had the bizarre adventures in Capa's book [*Slightly Out of Focus*, a book of his photographs, with text by him, about to be published].

After the war ended, he invented still another Capa, a

CAPA WITH GERDA IN PARIS

*"To me, war is like an aging actress—more and more
dangerous and less and less photogenic."*

Hollywood moving-picture director, whose principal reality was a weekly paycheck from Universal-International Pictures with the words "Robert Capa" on it; this charade was quite convincing until Capa's first option came up. He next invented a movie actor—an Egyptian pimp's servant in a movie called *Temptation*. Capa then invented Capa the writer; in this contrivance he will have been found out the minute *Slightly Out of Focus* is read.

Capa is so thoroughly an invention himself that no one can tell a story about him without adding the fabrication that is due him. Even the true stories about Capa have a fictional quality. There was the time, for instance, in March, 1945, when Capa was "sealed" at an airbase near Arras along with other famous correspondents, just before an operation by the 17th Airborne in which Capa was to participate. Capa appeared at the base public-relations office and announced that he wanted whiskey. The public-relations officer said that whiskey was not permitted on the base for twenty-hour hours before a mission. Capa asked to use the telephone. The P.R.O. threatened to pull the phone out of the wall if Capa reached for it; the base was under a blanket of absolute secrecy. Capa left. A few minutes later he returned and said casually, "I found a telephone."

A couple of hours later the chief public-relations officer from the headquarters of Lieutenant General Lewis Brereton landed at the field; his errand was to unload a case of whiskey for Capa. A couple of hours after *that*, a silver plane circled the field and landed, and General Brereton himself stepped out, brushed past the nervous commanding officer of the base, greeted Capa, and asked him if he'd got his whiskey all right.

Capa is not so perfectly invented that he escapes making mistakes. One of the qualities Friedmann devised for Capa was that of absolute nonchalance. Toward the end of the war, having seen terrible wartime sights in Spain, China, Spain again, France, the London blitz, North Africa, Sicily, Italy, France again, and Germany, he wanted above all things to cover the Armistice. "To me," he had said, "war is like an aging actress—more and more dangerous and less and less photogenic"; he wanted to take photographs of peace. One night he was playing poker at SHAEF headquarters while waiting for the Armistice assignment. A P.R.O. came in and said cryptically, "I've got a little job for you, Capa." "*Little* job?" said Capa. "Don't bother Capa. Capa is playing cards." The P.R.O. gave the "little job" to another photographer, and Capa missed the Armistice.

Despite all his inventions and postures, Capa has, somewhere at his center, a reality. This is his talent—which is composed of humaneness, courage, taste, a romantic flair, a callous attitude toward mere technique, an instinct for what is appropriate, and an ability to relax. He has the intuition of a gambler: on Omaha Beach, while crouching terrified behind a tank, Capa suddenly realized he would be far safer on the open sand than behind such a target, and he moved out into the clear. His courage is partly this apprehension of the odds, and partly innate; one of the finest tributes he ever got was from an enlisted parachutist of the 82nd Airborne, who, a moment before jumping into battle from his plane, in which Capa was taking pictures, said, "I wouldn't have your job for anything—too damn dangerous."

POSTSCRIPT   And so it proved to be. On May 25, 1954, while covering yet another war, Robert Capa was killed by an anti-personnel mine on a battlefield near Namdinh, in what was then French Indo-China, during fighting between the French and the Vietnamese.

Benjamin Weintraub

On the dark day when the Jews of Wilno were gathered into a ghetto, a tall, athletic, twenty-three-year-old man named Benjamin Weintraub sat down in his room in the presence of his wife and split the heel off his leather knee boot, cut a neat round hole in the inside of the heel, took his wedding ring off his fourth finger, put it in the hollow place in the heel, and nailed the heel back on his boot. The ring was gold and heavy. Inside it were engraved the date of his wedding, 5 iv 41, and the name of his wife, LIBA.

Later the same day the young couple were taken to the ghetto, which consisted of two miserable streets and was divided into two parts—one for "specialists," who could claim various skills, the other for "nonspecialists," who had no trade. Weintraub and his wife were put in the "specialists'" ghetto, and, although he was trained as a chemist, he was classified by the Germans, quite arbitrarily, as an electromechanic. There were twenty-three thousand people in the "specialists'" ghetto, and about twelve thousand in the other. The two streets were so crowded that the Weintraubs had to live like sticks of cordwood in a room thirty feet long by twenty wide, with nearly forty people. The ghetto was surrounded by a high wall and

---

"Prisoner 339, Klooga," *Life*, October 30, 1944.

was heavily guarded by German and Lithuanian S.S. and S.D. men. Every day Weintraub was taken out into the city with a party to do heavy labor—usually having nothing to do with electromechanics. The work was hard, but he found he was lucky to be doing it: five weeks after the ghetto was formed, all twelve thousand of the "nonspecialists" were taken out to a place called Ponary, twelve kilometers from Wilno, and were killed by machine-gun fire. From time to time there were small "cleanouts" of specialists who were considered by the guards unfit or unruly. They would be taken out in small groups and would simply not return. Weintraub's mother, father, and two brothers were killed in these cleanouts.

Weintraub had recently come from a hopeful life, and that made the new squalor even worse. He and his wife reminisced: about the night they had first met at Jack's Sport Club and got on so well because she danced like a professional and he was immodestly willing to admit that he was the best dancer in their students' circle; of the times they went skiing together in the hills and woods near Wilno; their swims together at the swimming club, tennis on the public courts, volleyball at the university—a healthy, noisy life. He recalled the things he had done well: the day he won the eighteen-kilometer race at Neuwilno in 1938, his having graduated second in his class at the secondary school, his skill in basketball at Wilno University. They talked of the futility of all the ambition he had had—his youthful desire to be a great concert pianist and his hard studies at the Wilno Conservatory of Music, then his more sensible decision to make a decent living as a chemical engineer and the years of preparation at the university. He teased her about how hard he had tried to teach her to sing, sitting at the piano in his own bedroom and struggling with her tone deafness, always finally giving up and playing Beethoven sonatas for her. He told her again and again of the wonderful trip to Finland he had taken as a boy of thirteen alone with his father, and of the incredible waterfall there called Immatra. They remembered their wedding party, only five months before they had been taken into the ghetto. She chided him about his stubbornness, for when she had moved into his family's five-room apartment at 2 Teatralna Street, he had not let her change a single thing in his room; he had a "sports corner" there crowded with pictures of athletes, and a "nature corner" with pictures of the Polish countryside in all the seasons.

There had been a time, Weintraub also recalled, when death had been an entertainment, in murder mysteries, his favorite form of reading. . . .

A ll that life soon faded. Memories of it gave way to a new and absorbing study: how to get away? News had filtered into the ghetto of Jewish partisan groups in the woods near the city, and all in the ghetto dreamed of escaping to them. Weintraub was rather slow to work out a plan, and then it was not a shrewd one.

There were Jewish police in the ghetto, and he thought that if he could obtain a ghetto policeman's uniform, he might somehow bluff his way past the swarm of S.S. and S.D. guards at the main gate. He finally managed to steal a uniform, and on September 6, 1943, two years to the day after being taken into the ghetto, Weintraub, disguised as a ghetto policeman, walked with his wife to the gate. They stopped a few minutes, trying to decide what to do, and as they waited, the car of the ghetto's ranking S.D. man, Unterscharführer Kietel, approached the gate to go out. The car stopped for a moment for a guard check and for the gate to open. Weintraub whispered for his wife to jump on the spare tire in the rear. He said he couldn't go out in uniform because he would be spotted too easily. Liba jumped on and clung to the spare. The car started up. Weintraub quickly turned away. About fifty yards beyond the gate, the street curved to the right. Looking back, Weintraub saw his wife drop off just before the curve and dart into a side street. That was the last he saw of her.

Weintraub learned two lessons from Liba's escape. Thinking it over, he remembered that Unterscharführer Kietel drove out every day at precisely the same hour, almost to the same minute. The first lesson this taught him was that these Germans were so methodical, so precise, that he might be able to use their precision against them. The other lesson was that an escape had always to be planned from beginning to end. He had not even thought what he would do beyond the gate.

There were at this time fewer than two thousand Jews left in the ghetto. On September 23, 1943, they were taken to a camp in a pine forest near a town called Klooga, in Estonia. Klooga was a labor camp. When the prisoners arrived, there were signs denoting various professions stuck in the sandy soil in front of a barracks. The Jews were told to group themselves around the signs according to their skills. Weintraub had learned from the experience of the "nonspecialists" the importance of declaring a profession. Seeing all the pine woods around the camp, he went to the sign for carpenters.

To inhibit escape, a barber ran clippers in a straight, naked line from the middle of each man's forehead to the nape of the neck. The prisoners were given unmistakable striped blue canvas shirts and jackets or coveralls. And they were given numbers. From this time forward Benjamin Weintraub was No. 339, Klooga. A cloth label on his shirt declared his number. On the label, too, was a star of David.

No. 339 at Klooga and all the other unlucky numbers got up at 5 a.m., had a single cup of burnt chestnut ersatz coffee, started work at six and had a half-hour rest at noon, during which they were given an unvarying bowl of soup, worked on until dark, and then were given a few slices of bread and twenty-five grams of a margarine which stank so that many were unable to eat it.

The work varied. The prisoners were set to building

wooden sheds and shops. Later they made concrete blocks and tank obstacles. Some made wooden shoes for shipment to Germany. Some cut wood. Some loaded the camp's products into freight cars on a siding about half a mile from the camp.

There was always too much work, there was never enough sleep, and the craving for food was constant and sickening. But the worst thing of all was the mental depression the prisoners felt. Their guards were trained in impersonality and seemed to take pleasure in hurting flesh and bone. The prisoners gradually lost all hope. The urge to survive drove some of them to degradation—they informed against their fellows, some even curried favor with their tormentors.

No. 339 was outstanding among the prisoners. The superiority at skiing, swimming, and basketball of which he had once boasted so immodestly had trained him well for the camp. He kept initiative and even a kind of hope long after the others lost it. Since he was strong and apparently so cheerful, the Germans began to trust him and put him in command of work parties.

He rewarded their trust by planning day and night to escape, not alone but with many others. At first he simply observed the daily habits of the Germans—where they walked, their punctual hours of changing guards, of eating, and even of going to the bathroom. Then he began small reconnaissances. He would sneak out of his barracks at night and walk around awhile, feeling out the vigilance of the guards. Gradually he widened his movements.

He began going out through the wire at night at a place where sentries left a gap in their patrol, and he would make his way to the town of Keila, twelve kilometers from the camp. Then he began to have luck. He met some Estonians who were willing to risk their lives by giving him bread, butter, and cheese.

Others, on his instructions, began sneaking out, too. Several were caught and soon disappeared. The Germans said they had "gone to Riga." A terrible whisper went around the camp that there was a gas chamber and crematorium at Riga. "Going to Riga" became the metaphor, among the prisoners, for death.

Many lost the will to live and virtually starved themselves to death; when they became too weak to do any kind of work, two German doctors, named Bottmann and Krebsbach, put them permanently to sleep with a drug called evipan. Bottmann was not a very good doctor and probably knew it, and very likely it was an inferiority complex which made him, one day, flog a Jewish surgeon named Ovseizalkinson within an inch of what was left of his life. The Germans devised an ingenious whipping cradle whose straps and buckles placed victims in the best possible position to have one man sit on the head while the other whipped the buttocks. For the slightest offenses prisoners were given twenty-five lashes. The number twenty-five, like the word "Riga," came to have an awful significance among the prisoners.

There were a few cases of wanton cruelty. One winter night, when a number of Jews built a bonfire outdoors to warm themselves without having asked permission, Unterscharführer Gendt went berserk with an axe. He killed, among others, a man named Dr. Fingerhur, who had been one of Wilno's outstanding gynecologists. One of the guards had a vicious dog which he occasionally sicked on prisoners. One day some dreadful-looking shadows of people limped into the camp and said they were survivors of a typhus epidemic at another camp near Narva, hundreds of kilometers away, and that the Germans had made them walk all the way along the coast to Klooga. They described how S.S. guards had disposed of habitual stragglers by drowning them in the sea.

Practically the only things that kept the prisoners alive now were a sense of common fate and a lingering defiant sense of humanity. They exchanged occasional messages that symbol-

ized these senses. For instance, on Liba's birthday that year
Weintraub was handed a note by a guard. It read, "To Prisoner
339 from 359, 329, 563, and 350: We, your comrades, greet you
on this day and hope that you may see your wife as soon as
possible and that you may then live at her side until her blond
hair turns to gray."

The hopes that 339 had for an escape were jarred one freez-
ing day early that year. He was walking through the camp with
a long board on his shoulder when his right foot slipped on a
patch of ice and brought him down. His weight fell on the
right leg and broke it badly just above the ankle. He was in
bed for two and a half months.

When his leg mended, No. 339 was afraid he might have
lost his contacts in the village of Keila, but he found that he
was able to pick them up again quickly. He was lucky particularly in gaining the trust of a man named Karl Koppel who
lived at 58 Hapsal. Koppel was a great help to 339. He managed to get some pistols and some ammunition. He gave the
pistols, one by one, to 339. Koppel provided fifty rounds of
ammunition per weapon. When he got each pistol back in the
camp, 339 went in the dark to the woodpile, only a few feet
from the barracks, hauled out a log from low in the pile, took
it into the barracks to his bunk, scooped out a hollow with a
chisel stolen from the carpentry shop, put the pistol in it, and
then took the log back outside and returned it to its place in
the pile.

Koppel had given 339 only seven revolvers when a miscalculation upset the whole plan. The miscalculation 339 made
was not of his adversaries but, ironically enough, of his fellow
Jews. He told too many. The word spread. With the help of
the whipping cradle, the Germans found out a few names.
Then, apparently at random, they made a list of almost five
hundred Jews. Perhaps they were uncertain who the real leaders were; perhaps the Germans needed manpower too much.

At any rate, none was executed. Instead, all five hundred were taken to another camp, at Lagedi, about fifteen kilometers from Tallin.

Here 339 had to start the whole process from scratch. This time he told only his most trusted friends. Ironically, the camp that was intended to punish the escapists turned out to be less severe than Klooga. The S.S. man in charge was no less harsh personally than the S.S. man at Klooga. The difference was that he had just been recalled from the Russian front. He knew how the war was going. He had heard about the Moscow declaration on war criminals.

Early in September of that year, the Russians launched an attack against the Baltic States. No. 339 and the others were given no war news at all and they did not know what was happening when, on September 18th, thirty trucks driven by S.D. men came to camp. That day most of the men were out constructing anti-tank bunkers for Tallin. No. 339 was doing some work in the camp with eighteen other men.

The nineteen prisoners in the camp were gathered together near the front gate. The S.D. men began to argue. No. 339 knew enough German to understand that they were arguing whether to take the nineteen right away or wait for all the prisoners to come back in. He heard the word "Riga" and the word "Klooga." He saw that the guards were taking part in the discussion and that all the Germans were ill at ease and confused.

He was standing near the gate. At a peak in the argument he bolted. He ran straight across the road, where the trucks were waiting, into some woods. Then, banking on the thorough Germans to comb the woods, he doubled back and went into the back door of an Estonian house that stood only a few yards from the camp gate. He persuaded the Estonian who was there to lend him a coat and cap. He took up a piece of material, a needle, and some thread, and told the Estonians to say that he was a tailor who worked there. He thought that if the house was searched the job might be done by one of the visiting S.D. men, who would not recognize him.

In a few minutes he looked out of the window and saw his eighteen comrades being bundled into a truck. The truck drove off.

The others came back from their work after about two hours. They were not marched into the camp at all but were lined up in groups of about thirty beside the trucks on the road. This time the thorough Germans took no chances. The drivers and guards formed a huge ring around the trucks, the prisoners, the road—and the house in which 339 was trying to hide. Eventually some of the camp guards came into the house, recognized 339, and took him out.

Something made 339 edge his way to the last truck. That instinct saved his life. The last truck left at about nine o'clock in the evening. Along the way it broke down. After it was repaired, the driver and guard were at a loss what to do. They inquired of some officers they met along the road. The officers suggested that they take the truckload to Tallin jail.

The truckload of prisoners arrived at the Tallin jail early in the morning and slept there a few hours. In the morning they were bundled back in the truck and driven to Klooga.

When they reached the camp they saw that all of the camp's three thousand prisoners had been gathered in the barbed-wire-enclosed yard behind one of the barracks. The truckload including 339 was put in the enclosure, in a group consisting entirely of men brought from Lagedi. No. 339 asked a guard what was going on. The guard said they were being taken to Riga and to Germany. So they were "going to Riga" at last. A few minutes after his truckload arrived, 339 saw, off in the underbrush some distance away, a line of about three hundred men carrying logs. He asked one of his friends who had arrived from Lagedi with the earlier trucks the night before what the logs were being carried for. The friend said he did not know, that early that morning the Germans had picked out the three hundred strongest men in the camp, had given them a huge breakfast, and had taken them out to work.

The breakdown and late arrival of his truck kept 339 out of that working party. That is how the instinct that had made him get in the last truck saved his life, for not one of the strong men carrying wood survived that day.

No. 339 asked the guard where the men were carrying the wood, and why. The guard said that the wood was needed in Germany. It was going along with the prisoners to Riga and Germany. The prisoners, he said, were loading the wood for Riga.

The prisoners were loading the wood for Riga only in the symbolical sense of the word. They were taking it to a clearing in the woods about half a mile from the rear gate of the camp. There they were ordered to construct curious platforms. First they laid four heavy logs in a square. Then they filled in the square with pine boughs. Then they scattered small kindling wood among the pine boughs. Next they put long crosspieces across the square, and across these they laid shorter logs until there was a kind of floor. In the center they put up four poles to form an area about a foot square and kept the space inside that little area free of sticks and boughs. The platforms, of which there were four, were about thirty feet square.

This work took quite a while. In the enclosure, 339 grew suspicious. At noon promptly, the methodical Germans fed the prisoners in the enclosure. But the others did not come back for lunch. No. 339 asked the guard what was holding them up. The guard said, "Perhaps they have decided to take them straight to Riga without coming back here."

The men at the platforms must have been terrified at what was happening then. They were being divided into groups of thirty. The first three groups were ordered onto three of the

platforms and were told to lie prone. When they were all
down, S.S. men with revolvers stepped onto the platforms and
shot those who were lying there, one by one, in the back of the
head. Those who tried to run away or tried to resist were shot
in the face or stomach.

As soon as all the men on the platforms were shot and before some of them were dead, the others were ordered to build
another layer to the platform right on top of the bodies of their
companions. Still no boughs or sticks were put in the little
square in the center. The Germans had thought of everything:
that was to serve as a chimney, to give the fire some draft.

As soon as he heard the first shot in the enclosure, 339 knew
that the Germans were determined to kill every Jew, Russian,
and Estonian in the camp. He was frightened, but he tried to
think clearly. One thing he knew; this would be his last chance
to try an escape.

While the men out at the platforms were building the second layer, 339 began to plan. There were just two permanent
guards in the enclosure. Others came and went. The two in
the enclosure had tommy guns and walked back and forth in
front of the two large groups. The guard in front of the women
looked across at the smaller Lagedi group really carefully only
when he was walking toward it. It took him about twenty
seconds to make each lap. The nearest door of the U-shaped
barrack was about sixty feet away. It would take perhaps ten
seconds to run to the door and disappear to the left up the
stairs.

Fortunately he had explored every inch of the barrack many
times. He knew of a trap door through which he could get
above the ceiling of the attic. He would go completely around
the three sides of the U above the ceiling. At the other end of
the building, he would drop down to the top tier of bunks, run
around a pile of window frames there, pull them up into a
crude barricade, and crawl through in the dark to a hollow

chute that led down to the next floor. This was large enough for one person to hide in, and it was dark. Beyond that, 339 could not imagine anything.

Out at the platforms the second layer was ready, and three more groups were ordered to climb up. The S.S. men followed and began putting their pistols to the backs of the victims' skulls.

When the noise of the second group of shots was heard in the enclosure, panic broke out. Women began shrieking. There was a commotion among the men. No. 339's friends looked at him to see what he would do. In the excitement over the shooting, he ran.

He made the door all right. As he ran up the stairs he heard the sounds of footsteps behind him, and he tried to run faster. Then he realized that there were many footsteps, and that he was afraid of being followed by only one guard, or at most two. He looked back. Something he had not foreseen had happened. Many other prisoners were following his lead.

Quite correctly, the guards out in the yard held their positions with their tommy guns aimed at the bulk of the crowd. But before they could get it under control, well over a hundred people had run into both doors of the building. About forty followed 339 over the course he had planned. By the time they all got behind the barricade of window frames and in and near the chute, the place was a mass of terrified flesh.

All those who had run into the other door of the barracks— on the ground floor, three flights down from 339 and his followers—tried to hide on that first floor. They threw themselves under bunks, cringed in corners, and climbed onto upper bunks.

The guards called out for reinforcements. These entered the door on the ground floor under 339's hiding place. One of 339's companions had cut an electric-light wire and caused a short circuit, so the barracks were all dark. Apparently the S.S. reinforcements were conscious of death themselves that afternoon, because 339 heard two German voices say, in tones that seemed to express fear of the dark, "Are there any guards in there? Come out, you people."

There was a silence. A friend of 339's named Dondes Faiwusz, who had run through the kitchen shed inside the U of the barracks and into a window on the ground floor, saw what happened next. Two S.S. men entered the main room on the ground floor, where all the runaways were trying so pathetically to hide in exposed places, and they sprayed the room, one to each side, with tommy-gun bullets. Up on the third floor the forty men heard a great deal of firing—enough, they later learned, to have killed eighty-seven of their fellow prisoners. It was hard for 339 and his packed-in companions to restrain themselves from crying out in their panicky conviction that the Germans would come up and find them and spray them with bullets, too.

But after the firing downstairs, and the screaming and groaning that followed it, subsided, 339 and his friends could hear only distant sounds—shouts in the courtyard, more shooting far away.

The shooting came in periodic flurries—as new layers were finished on the platforms. In midafternoon there was an increase in the firing. Apparently the S.S. men thought they would never get finished, using only the platforms, so they herded seven hundred people into a barracks, shot them there one by one, and set the building afire. No. 339 and his fellows were lucky that the Germans did not choose their barracks. The smell of burning wood and flesh raised their hair on end. They thought their building might be burned.

The shooting and the smell of burning went on until two

or three in the morning. Then there were sounds of German voices and trucks and cars driving off. Then there was silence.

No. 339 and the others could not be sure that all the Germans had gone. Nor could they be sure that they would not come back the next morning and hunt them out. The stench of burning flesh and the sound of screaming people were so fresh in their minds that they crouched absolutely still all night without whispering.

The group of forty stayed in their dark hole for five days and nights. On the second night some of them sneaked out, as they often had done, and stole bread from the camp commissary. But they did not dare look around much. They went back up to the attic.

On the fifth day one of the men ventured out. The camp was deserted. He saw a Russian airplane overhead. He ran trembling upstairs to tell the others of their deliverance. A few hours later the first Russian soldier came into the camp.

No. 339 thought first about the new life he could now begin. He took a scrap of paper and he wrote a letter he intended to give to a Russian officer:

To the Consul of the American States in Moskau.

Dear Consul!

I stayed from thousands. I have lost my parents and brothers. My wife remained in Wilno and I have no news from her. The only one who remained is my father-in-law, an American citizen who is now living in New York and [with] whom I want to communicate about myself. I had no other chance and I am forced to ask you and I am sure that you will not refuse me. Please send this telegram: Samuel Amdurski, Federal Food Corporation, New York. During a year no news from Liba and Bertha. I am in Estonia. I will do all to find them out.

Benjamin

Then 339 thought about the life he had had. He sat down, pried the heel off his boot, and found his wedding ring there. He tried to put it on his fourth finger. Three years of manual labor for the master race had thickened the fingers that had once played Beethoven and measured chemicals into test tubes. He could not get it on. He put it on his little finger. It just fit.

POSTSCRIPT   About a week after the culminating events of this story, I was taken to Klooga with other correspondents then based in Moscow. With the help of a Polish-English dictionary, Weintraub and a couple of his friends laboriously told me his story. As it turned out, he then gave me the letter he had written, which I delivered to the American consulate on my return to Moscow. Some weeks later, back in the United States, I got in touch with Mr. Amdurski and learned that both Benjamin and Liba Weintraub had written to him. With his help the couple was eventually reunited.

Bernard Baruch

N O T E : Bernard Mannes Baruch (1870–1965) became famous in the first half of the century as an adviser to Presidents. The legend, exuberantly cultivated by him, was that he sat on a bench in Lafayette Park, across from the White House, and waited for Presidents or Cabinet members to happen along, join him, and ask him what they should do. Sometimes this actually happened. Perhaps because starting from nothing he had amassed a huge fortune, he was considered uncannily shrewd, and his counsel was indeed sought—or, in some cases, fought off—by Presidents from Woodrow Wilson to Dwight Eisenhower. His actual public service was limited; he was on the War Industries Board during the First World War, and after the Second World War was United States representative on the United Nations Atomic Energy Commission. But he was happy to give advice whenever it was sought, and often when it was not. Many influential people took him very seriously. As to money-making, he told me one day that it was just a faculty. "Some men," he said, "can make funny faces, others can make fools of themselves, others can make money. How can you define a talent? What makes one fellow able to stand up in the ring and belt the daylights out of someone else? What makes another so good at standing on his head, another able to cut such fancy curlicues on ice skates, and another so clever at saying 'Blah-blah-blah'?" He did in truth have an aston-

---

"A Day at Saratoga," *The New Yorker,* January 3, 1948.

ishing gift for buying at the bottom of the market and selling at the top. This talent, it appeared, made him healthy, wealthy, and, in the popular view, uncommonly wise.

Dew was heavy on the grass beside the long row of stables. A thin blue plume of smoke stood up from the chimney of the mess shack across from the stables, and the early sunlight glistened on the tents of the swipes and exercise boys ranged along the outer edge of the field beside the mess shack. Few sounds broke the stillness of the morning—stamping in the stalls, muffled human and equine coughs now and again, occasional ejaculations and sharp bursts of laughter from the boys, and a distant jubilee of peepers in some flats not far from the track. Many of the stalls were empty; this was the last week of the Saratoga season, and quite a number of horses had already been shipped to other tracks. It was about eight o'clock. Robert J. Kleberg, Jr., owner of the King Ranch, in Texas, of Assault, and of all the horses in these stables, sat alone in a garden chair under a brilliantly colored and incongruous beach umbrella, up toward one end of the row of stalls. Max Hirsch, Kleberg's trainer, stood under a tree talking with some of the exercise boys. Hirsch, a sharp-faced man with glasses, was wearing a gabardine shooting jacket, with a shoulder patch to couch the butt of a gun; he kept his hands in his pants pockets and his shoulders hunched, and talked in a husky voice. A black mongrel dog lay by the trainer's feet.

A Cadillac limousine drove up the road that led into the Kleberg stable area. It stopped on the grass not far from the mess shack. "Here's the boss," Hirsch said, and turned and walked toward the car. The dog followed him. Kleberg stood up and also approached the limousine. A chauffeur got out and opened the car door. A huge old man stepped out of the car and, behind him, a young woman. The old man—Bernard

Mannes Baruch—straightened up and stood like a general reviewing troops. He had on a single-breasted suit, a topcoat parted in front enough to show a Phi Beta Kappa key hanging from a watch chain, and a gray, snap-brim hat. He wore a white plastic hearing aid in his right ear.

"Hello, Boss," Hirsch said.

"Hello, Max," the old man said. He shook hands with the trainer and then turned to receive Kleberg. "Hello," he said. "Hope you don't mind our coming out to look things over."

"Delighted to have you," Kleberg said.

"This is Navarro, my nurse," Baruch said.

Hirsch asked, "Want to look at the horses now, Boss, or would you rather have your breakfast first?"

Baruch slapped his stomach and said, "I'd better have a bite first. Otherwise, I might eat one of your horses." He laughed. He had got up, in the Gideon Putnam Hotel, an hour earlier, quartered and eaten three oranges, worked fifteen minutes with dumbbells, taken a cold bath, dressed, and driven out to the track; and he was hungry.

A girl of about twenty, in blue jeans and a tweed jacket, with her hair tightly braided and pinned up on the back of her head, came out of the mess shack. Kleberg introduced her to Baruch as his daughter Helenita, and Baruch stepped right over to her and said, in deep Southern tones, "Well, Miss, I see you like to ride."

"I do, yes," she said.

"Do you do any shooting?"

"A little."

"What kind of gun do you use?"

"A four-ten."

"A four-ten!" Baruch put his hands over his ears and made a face that suggested he had never before in all his seventy-seven years been the recipient of such astounding news. "Do you realize," he asked Miss Navarro when he had recovered,

"that a four-ten has a muzzle no bigger than *that*?" And he
made a circlet less than the size of a dime with his forefinger.
"You must be a formidable shot," he said to Miss Kleberg
gravely.

"You ought to see her father," said Hirsch. "I've seen Mr.
Kleberg stick his left hand out the window of a moving automobile and take the head right off a turkey with an automatic."

"I remember," Baruch said, "a man named Wingfield,
George Wingfield. *He* was a man with a gun. He started out
as a jockey. Then he was a gambler in Western mining camps,
and a prospector. One day, he stopped in at the bank in Win-
nemucca, Nevada, and asked George Nixon, the fellow who
ran the bank, for a stake of a few hundred dollars. Well, Nixon
and Wingfield got to be partners, and Nixon became a senator.
On the afternoon of the twenty-eighth of December, 1906
(I believe it was), William Crocker, of San Francisco—he had
a pointed beard; he was a great believer in the West, a great
optimist—came into my office in New York with Senator
Nixon and said Nixon needed two million five hundred and
seventy-eight thousand dollars for a gold mine he and Wingfield were developing. Goldfields Consolidated, it was called.
Nixon made a noise like a dividend, so I put up a million and
got involved in the enterprise myself. The first time I saw
Wingfield was when I went out to Goldfield quite a bit later
to look the property over. He was carrying five revolvers—two
here, two here, and one here. He also had four Pinkerton de-
tectives with him. Wingfield told me he'd been having labor
trouble with some of the I.W.W. boys in his mine. One reason
was a company rule he had, to the effect that the men working
in the high-grade mines had to strip as they started home, and
then they had to jump over a bar, so that any nuggets of gold
they might have hidden under their arms or between their legs
would fall on the floor. The I.W.W. had beaten up Wingfield's
superintendent and some of his foremen and left them out in

the desert. Wingfield had ridden out himself and brought the men in and walked right through a mob of the strikers in front of the bank. He was afraid of nothing. When the strikers tried to knock out a newspaper he published by frightening the newsboys and distributors off the streets, Wingfield went out and peddled his papers himself. One of the strikers waylaid him, but Wingfield knocked the man out with the butt of one of his guns. As I say, Wingfield was the best shot I ever saw. Out at one of the mines, someone would throw a bottle up, end over end, behind him, and he'd wheel around and get one of his guns up in a single motion and break the bottle. Now, that's shooting. . . . I'm hungry! Let's eat!"

Max Hirsch opened the door of the mess shack; Baruch bowed to Miss Navarro and let her pass in ahead of him; Baruch and Kleberg followed; Miss Kleberg went off to exercise a horse. The shack had two small rooms—a dining room and a kitchen. Two places were set at a round table; the Klebergs and Hirsch had eaten earlier. Baruch took off his hat but not his topcoat, and sat down, along with the others. A fat, smiling Negro woman served cuts of melon.

"That's a fine girl, your daughter, Mr. Kleberg," Baruch said as he shook a great deal of salt on his melon and began to eat. "A fine, pretty girl. You know, I have reason to remember her grandfather on her mother's side. He was a member of Congress, as you know. Congressman Campbell."

Kleberg smiled and nodded.

Baruch ate with relish and said, between mouthfuls, "He took part in the 'leak investigation.' First time I was ever investigated. Let's see—it was in January, 1917. The month before that, there had been a series of peace rumors, and with each one the stock market broke a little, and each time it did, I sold short and made some money. I made five hundred thousand

dollars one day. A rumor got around that I had made my
money on the strength of some information from the White
House, supposedly a leak of some peace negotiations. So these
congressmen called me in to investigate me. I got them in the
palm of my hand at the very beginning. They asked me my
name and address, then they asked me my occupation, and I
guess they expected me to say I was a banker, or something
dignified like that. I sat up straight and said I was a speculator.
That had 'em. Then I went on to tell them I made my money
in perfectly legal ways—just by being faster than the next fellow. For instance, on December 16, 1916 (I believe it was), I
was standing at the ticker reading a news report of a speech by
Lloyd George. The first part of the story was full of determination; the British would carry on, they'd fight to the last man,
and so on. Then the word 'but' came over the ticker. I didn't
have to see any more. I knew that whatever followed that 'but'
would start another rumor and peace scare and a decline. So
on the strength of that one word I immediately sold heavily,
and that was the day I made half a million. Well, through all
the investigation your little girl's grandfather was very courteous and understanding, but there was this other fellow—I
forget his name, he was some sort of a radical from the Northwest—"

The cook brought Miss Navarro and Baruch plates with several huge, fat pancakes on them, and coffee. "Ah!" Baruch said.
"Flapjacks! Fine, fine! Please pass the butter, Navarro. Now
the molasses, please. Fine, fine! ... As I say, this other fellow
was extremely obnoxious, trying to be as unpleasant as he
could. Then, all of a sudden, in one of the afternoon sessions,
I noticed he was getting polite and seemed to be very good to
me. After the session—some more molasses, please, Navarro
... thank you—after the session, Lacey, my faithful attendant
for twenty-odd years, was approached by a woman who said
she was this harsh congressman's wife, and she asked if the

BARUCH ON HIS PARK BENCH

*"We can fix the world. We've got to believe we can,
and then we will."*

man who was being investigated was a son of Belle Baruch, from down in Camden, South Carolina. Lacey said I was. 'Then I'm going to tell my old man to lay off,' the lady said, 'or else I'll tear his eyes out. No son of Belle Baruch could ever do anything wrong.' He laid off, too. When I got back to New York, I told Mother—she was then sixty-seven—what had happened. You must understand, Mr. Kleberg, that my mother was a remarkable woman. She was very beautiful, and she had a pure and serene heart. She always endeavored to instill into her children lessons of tolerance and kindliness. 'If you can't say anything pleasant about a person, keep your tongue between your teeth,' she'd say to us, and 'If you touch pitch, it'll stick to your fingers.' She was active in all kinds of charities. Whether she worked for the benefit of the Montefiore Home or the J. Hood Wright Memorial Hospital—whether it was for a Jewish or Protestant or Catholic organization made no difference to Mother so long as she felt she was doing some good. Late in her life, the people who used to work with her on these charities called her *'la Grande Duchesse'*.... More coffee? Thank you, yes, I will.... Well, when I told my mother what had happened during the investigation, she said, 'Now, let me see, let me see.' I could tell she was trying to think of the nicest thing she could say. Then she told me that when she and Father—he was a remarkable person, too—lived in Camden, there were only four or five Jewish families there: the De Leons, the Levys, the Baums, and the Wittkowskys, as I remember it. Then another Jewish family immigrated to this country and moved to Camden and opened a bakery. And Mother said that one day she saw the baker's wife breast-feeding her child in the open street, and Mother told her, in the gentlest sort of way, that customs were somewhat unusual in the Southern part of the United States, that there were certain kinds of unnecessary modesty, that it might be better to nurse the child indoors, and so on. Always after that, the baker's family thought Mother was an angel. And this congressman's wife was the baker's daughter. You can see from this how kindness always comes home again."

By this time, Baruch had cleaned his plate and had finished his second cup of coffee. "Now!" he said. "Is Assault going to beat Armed?" Kleberg and Hirsch and he talked awhile about various Kleberg horses, and then they decided to go out and look at some of them. As they stood up to leave, Baruch whispered to Miss Navarro and she opened her purse, took out a five-dollar bill, and gave it to him. "Best flapjacks I've had in a dog's age," he said to the cook, who was clearing away the dishes, and he handed her the bill. "Always glad to see *you,* Mr. Baruch," she said. "Come back real soon."

The three men and Miss Navarro went outside and stood for a time watching the exercise boys walk a number of horses in blankets around and around a tiny oval. Presently, Baruch pointed at one of the handlers and said, "See that fellow over there—the one in the mutton-pie hat? He used to work for me. There's a fellow, a few years ago he was down, both mentally and physically, way down lower than a snake's belly. I got ahold of him and took him down to Hobcaw Barony, my place in South Carolina, and he used to go shooting with me. He couldn't hit a flying barn, but he'd tramp all day and he'd try. Bit by bit, he began to get feeling better, and now look at him. He's on top of the heap." Suddenly, Baruch's voice became a few tones deeper and its resonance increased; a seriousness and persuasiveness came into his face. "You know, it's the same way with nations as it is with men. We, as a nation, can't let all this get us down. Now, Joe Kennedy—the former Ambassador, you know—he'll say to me, 'Oh, it's all gone to hell in a bucket, and you know it, Bernie.' But he doesn't believe that: Joe's got a sense of humor, he's pulling my leg. None of us believes that. We've got to *think* we can lick this thing, and then, by God, we will lick it."

The conversation swung back to horses, and Kleberg suggested that Baruch might like to see Bridal Flower, a horse that, Kleberg remarked, was a beauty all alone on the track in morning workouts but not yet calm enough in races with other horses. One of the swipes led the horse out of her stall; she was a slight filly, nicely proportioned and nicely named. Kleberg said to his trainer, "Max, tell Mr. Baruch how fast you think that horse'll run a mile one of these days."

The trainer, patting his dog, said, "Bridal Flower's a horse that can go. She'll go out there sometime and break the world's record."

"Don't talk to me about world's records," Baruch said. "I got myself badly burned by a world's record once. I had a horse called Knapsack, a dandy horse. I had high hopes for Knapsack. One day, he was up against a fast thing—I think it was called Cherry Pie—a very speedy animal, but I really thought Knapsack could win the race, so I sent a boy to put a bet on him. I told the boy to put twenty-five thousand on the nose on Knapsack, but when he came back, he said he was terribly sorry, he'd made an error, he'd put thirty-two thousand on my horse. I said, 'That's all right, son, we all make mistakes.' At that point, I could afford to be tolerant, because I was sure I was going to win. Well, they ran the race, and Cherry Pie broke the world's record and beat Knapsack by the whiskers on the end of his nose. But he had to break the record to do it. That's the reason I don't like to talk about world's records. Let's talk about something else!"

Hirsch had a new subject all ready. "Want to see a remarkable dog do some work?" he asked.

"I always enjoy watching a good dog," Baruch said.

"Well, take a look at this," the trainer said. He took a quarter out of his pocket, rubbed it hard between his thumb and forefinger to get a scent on it, and scaled it nearly fifty yards across the road toward a field of tall grass and goldenrod. The mongrel sprinted off as soon as the coin left Hirsch's hand. As the quarter fell toward the field, it hit the white fence along the road and ricocheted into the grass at the edge. The dog, evidently judging his run by the coin's early flight, ran on under the fence into the field, sniffed about there for some time, worked back toward, and then back under, the fence, and finally found and retrieved the quarter. Next, Hirsch hung a handkerchief over a branch of a maple tree, some ten feet off the ground and almost two feet out from the trunk. He led the dog to a spot about thirty feet from the tree and pointed to the handkerchief. The dog spurted toward the tree, literally ran up the trunk on his momentum, snapped the handkerchief off the branch with a backward lurch, twisted in midair, and landed on his feet. Kleberg now threw a coin well out into the field of grass and goldenrod, and while the dog darted back and forth in the tall growth trying to find it, Baruch walked over with Hirsch and leaned on the white fence, watching, entertained by the dog's earnest money-grubbing.

During Baruch's absence, Kleberg asked Miss Navarro, "How's the old man's health? I haven't seen him for several years, but he looks every bit as well as he did the last time I saw him."

Miss Navarro, who has been Baruch's nurse for two years (since a mastoid operation, when he was seventy years old, Baruch has had a nurse, mainly to supplement his own firm self-discipline with a nurse's admonitions and attentions), is a broad-faced, handsome, calm, good-natured woman. "He's never been better in his whole life," she answered. "You know, he was a prizefighter when he was a younger man, and he still eats like a prizefighter. Yesterday at lunch he had three fried eggs, three slices of ham, lots of vegetables and bread, and three totally different and distinct desserts. You saw him at breakfast.

He weighs two hundred and two pounds, but of course he's got the frame to carry it. He thought he had a little gout a couple of years ago, but I told him not to be silly, all the matter with him was that he was just like a woman—he bought his shoes too small, to make his feet look better. So then he got some good big shoes and everything's been fine ever since. He's as strong as an ox, and I think he'll live to be two hundred years old."

When Baruch and Hirsch walked back to the others, after having given the dog two or three more trials, Baruch said to his host, "I was just saying to Max that I've never seen a finely bred dog that was really good. I've known a lot of dogs in my time: I remember an English mastiff named Sharp that one of my father's patients gave us when I was a boy, and then we had a bulldog named Fierce, and later De Lancey Nicoll gave me a big brown setter named Dewey—he was a great dog; that dog actually knew what you were talking about; he could even catch crabs in shallow water—and I had a shepherd dog named Peter, and many others. But I've always had more success in the hunting field with scrub dogs than with highly bred ones. The thoroughbreds are fine on points and they move beautifully, but they haven't got the nose of the hybrids. I had an old fellow down at Hobcaw and every time he saw a thoroughbred, he used to say, 'He can't find nothin', he can't smell nothin', and he ain't good for nothin'.' Is there any thrill greater than hunting behind a good dog, Mr. Kleberg? By God, if there is, I don't know it!"

Miss Navarro reminded Baruch that he had a ten-o'clock appointment at the mineral baths. He walked toward his car.

"Come out again some morning," Kleberg said.

"All right," Baruch said. "I'll come out and we'll sit under that umbrella over there and fix up the world. Remember that time in '40 we sat in that very spot and figured out how to beat inflation?"

Kleberg laughed and said, "I certainly do. I wish they'd

taken up some of our ideas! But if we can't fix the world this time, at least we can talk about horses."

In the car, Baruch said to Miss Navarro, "Did you hear what that young man said? He said, 'If we can't fix the world.' I don't like to hear the young men of this country talking that way. We *can* fix the world. We've got to believe we can, and then we will. . . . A nice-looking filly, Bridal Flower. . . . Imagine that girl shooting a four-ten! . . . What a fine fellow Max Hirsch is! . . ."

Baruch stopped in at the Gideon Putnam just long enough to see whether a call had come through from a Mr. Buzzy Appleton, a gentleman with a number of business interests in New York City [i.e., his bookie] who, all through the Saratoga meeting, had been giving Baruch advice on the horses. The call had not come, so Baruch drove to the Washington Bath House, indulged in a mineral bath, suffered a massage, and fell into a deep sleep, which lasted for a little more than half an hour. This nap made him late for an eleven-o'clock appointment with a man named Crampton, and when Baruch returned to his hotel rooms, the caller was waiting for him.

The living room of Baruch's suite was a large room in the northwest corner of the hotel. It was a standard hotel room, overstuffed and mass-produced, except for one small cluster of furniture at one side of the room. Upon this group Baruch had placed his stamp. It consisted of three chairs—a thronelike leather-upholstered wingback, for Baruch, and two wooden basket chairs, very nearby, for collocutors—and a drum table crowded with papers: letters, among them one from Secretary Marshall congratulating him on his seventy-seventh birthday; copies of the *Morning Telegraph* and the *Daily Racing Form;* a pocket-size murder mystery; and various notes and scraps. On entering the room, Baruch took off his hat and coat and sat down at once in the leather chair. "Sit over here where I can hear you," he said to Crampton, and he leaned forward and pulled one of the wooden chairs to within a couple of feet of himself. Crampton sat in it. "What can I do for you?" Baruch asked in a rather forbidding way.

Crampton was interested, he said—

"Talk louder!" Baruch said. "I'm a little deaf." He took the microphone of his Zenith hearing aid out of his vest pocket and held it up in front of him.

Crampton, somewhat confused, said he had said he wanted to interest Mr. Baruch in buying some shares in—

"What did you say?"

Crampton began again, and this time he managed to get fairly far into his case before Baruch said, "I don't really care about money. When I made my first million dollars—I was about thirty then—I went to my father, and I was pretty excited, as you can imagine, and I asked him if he wanted to go down to the bank vaults and *see* the million, the actual securities and bankbooks. My father was an extraordinary man, Mr. Crampton. My father had the finest collection of natural faculties of any man I ever knew, and he constantly improved what he had. He was able, by reading and by study, to assimilate anything, and he had a mental machine that was able to take in whatever was good and reject what was bad. He was a handsome man, too—six feet tall, slender but straight, with a dark beard and mild blue eyes that looked straight at you. A very imposing personage. He was a doctor and he worked all his life for his fellowmen. His passion was physical therapy. He conducted some of the first experiments in hydrotherapy, and that's why I'm so interested in this spa. People think I'm up here to see the races. Actually, I'm preparing a report for Governor Dewey on the baths. Well, when I asked my father if he wanted to see my million dollars, he said, 'No, son, I'm not interested in your money. I'm only interested in what you are going to do with it.' Father also used to say, 'Son, remember that there is no such thing as gratitude. Do things for your own satisfaction, and that means: do them well.'"

The telephone rang. Baruch shouted to Miss Navarro, who was in the next room, "See if that's Buzzy!" It was not Buzzy, Miss Navarro reported, but someone from a charitable organization, asking Baruch to make a speech. Baruch told her to find out when the speech was to be. It was, she said in a few moments, to be the next day. "Tell them I can't do it!" Baruch shouted. "Tell them that I have to prepare my speeches carefully." He turned to his visitor and said, "People believe in me, Mr. Crampton. They think I'm honest and they listen to my advice. They think I'm always right. That's the greatest satisfaction I've had in life—being right. But it's a heavy burden. I can't get up in public and say the first thing that comes into my head. I have to study things out. . . . Let's see, where were we?"

Crampton hurriedly presented a couple more of his ideas, and then Baruch said, "The only way you can succeed with a proposition like yours is by hard work—hard work and courage. You've got to be ready for anything and fearful of nothing. I believe I can say I'm afraid of nothing. I used to be a fighter in the ring, and I wasn't afraid of taking a beating. I'm not afraid of death. Some people think I'm an old man (I'm younger than most of them, really), but I'm not afraid of dying. What is it that Horace said—*'Pallida mors . . .'?* I remember the translation:

> With equal steps, pale death advances
> upon the hovels of the poor
> And upon the turrets of the mighty . . .

I haven't been afraid of death since I saw my father die. In his very last days, he said he wanted to die without rites. He didn't want the prayer 'Shema' recited when he died—that's a Hebrew prayer: 'Hear, O Israel, the Lord is our God, the Lord is one,' and so on. Father said he didn't think he wanted to try to fool God at the last minute. Just before he died, my brother Hermann stood over him saying, 'I'm Harty, I'm Harty'—for Hartwig, another brother. Hermann was testing Father, you see, to find out whether he was *compos mentis*. Father just shook his head—he *always* had a clear mind—and closed his eyes and died easily. That was all. I've never been afraid of it since then. . . . You were saying?"

Crampton made another start. After he had spoken a couple of sentences, Baruch said, "I forgot to add that along with courage you've got to have a sense of justice and fair play if you want to succeed. I have a terrible temper, Mr. Crampton, though I never can remember to *stay* angry. Nothing makes me madder than something that isn't fair. See that bump?" Baruch made a fist of his right hand, put it under Mr. Crampton's nose, and pointed with his left hand to a large irregularity—apparently an ill-knit broken bone—on the back of the right hand, just behind the knuckle of the third finger. "I got that because of a bit of foul play. It was eleven years ago, in 1936. I was driving to my apartment in New York in a taxi, crossing Fifty-seventh Street. Just as we approached Fifth Avenue, some fellow slammed his car across in front of my cab and nicked our fender. The driver of this other car got out and walked back, swearing at my taxi driver. My man was getting out to talk back, and the other fellow slammed the front door of the cab shut on my driver's hand. It crushed the fellow's hand painfully. That made me mad, and I put my head out the window and said, just as severely as I could, 'You ought to be ashamed of yourself!' The fellow said, 'Yeah? You get out here and I'll do it to you, too.' Well, I unbuttoned my coat. Then I thought, If I get out on that side, *I'll* have a crushed hand, too. So I moved over and got out on the other side of the cab and snuck around behind"—Baruch stood up and began walking stealthily in a circle around the room—"and I may as well tell you I used to be a pretty good boxer. I got some pointers, in my younger days, from Joe Choynski and Fighting Bob Fitzsimmons down at Woods' Gymnasium, on Twenty-eighth Street, the south side between Fifth and Madison. So I came at this fellow on the run"—Baruch began to trot across the room, with his fists clenched, left hand forward, right hand drawn back a little—"and when I reached him—*ungh!* Right on the point of his chin! Luckily, he had a glass jaw and he went down flat on the pavement, out cold. A policeman came up, who'd seen me going by that corner for years and knew me. He said, 'Anything I can do to help you, Mr. Baruch?' I said, 'Yeah! Pick that son of a bitch up so I can hit him again.' Excuse me, Mr. Crampton, I was pretty angry. The cop said, 'If I was you, Mr. Baruch, I'd get moving before some flatfoot comes along here that doesn't know you.' So I moved along." Baruch sat down. "That happened when I was sixty-six. I've always kept myself in pretty good condition. Good health is terribly important, Mr. Crampton. If we could just get a nation of people healthy at both ends—clear minds and sound dogs! . . . Forgive me for interrupting. Go right ahead."

Rather hastily and somewhat inarticulately, Crampton again began pouring out information. "You can't start anything with any hope of succeeding," Baruch soon said, "that is, until you've made a study of every possible fact. That's all that matters— facts, facts, facts. When I was on the War Industries Board, in the first war, Woodrow Wilson used to call me 'Dr. Facts.' President Wilson was my first hero, Mr. Crampton. He became my hero long before he was President, because of his policy of democratizing the eating clubs at Princeton. You see, I grew up a poor boy. When we first moved to New York, we lived in the attic of a boardinghouse at 144 West Fifty-seventh Street. I went to City College. I had it all planned out to go to Yale. I was going to work my way by waiting on table. But my mother didn't want me to leave home, so I used to walk to college. I was a great big fellow and a fighter and not afraid of anything, but I wasn't elected to a Greek-letter fraternity. I don't think it was because I was disliked. I think it was because I was a Jew. I think so. Though I can say that that has never militated against me. Somehow, people have been very courteous to me. I give courtesy to everyone, and I get it." Baruch sat up a little straighter and spoke, suddenly, more forcefully. "I demand courtesy!" He leaned back again. "I come from good stock. On my mother's side, I am seven generations American from a Spanish and Portuguese line. My father was an immigrant from Prussia. I think he must have been partly of Polish descent, because of his blue eyes. I remember, once, riding out to a farmers' convention in Chicago with Clemenceau, who was then visiting America, and he said to me, 'The Polish Jews are very great people,' and I wanted to ask him why he thought so, but just then the train stopped and there was a crowd on the platform yelling to see the old Tiger. He went out and waved to them, and when he came back, he sat down and said, *'Oui, mon enfant.'* I was just going to ask him my question when he said, 'Tell me about your George Washington. Is it true he was not an educated man like Wilson?' But before I could answer him, he nodded off and was fast asleep. . . . Go on, Mr. Crampton, go on."

Crampton's salesmanship was interrupted again by the telephone, and this time Miss Navarro shouted that it was Buzzy Appleton. Baruch said, "Excuse me, sir. This is an important call I've been waiting for," and went into the next room. Crampton could easily hear Baruch's loud shouts into the phone: "That you, Buzzy? . . . Say! I got out on your last one yesterday. That horse named Aralak. . . . Sure I had him! You told me that whenever you gave me a horse with three stars, I could take out the family jewels and let myself go, and you had three stars on Aralak. I got out nicely. Any three-stars today? . . . Wait a minute. Navarro'll take them down. Thanks, Buzzy. Don't forget to call me tomorrow." As Baruch returned to the living room, Miss Navarro's quieter voice could be heard repeating the names of horses that Appleton liked that day.

Again Crampton picked up his raveled thread. He had spoken a few rather forlorn sentences when Baruch took a large gold watch from his vest pocket, looked at it, and said, "Nearly lunchtime. I can't be late for lunch. Now, let me see if I have your story straight." He proceeded to summarize Crampton's appeal. From the half sentences, the false starts, the strained recapitulations, and the blurted statistics that Crampton had squeezed into the half hour's conversation—scraps to which Baruch had scarcely seemed to listen—the old man now pieced together a succinct, pellucid, and persuasive sales story. "Yes, that's it! That's it!" Crampton exclaimed. "I didn't think—"

"I'll mull it over," Baruch said, standing up, "and let you know in a couple of days. Goodbye. Thanks for coming in."

Baruch went to lunch, in the hotel dining room, at precisely noon, with Miss Navarro. He ate three lamb chops, a hill of rice, some salad, and several rolls, and was getting into his third dessert—a slice of watermelon, following a dish of ice cream and a pastry—when he looked at his watch again and found that he would barely have long enough for his nap before post time for the first race at the track, and so, though still not exactly sated, he ate only five or six forkfuls of the melon before he asked Miss Navarro for two dollars, which he put under his plate for the waitress, and left.

In his bedroom, he lay down and slept until, twenty minutes later, Miss Navarro awakened him. He arose, fresh, and though the afternoon was fairly warm, he put on his topcoat. He gathered up his *Morning Telegraph* and *Daily Racing Form,* slung a binoculars case over his shoulder, told Miss Navarro to make sure she had Buzzy Appleton's list, and hurried out with her. His chauffeur drove him to the clubhouse at the track. Waiting for the elevator to the tier of boxes on the second level of the stand, he encountered an acquaintance. "Look at that!" Baruch said, indicating with a sweep of his hand the tables at which clubhouse patrons were eating and drinking, the general-admission crowd walking around on the cement apron in front, the straightaway of the track, the laborers with their tractors and harrows and water trucks preparing the soil of the stretch, and, beyond, the tote boards twinkling with chance. "This *is* a country," he said. "There's nothing philosophical or metaphysical about the difference between our country and others. People here can drive along and buy hot dogs wherever they want, cross state lines without permits, and come to this track and throw their good money after their bad with no one to stop them." In heavy accents of irony, he added, "Rotten country, isn't it?"

The acquaintance, a sportsman, who seemed not at all surprised at this patriotic outburst, countered Baruch's question with one of his own: "How you doing on the nags?"

"Fortunately, I put my mind to my work yesterday, and I prospered," Baruch said. He did not mention Buzzy Appleton's three-star recommendation, which had abetted the prosperity, but he remembered to knock on the wooden wall by the elevator door. The elevator came and, with Miss Navarro, Baruch ascended. He went to his box—in the fourth tier, at some distance to the right of the finish wire—and prepared himself for the day's work: focused his binoculars, folded his dope sheets and put them on the shelf at the front of the box, persuaded Miss Navarro to turn over to him a roll of cash, put his pince-nez beside the papers on the shelf, and riffled the afternoon's program, reading it through his tortoise-shell glasses. Presently, a man named Schuyler, with a red face, a felt hat the front of whose brim was turned upward, and a voice that expressed the most commonplace thoughts in an extremely confidential tone, presented himself and waited about for orders from Baruch. After the trumpet had announced the horses for the first race and they had danced out in front of the stands, and after Baruch had taken off his tortoise-shells and put on his pince-nez and had a good look at them, and taken off his pince-nez and put on his tortoise-shells and had one last look at the experts' opinions and at Buzzy's list, he leaned forward, spoke in a very low voice to Schuyler, peeled a fifty-dollar bill from his roll, and handed it to him. Schuyler, looking as if he had just been told the details of the trigger mechanism of the atomic bomb and was trying to look as if he knew nothing, went off to place the bet. In a few minutes, the race started. Baruch stood up and watched through his binoculars. His horse did not win. To Miss Navarro, he said, "Here, as elsewhere, the experts lead us astray. They know the words to deceive us."

During the afternoon, a succession of people dropped by Baruch's box. Some of the visitors were friends; some said they knew his son, or one of his two daughters, or a friend of his; one said he had admired Baruch's rubber report during the war; another wanted to shake his hand because of his atomic plan; some offered no pretext whatever. All of them asked his advice on the horses, and most of them annoyed him. "I know nothing about horses," he said to one visitor. "There are lots of experts on horses, but I'm not one of them. Of course, I've noticed that these noisy experts never have two nickels to rub against each other—but don't come to *me* for advice." To another, he said, "I've been in a lot of businesses in my day—ranching, gold mines, stocks and bonds—and I just tuck away what little I know and try to keep quiet. You find some men who think they know everything about everything. They succeed in one business and then they get up on their little dung-hill and shout about all kinds of things." To another, who querulously wondered whether a race just won by a long shot had been fixed, he said, "I've been in all walks of life and I've seen men under temptation. In the stock market. Here at the track. The big dog of truth eventually catches up with those who succumb. But I've never lost faith in human beings. I remember, when I was a kid, I read a story about a white man who fell into the hands of some Choctaw Indians, and they began torturing him to get some information from him. But he stood steadfast and said nothing. Integrity! See what I mean?" To hear his visitors, Baruch held up the little microphone of his hearing aid. When he tired of their questions, he simply shut down the rheostat on the microphone and put the contraption away in his vest pocket. After that, the visitors, unable to get through to him, went away.

Some of his callers he welcomed. Joseph P. Kennedy stopped by for a few minutes, and the two men joked about their losses. After Kennedy had left, Baruch mentioned Kennedy's son Congressman John F. Kennedy to Miss Navarro, then said, "The children of famous men generally have a hard time. They remain in the penumbra of their fathers. Not young Kennedy, though. He's stepped out." Later in the afternoon, Herbert Bayard Swope, in a straw hat and track tweeds, dropped by with rapid-fire information on developments in Geneva, prospects at Lake Success, the Republican outlook, and the next race. Later still, Alfred Gwynne Vanderbilt came to pay his respects and was treated to a recitation by Baruch of trout-fishing experiences in Canada, complete even to the names of streams and the locations of pools that used to abound with delightful speckled trout. When Vanderbilt had left, Baruch said to his nurse, "That young man's mother came down to Hobcaw once to hunt. She was the loveliest thing I ever saw. She had on a boy's costume and a little cocked hat with a feather, like Robin Hood's. She crept and crawled through the underbrush after those turkeys all day long. By God, she was a fine creature!" At about four o'clock, Baruch asked Miss Navarro, "Did you bring anything to eat?" She opened her handbag, took out something wrapped in pink tissue paper, removed the paper, and handed Baruch two large biscuits. At the same time, Schuyler arrived with some Coca-Cola. Baruch said, "Aha! Mr. Schuyler, you're a gentleman and a scholar. . . . Schuyler the scholar." Baruch wolfed his snack. Buzzy Appleton had not provided any three-star choices for this afternoon, and Baruch, though playing his bets secretively through the security-minded Schuyler, appeared to be losing. He stayed for the last race.

Baruch had offered Swope a ride back to the hotel. As Swope stepped into the car in the driveway in front of the clubhouse, he bumped his head on the top of the car doorway. "Abominable car!" he said, rubbing the top of his head. "You'll have to get a bigger car, B.M., if you want my patronage."

"If a man's head gets too big, no car will contain him," Baruch said. "I mean that generally. No reflection on yourself, Herbert."

Back at the hotel, Baruch changed into a dinner jacket and took a hearty dinner with Miss Navarro. Afterward, although he would have preferred to stay at home, he felt he owed it to the memory of Franklin D. Roosevelt to appear at a performance in Saratoga of a play starring Faye Emerson, Elliott Roosevelt's wife. He sat watching and thinking in the darkness of the theater through the first act, unable to hear a word of what was being spoken on the stage. At the end of the act, he returned to the hotel. He undressed, took a cold bath, and was in bed at ten-thirty.

Alfred A. Knopf

Some years ago, a few of Alfred A. Knopf's friends began to notice that he was dropping out of sight now and again, for several weeks at a time. When he returned after each disappearance, he seemed rejuvenated. He was garrulous then, and ate his food and smoked his cigars with an uncharacteristic abandon. During those periods he spoke of conditions in Washington and in the publishing business not as worse than usual but merely as bad. In other words, he was ebullient. His friends concluded he was secretly in love. I have long wanted to get to the bottom of this mysterious affair, and this volume gives me, at last, the cherished chance. I have sought out those who shared Alfred's secret, and they have told me what they know and have even, in some cases, let me see correspondence with Alfred concerning it. I hope that Alfred will not regard publication of this material as an invasion of his privacy, but merely as raw material for the biography that must someday be written about our era's most remarkable publisher of books. At any rate, the facts are in. Alfred is in love with the national parks.

It all began, it seems, in 1948. "The way Alfred first 'came upon a national park,'" writes Bernard De Voto, "was via

---

"A.A.K.'s Love Affair," in *Alfred Knopf at 60*, privately printed, 1952.

B. De Voto. He liked to go on automobile trips but had only done so east of the Mississippi. In connection with his business he had frequently been in the Far West, but only in the cities. He decided that for once he'd drive West and spend four or five weeks doing it. It turned out to be six weeks. He called on me for suggestions and it worked out in the end that I blue-printed the trip. We decided to do a limited trip thoroughly and I made it Montana and Wyoming. I wrote a long compendium—hotels, motor courts, where to buy ranch pants for Blanche, what to see, etc., etc. I wrote Newt Drury about him—that I was sending him to Glacier, Yellowstone, Teton, and the Badlands. . . ."

Newton B. Drury, then Director of the National Park Service of the Department of the Interior, wrote Alfred in April, 1948, saying that De Voto had told him about the projected trip, and offering to give any help he could. Alfred took him up on it, and when his itinerary was ready, he sent it down to Washington. Drury wrote letters to a number of superintendents and custodians, and sent Alfred some circulars.

"Well," resumes De Voto, "Alfred took my Handy Guide of 1001 Fascinating Facts of Indispensable Information along with him, traveled all the roads I'd specified, ate at all the places, etc. Rogers gave him the works in Yellowstone. . . ."

"During the morning of July 2, 1948," writes Edmund B. Rogers, Superintendent of Yellowstone National Park, "a distinguished-looking couple came into my office. They introduced themselves as Mr. and Mrs. Alfred Knopf of New York. The name, of course, was familiar, but I had never met them. They presented a letter of introduction addressed to the Superintendents of several national parks from the Director of the National Park Service. The letter was quite routine, the kind that we receive dozens of each year." It did not take Rogers long, however, to discover that this was no routine visitor. After an exchange of amenities, they started to explore each other.

Rogers soon learned that Knopf had lived his life in New York City and that his world had been books. While he had visited the West before, this was his first trip by car and his first visit to the national parks. He was discovering America, a land to which he confessed himself a stranger. He was deeply interested, but the land's terrain, philosophy, and mores were absolutely foreign to him. Rogers was excited by Alfred's excitement—was, he says, "eager to share his adventure"—and soon remarked that Alfred reminded him of Keats' "On First Looking Into Chapman's Homer."

"Finding that I knew something of this strange land," Rogers writes, "he seized me as his guide. I fortified myself with two competent aids, Joe Joffe, my Administrative Assistant, and Franz Lipp, a landscape architect from Chicago who spends all his spare time and more than his spare money in photographing Yellowstone, and the five of us had lunch together. The philosophy, the hopes, the successes, and the failures of the National Park Service were explored into their darkest corners. Time disappeared under a barrage of questions from them both which came faster than the answers could be made."

Lipp had been with the Knopfs since the night before. Some time previously, he had corresponded with the publishing firm about the possibility of their doing a book of his photographs of Yellowstone, and a week or so before, he had received a telegram telling him to look for the Knopfs at the Canyon Hotel, in Yellowstone, early in July. When they had arrived at Canyon, he had met them and they had dined together. "Both the Knopfs were exceedingly interested in almost anything," the landscape architect writes, "and in particular, Mr. Knopf showed quite a knowledge of Rocky Mountain flora, which during their visit was about in its prime." The following morning the Knopfs and Lipp had driven from the Canyon Hotel over Dunraven Pass, down to Tower Falls, and then to Mammoth, the site of Rogers' headquarters. After the lunch in the Mammoth Coffee Shop, Rogers took the party in the No. 1 Government Car down to Gardiner, "in order," as Lipp says, "to introduce the antelopes. These enchanted Mrs. Knopf in particular, who compared them to the chamois of the Alps. There were not too many antelope in this region at that time, but the ones we saw gave a very good display of their galloping, which delighted both of them."

Since the Knopfs were game to see more of Yellowstone, they went on, with Lipp, first to Norris Geyser Basin, then to the Lower Geyser Basin, where they seemed enthusiastic about the Paint Pots, and to Upper Geyser Basin, to see Old Faithful. "I had a little bit the impression," Lipp writes, "that they were not too impressed by the display of Old Faithful, but were rather very much impressed by the number of people (mob) from all over the country, gathered around it." Next they drove over to West Thumb, around Lake Yellowstone, and by way of Hayden Valley back to the Canyon. "At this point," writes Lipp, "I have to make a confession. As much as I have been out in Yellowstone, I never before made a trip around the entire loop, which is about a hundred and fifty miles, all in one day. I didn't realize how completely punch drunk one becomes by getting all these very different impressions of all the different phenomena and sights. It resulted in a complete case of fresh air poisoning." Alfred, however, seemed to take things pretty much in his stride. At dinner, watching the dancers, he remarked dryly that the standard of tango dancing in the West did not come up to that of New York. He and Blanche decided to stay on a couple of extra days.

Superintendent Rogers writes, "The visit of the Knopfs to the Yellowstone, which we playfully refer to as the 'Education of the Knopfs,' is one of my cherished adventures in the Park Service. If we gave them anything, the Knopfs gave us much more. We need, every so often, some fresh, alert, and penetrat-

ing mind to drive us into taking inventory and appraising ourselves and our concepts and our effectiveness."

After Yellowstone, De Voto writes, the Knopfs "stayed on a
dude ranch in Jackson Hole for more than two weeks. Alfred
took thousands of pictures . . . and the result was he fell in love
with the West and especially the parks. When he got back, he
was like a kid who had met Santa Claus and made the rounds
with him. Why hadn't anybody told him about this scenery?
Why didn't people in the East know about it? Why were
Americans so damn ignorant of their country? He must have
made quite a nuisance of himself at dinner parties in New
York that winter, for he couldn't talk about anything else.
'Benny,' he said to me once, 'I'm fifty-six years old and I never
suspected this stuff existed. I'm never going to Europe again.'
As a matter of fact he's been to Europe only once since, and he
was a man who thought nothing of going two or three times a
year. He was outraged because there weren't books about the
parks—and we know what followed from that."

Immediately after Alfred's return to New York, he wrote
Director Drury two letters on the same day, one a terse thank-
you note, saying, "Mark me as a most enthusiastic friend and
admirer of the National Park Service, and call on me whenever, or if ever, there is anything I can do to help you." In the
other, he said, "I would like awfully much to get written and
to publish a really good book on the National Parks. But I
haven't an idea where to look for a writer and would welcome
any suggestions from you." Alfred said he had in mind something larger, more comprehensive, and written at a considerably more sophisticated level than anything that had been done
previously on the parks. Then, as De Voto noted, he began
filling whatever ear he could with the news that the West is
magnificent, the parks are magnificent. He had a talk with
Drury about the book project in New York on August 27th.
On October 19th, about three weeks before an election in

ALFRED KNOPF IN PARADISE

"I never suspected this stuff existed. I'm never going to Europe again."

which Alfred, along with some other people, assumed that Thomas E. Dewey would be elected President of the United States, Alfred wrote to the Republican candidate about the National Park Service, and enclosed a Marquis Childs column on the subject. A few days later, he wrote to *The New Yorker,* "I was astonished to find the enclosed advertisement for Yellowstone Whiskey in the pages of your learned family journal. Surely you would not want to spread the notion among your readers that the Teton Mountains and Jackson Lake are in Yellowstone National Park, or would you?" An apologetic letter came from the advertising agency that had prepared the copy, and Alfred wrote back advising the copywriter to go and see the park for himself, and while he was there, to call on Mr. Rogers, the Superintendent, at Mammoth Springs; that would straighten him out. In January, 1950, at the time of hearings on the federal budget, Alfred, having been urged by no one, wrote to sixty-odd "gentlemen on Capitol Hill," members of the House and Senate Appropriations Committees, about the National Park Service, saying, "I cannot think of any dollar of the citizen's money expended by the Federal Government for which the citizen gets, or at any rate can get if he wants to, a finer return"; and asking, therefore, that the respective committees would "deal in a free and generous spirit with the National Park Service." The letters were not multigraphed.

In the meanwhile, several people connected with the Park Service had been making suggestions as to who should write the book Alfred wanted to publish; and De Voto, a member of the National Park Service's Advisory Board on National Parks, Historic Sites, Buildings, and Monuments, had also been consulted. Almost everyone agreed that the best possible candidate would be Freeman Tilden, author of *A World in Debt,* who was thoroughly familiar with the parks and had done some writing about them. By the next June, Tilden had signed a contract for the book. Its preparation took more than a year. "Although I have met Alfred occasionally over the years of my writing," Tilden writes, "the Parks book is the first on which he has been my publisher. So far as I am concerned, Knopf the Publisher is a man of few words. An instance: when this Parks book was finally from the printer and he showed me a copy in his office, I said, 'This is certainly a beautiful book.' He said, 'Yes, too beautiful.' I gave way to thoughts one day, in his sanctum, that I foresaw, as a concomitant of the book I was doing, that it might be the basis of a supplementary reading book for the grade schools. He said, with neither sourness nor sweetness, 'Maybe you had better finish this one first.' He is the first publisher I ever had who never uttered a saccharine word to me: I incline now to think that is the basis for the best relations between writer and publisher. Anyway, I like it so." And in the end Alfred liked Tilden's book; he read the manuscript, he wrote Drury, "with great interest and great pleasure."

In the summer of 1949, Alfred was not able to get away on a trip to the parks. In June, however, he met Horace Albright, now president of U.S. Potash Company, who was many years ago Superintendent of Yellowstone and who preceded Newton Drury as Director of the Park Service; the resulting friendship intensified Alfred's interest in the parks. Through Albright, Alfred eventually arranged for the publication of a second book on the parks, a biography of Stephen T. Mather, the pioneering spirit in the founding of the national parks, by Robert Shankland. By the next spring, the Knopfs were off again—to Natchez Trace Parkway and, on the way back, the Blue Ridge Parkway. On June 12th, the Secretary of the Interior, Oscar Chapman, wrote a formal letter to Alfred inviting him to join the Advisory Board on National Parks, Historic Sites, Buildings, and Monuments of the National Park Service. Accepting delightedly and as formally as he could, Alfred could not resist adding this note to the Secretary: "I know how busy you are, but I hope you will find time at least to glance at a book which my office sent you a while back—*America's New Frontier*, by Professor Morris E. Garnsey of the University of Colorado. I suspect it of being a book right up your alley." The Secretary's only answer, on July 28th, was a packet containing Form 57, which is an Application for Federal Employment; a waiver of compensation; a fingerprint chart; an affidavit regarding strikes against the United States Government; an oath of office; and a request for loyalty data—none of which could be considered right up Alfred's alley. Writing Director Drury in August, Alfred exclaimed, "When I received from Secretary Chapman the budget of forms which I have to fill out, well—words fail me!" Words didn't fail Bernard De Voto, who at the same time was having trouble, because of the intricate paperwork involved, collecting expenses for trips he had taken for the government. "I seem to have run afoul of the accounting office again," he began a long letter of protest to Drury; and his letter to Herbert Evison, the Chief of Information of the Park Service, ended, "If the United States wants my service any more, it can damn well send a car for me." (He relented, of course.) In October, when Alfred returned from a brief trip to London, he found "a lifetime's reading" had been sent him from the Park Service. On the subject of red tape, he wrote Drury, "I doubt that I'll be as ornery as Benny. It is clear that people by and large are taking lying down this creeping paper attack on them. Without papers today, the citizen literally does not exist, but that's an old story, for he ceased the kind of existence he was used to in September, 1914, and will never be able to get it back. What I do object to is paying the wages of the kind of people who first have to devise these questionnaires and then check them when they come back. Also, as a publisher who wants paper to print good books on, I object to the amount of paper that these petty bureaucrats consume at my expense."

Eventually, Alfred enjoyed the meetings of the Advisory Board, and contributed much to them. One of his fellow members, Charles G. Sauers, Superintendent of the Cook County Forest in Illinois, writes, "I came to meet him in Drury's office and first thought him a brusque person, when, as a matter of fact, he was simply being, as usual, quiet and being, as always, a most accomplished listener. To sit with Alfred at our board meetings, one comes to know his size. His deep sense of orientation, his ability to utilize experience in an orderly manner, his willingness to listen, and his curt and realistic summations are effective indeed. The Advisory Board is composed of eleven members, largely historians, archaeologists, historian-architects, biologists, and the like. Knopf, the publisher, brings to the table a broader perspective and a lifetime of successful experience in the observation and practice of the fine arts. His imperturbability and the feeling of steadiness he conveys are sometimes shoved aside by flashes of unconcealed contempt for irresponsible and half-baked proposals. It is a treat to sit at conference when Knopf and De Voto are in disagreement. Bernard makes one of his headlong proposals, brilliant and tense. Alfred smokes his cigar, handling it with the care its quality deserves, never chewing it. He listens intently and at the same time seems to ruffle through the card index of his mind. He then moves in to analyze the proposal and state his opinions, always with brevity. What a duo!"

Toward the end of 1950, Alfred was in frequent correspondence with Drury and others about the format, wrapper, maps, and so on, for the Tilden book. He asked Drury to write an introduction. In the meantime the book on Mather was made ready for publication and other books on various phases of conservation were in the works. In February, 1951, Alfred and Blanche drove down to the Everglades National Park in Florida. The book about Mather was published in April; the Tilden book in June.

That spring Alfred was also planning his most ambitious exploration of the parks—and indirectly, of himself and of

America. With the help of Horace Albright and others, he arranged a very stiff program—Crater Lake, Lassen, the redwood country, Yosemite, and Sequoia and Kings Canyon, with business stops in Portland, San Francisco, and Los Angeles sandwiched in, all to be accomplished between August 21st and September 12th.

The visit to the redwood country was with Newton Drury, who had retired as Director of the Park Service the previous April and had returned to his native California. Alfred and Drury met at Redding, and drove through dreadful heat over an abominable road, narrow and curving—with Alfred, at the wheel, venting scorn for California drivers—down to the coast. They spent the night at an auto camp at Orick, and when they sat down to eat in a roadside beanery, Alfred pulled out and uncorked a bottle of wine he had brought along for just such a fearful emergency. The next day, driving hard from forest to forest, they took in, more than once, the breathtaking massed effect of pure stands of *Sequoia sempervirens* and *Sequoia gigantea*. Alfred snapped many pictures; he seemed impassive in the presence of trees four and five thousand years old, and there were times when Drury was glad he knew him well enough to realize he wasn't bored—far from it. He also knew him well enough not to tell him what to look at. They wound up, after a long day, at San Francisco.

After several days' work in San Francisco, Alfred drove with his old friend Floyd H. Nourse to Yosemite. There the superintendent, Carl P. Russell, and his assistant, Ralph Anderson, escorted the pair into the Yosemite high country, to Tioga Pass, down Leevining Canyon to the Mono Basin, and on to the ghost town of Bodie, once the mining center of the Mono Lake region. Dr. Russell thought Alfred particularly enjoyed wandering around the ruins of Bodie; he inspected the old church and ate a box lunch on the front stoop of a long-abandoned home. They returned by way of Bridgeport, where they went into a typical country store, drank soda pop, and chatted with the Mono County people who were shopping, and with a local character named D. V. Cains, whose family had lived in living Bodie. The next day Ralph Anderson took Alfred and Nourse to Glacier Point and the Mariposa Grove of Big Trees. On the way to Glacier Point they overtook a party of three women stranded by the road trying to change a tire. Alfred was all for helping them. The three men did the job in record time, then posed for a snapshot at the request of the woman driver. "At Glacier Point," Dr. Russell writes, "Mr. Anderson looked up the Stuart McCorkles, distinguished visitors from Austin, Texas, and Mr. Knopf was as interested in meeting and advising these people as was Mr. Anderson." Alfred, Nourse, and Anderson picnicked under a Jeffry pine tree near Sentinel Dome and leisurely returned to Yosemite Valley by way of a section of the old Glacier Point Road. All through the two days, Alfred had spoken with mounting anticipation of the next step on his itinerary—a pack trip in Sequoia and Kings Canyon National Parks, where he was going to rough it. He told the others that Superintendent Eivind Scoyen had warned him that the weather might be very cold, and to come well supplied with long johns; and he spoke of what a contrast it would be to go straight from a pack trip in winter woolies in the high country down to Hollywood, where he was to escort Ethel Barrymore to a dinner party with his brother.

The pack trip in Sequoia National Park was the climax of Alfred's explorations. "Let me say," Superintendent Scoyen writes, "that the High Sierra of these parks is very rugged terrain. Our elevations run from 1,400 feet to 14,495 feet at the summit of Mount Whitney, highest point in the continental United States. We have ten peaks over 14,000 feet, and scores over 13,000. The parks include three of the great canyons of the United States—those of the Kern, South, and Middle Forks of the Kings River. We have somewhat in excess of 400

lakes, and less than a dozen of these occur at an elevation below 10,000 feet." Alfred had only four days and three nights to
devote to this forbidding terrain, which meant that Scoyen was
faced with the choice of traveling far and hard each day, or just
biting into the edge of the mountain country. In the end, he
compromised between the two extremes.

The trip started from the Wolverton Corrals, near the Giant
Forest, at an elevation of 7,000 feet above the sea. The party
consisted of Scoyen; Alfred; Clarence Fry, a retired Ranger and
an old-timer, whom Scoyen took along mainly because of his
wide knowledge of the flora and fauna of the parks, and who,
though he never went beyond grammar school, could name
any of the several hundred plants in the parks accurately by
their Latin names; Ray Rundell, Scoyen's chief clerk; and, as
packer, Lou Gannaway, who enlisted in MacArthur's 2nd Cav-
alry Division to take care of horses, was "motorized" into a
radio operator, served all through the South Pacific campaigns,
and then returned to packing in the High Sierra. Each of the
five men, of course, had a saddle horse, and there were five
mules to carry dunnage, equipment, and supplies. Early-
September weather in the high country could be tricky, and "I
am sure," Scoyen writes, "that Alfred would have been rather
startled if he had discovered the details of a bundle consisting
of sweaters, woolen socks, overshoes, mittens, ear muffs, etc.,
that I took along to handle a weather situation that could normally be expected." As it turned out, the weather went to the
opposite extreme; it was unusually hot.

Leaving Wolverton, the party rode to the Ranger Lakes. The
trail was good until they reached the pass across the Great
Western Divide, known as Silliman Pass. From there down to
the lakes, they had to pick their way; the going was rough at
times. Even the most experienced riders, Scoyen says, spend a
good deal of time, when they get off the main trails in the High
Sierra, dismounted and leading their horses. Alfred did pretty

well. "On that first day out," Rundell writes, "we had to call him 'Al,' because he became one of the gang immediately. From observations of a rider bringing up the rear of four mountain men followed by a string of pack mules, I could only admire the grit, determination, and posterior suffering of Al Knopf in conquering western riding on a western horse, over trails made for squirrels instead of men and horses. I began the trip well reinforced with heavy leather chaps. Al, however, had rather light clothing, I thought, for his comfort in warding off saddle torment. Al rode a horse named 'Jim,' who was very tall and took long strides. He was a gentle, plodding beast, but appeared somewhat rough riding, having action in navigating rocks and rough spots not unlike the motion of a camel. Such navigation for Al, who had not ridden for some time, produced considerable anguish for several hours. However, I noticed that by bracing one hand on the cantle of the saddle and the other on the pommel, he was able to produce a posture similar to that of vaulting a fence, so that the horse and saddle could rock violently with no special damage to Al." The party found a pleasant place to camp at Ranger Lakes. Before nightfall, they caught some fish. "Alfred told me," Scoyen writes, "that he had never in his life slept in a sleeping bag, therefore we gave him some instructions on how to make up his bed and assisted him this first evening. However, this did not extend to blowing up his air mattress—wind and not experience is required for that." After all the warnings about winter weather, the night turned out to be hot—"the warmest, I believe," Scoyen says, "I ever spent in the mountain country. I am quite sure that Alfred was not very comfortable in his fine eiderdown sleeping bag." Day's log: ten miles; climbed from 7,000 feet to 10,000 feet; camped at 9,000.

The second day the party made its way through an area known as the Roaring River section and over into Deadman Canyon. "This was really a very hard day even for some of the experienced mountain men in the group," Scoyen writes, "and Alfred must have suffered a good deal." Among other things, the temperature was at least twenty degrees above normal, and the trail was unpleasantly dusty. But the party made a wonderful camp that evening in Deadman Canyon beside a mountain stream on the edge of a beautiful meadow. The serrated walls of the canyon on both sides rose up 3,000 feet. Day's log: sixteen miles; dropped from 9,000 feet to 7,000; camped at 8,200.

"The next day," Scoyen writes, "we ran into one of those things that travellers with a pack outfit in the mountains dread, but which occur quite frequently—lost stock. Usually the packer gets up at daylight and brings in his string. This is based on two things: first, in the mountains you start operations about daylight, and also your stock will start to wander about that time, just as a matter of principle. We waited about two hours and the packer had not yet returned from his search. Finally he did come back and said he had followed the tracks of mules and horses which he figured were those of our outfit on up the trail for about four miles. However, he came in sight of another camp and, of course, was disappointed to find he had been following the wrong tracks. As soon as we learned what had happened, we started to circle the area where our horses and mules had been grazing, and finally 'cut' their sign. Following them, we found they had gotten through the fence on the down stream side of our camp and were grazing peacefully along the trail about a quarter of a mile away!"

The mountain men had promised Alfred that with an early start that third day, they would be able to find him some very good fishing in the evening. But under the circumstances they did not start moving until about ten o'clock and reached camp late, at five in the evening. The trip was up Deadman Canyon, named for a sheepherder who died there seventy years ago, and over Elizabeth Pass, the location of the story in Stewart Edward White's *The Pass* and named for his wife. Heavy floods of the year before had done a lot of damage to the trail in the canyon, and much of it had not been repaired. The going, therefore, was slow. Finally the party reached the top of the pass and then went down to the headwaters of the Kaweah River and camped at a place called Lone Pine Meadow. By that time Alfred had lost all interest in an additional three-mile ride to a lake that was famous for its golden trout. Rundell says, however, that "he [Alfred] prepared a fine evening meal with the touch of a German gourmet." Day's log: ten miles; climbed from 8,200 feet to 10,200 feet; camped at 9,000 feet.

"The next morning," Scoyen writes, "which would be our last day on the trail, when everyone woke up, of course his first thought was, 'Where is the stock?' Looking around, we saw them high up on the mountainside above camp. Rounding them up was easy, because Lou Gannaway merely let out a few cowboy yells and in a very short time they all came trotting into camp." That day the party rode back to Wolverton. The Great Western Divide stood at their east as they rode, its peaks rising to 12,000 feet; and mountain slopes broke sharply downward from the trail 5,000 feet into the canyon below. Much of the solid granite around them had been given a high polish by ancient glaciers. As they went downstream, the country became much less rugged. "We were all more or less relaxed," Rundell says, "in the belief that the most hazardous trails were behind us. We were going down grade when suddenly old Jim's right front foot slid and wedged between two solid rocks in the trail. I saw him step once with the other three feet, and then the horse seemed to catapult the man off the trail. The horse remained upright, but Al was thrown to the ground close to the horse's front feet. Neither moved a muscle for what seemed an eternity. The rest of us froze in our saddles for a second so as to prevent exciting old Jim; but he and Al had the situation well in hand with a silent air of nonchalance until Clarence Fry could reach them, while I attempted to keep the other horses quiet. It so happened that the embankment was overgrown with grass and brush which broke the fall, and Al was none the worse for the experience. Considering the country we had been over, the odds for such a thing happening at a place where serious consequences did not result were at least 100,000 to one. Major credit must be given to Jim, who showed that he was a mountain horse of many years' experience. Most animals, including man, thrash about wildly when they suddenly find themselves with a foot trapped. However, old Jim stood still until the foot was freed. If he had moved at all, most of the footprints would have been on Al."

"The trail was so dusty," Scoyen writes, "that I was in the habit of riding far enough ahead so that the air would be clear by the time Alfred came along, therefore I did not see this particular accident and knew nothing about it until the party caught up with me some time later. To say that Alfred was lucky is certainly a mild statement of the situation." The party went on without event over the High Sierra Trail and reached home at three o'clock. Log: sixteen miles, from 9,000 feet to 7,000 feet.

The story is not yet complete. Alfred is still disappearing from time to time. As this is written, he is off in the Southwest, visiting parks. "Incidentally," Superintendent Scoyen writes in April, 1952, "I have just received a postcard from Alfred mailed to me from Big Bend National Park, in which he states he has gone back into the mountains again and observes the trails are not nearly as rugged as he found them in these parks. I have spent considerable time in Big Bend also, and assure you that Alfred's judgment on the matter is sound. However," Scoyen adds, "he did not indicate his preference." The trips are not just jaunts now. Alfred is beginning to dig deep. He seems to be exploring not merely terrain, not merely history and inheritance, but something more complex; something to do with our past and our future that has become important to him and that he, as a publisher, would like to make important to others. It is nice to see a man of sixty grown so young. "A thing you have to say of Knopf," writes Freeman Tilden, "is that he is integral. He doesn't try to be several other people, and if he doesn't feel in the mood, he doesn't invent emotion. We have in the parks, the primeval parks, many look-offs at the roadsides that we facetiously call Oh and Ah. Alfred can take in these surprising tours de force of Nature without saying 'Oh' and 'Ah.' But he feels the impact where it does him and the Park Service the most good."

Janet Train

In a mixed white-and-Negro neighborhood in a small city in southern Illinois, huddled next to a corner grocery store, a one-story, two-family tenement stands. Its bricks are old and spalled; the mortar crumbles between the uneven courses. The once-white paint on the wooden sills is cracked, and the screens are rusted and torn. A narrow alleyway between the store and the house leads to the back door of one half of the tenement; the front door is never used. Along the rear of the house runs a sagging wooden porch roof, but no porch; on the bare ground beneath the roof are piles of rubbish— empty tins, broken dishes, discarded parts of a cheap clock, a rusted toaster, a burst bag of hickory nuts. A sheet of moldy pressboard is nailed over the back door to keep out the hostile wind from the plains to the south of the city.

Inside are but two rooms, a living room and a kitchen, both of which double as bedrooms, and both of which are in disorder. In the former stands an ancient oaken rocking chair; a bureau, on top of which, besides a small radio, is a slovenly heap of toilet articles and clothes that want mending; a dirty, broken-down couch; and a cot heaped with bedclothes. The

"Intelligence, Choice, and Consent," No. 7 of *Education in the Nation's Service: A Series of Articles on American Education Today,* Woodrow Wilson Foundation, New York, 1959. Some of the names in this essay were changed.

linoleum on the floor is worn through to the fabric and even to the underlying wood in many places, and the plaster on the walls is cracked and falling. There are no pictures. The whole house is warmed by a small space heater, on which is balanced a spoked laundry rack draped with damp sheets and under-clothes. The floor is littered with shoes of several sizes, a pair of moth-eaten felt slippers, a wastebasket full of papers and garbage, and bundles of lint which stir in the drafts. In the kitchen, besides a stove and sink and table, there is a big roll-away bed, which for a long time has neither been rolled away nor even made.

Here and there, under beds and seats, in corners, wherever they can be tucked away from the pattern of traffic of the family of five that lives in this unkempt rented house, are a number of cardboard cartons containing treasures that are something of a surprise in this place.

They are books, scores on scores of books.

In this poor home lives Janet Train, a girl of twelve, who may be very bright. The books are hers. She seems to have enough intelligence to go eventually to college. She might well become a journalist, or possibly a medical doctor. She might make a fine teacher. Above all, she could become a discriminating voter.

But at the moment—even though this sixth-grade slum girl is being educated in a school system with a full intelligence-testing program, and though she lives in a city where a Youth Development Commission has been set up by a team from an outstanding university for the purpose of discovering and freeing young people's talents—her chances of going to college, of becoming a writer or doctor or teacher, seem very poor indeed. She is a leading candidate for the American talent scrap heap.

Far worse—if one has in mind the health of our democratic

society—she is not being given anything like adequate preparation for making those crucial choices, for giving those thought-out consents, that are the essence of our freedom.

The facts on the annual talent losses in the United States— on the failure of our schools and colleges to meet the growing demands of our society for expert physical and social scientists, engineers, medical specialists, psychologists, and teachers, as well, alas, as for poets and senators and prophets and wise men—have been advertised widely in recent years. But these advertisements have mostly been in the name of a negative: a perceived slippage of the United States in technological competition with rival nations.

The root of the waste of American talent lies paradoxically in a fantastic betterment of American society—in the expansion of its education, in less than two handfuls of decades, from a privilege for the very few to a facility for the very many. Since 1870, while the total population has about quadrupled, secondary-school enrollment has been multiplied more than eighty times. At the beginning of this century only one in every five American youths attended high school; now four in five do. At the beginning of the century only one young man or woman in fifty went to college; now one in five does.

As our school system expanded, our educators pitched their teaching to the mythical average student. Actually this tendency, founded on our pervasive belief in equality, has a long tradition here. "A middle standard is fixed in America for human knowledge," Tocqueville wrote early in the nineteenth century. "All approach as near as they can, some as they rise, others as they descend." The aim of our more recent mass education was to lift the whole mass, and lifting the mass seemed to require paying regard to the center of gravity, in order that balance might be maintained as the mass rose. The application of this method in mechanics leads to equilibrium; in education it has led to mediocrity.

Janet Train's intelligence has been repeatedly measured. The I.Q.s assigned to her have been, as will be shown, practically meaningless. But what is significant about this child of the slums is her consistency in one area of ability: on every standard intelligence test she has taken since her first-grade year, she has stood in the top one per cent in the whole country in verbal ability for her age. She is an avid reader, a hoarder of books. She uses language clearly and correctly. She can study, assimilate, remember. In a time when grammar is rather out of fashion, hers is good. She spells accurately. She knows what words mean, and she likes to use them.

But nothing is being done about Janet Train's evident talent for the only means we human beings have of understanding one another. Her intelligence—the first essential for considered choices and wise consents in a democracy—has been ill served.

W hat is intelligence? What is an I.Q.? How can we know what Janet Train has in her head?

Psychologists have given many definitions of intelligence: "capacity for learning," "the power to deal with novelty," "relational thinking," "the force which produces adequate performance, right solutions, correct learning." Intelligence is able to put together, to build; it is, as one psychologist has said, the "capacity for the right completion of complex forms, both material and immaterial, from fragments." Thus intelligence builds a dinosaur's skeleton from a few bones; but we must beware, for intelligence also built the Piltdown man, a forgery, from spurious fragments. In other words, intelligence is not in itself right and good. It is capable of breathtaking forgery, magnificent lies, prodigies of evildoing. Yet it is also the instrument that human beings must mainly use to better themselves, for without it they could not make plans.

Leta Hollingworth, who was one of the first American educators to show concern for able students, once reduced all this to a homely and wise definition: "Intelligence learns how to do and how to get what is wanted."

This is a proper emphasis. What is wanted comes first; the capacity to get it is secondary. Intelligence without desire is of no use to society—and this may be the trouble, up to now, in the case of Janet Train. It may also be one reason why the I.Q., as such, is in rather ill repute these days in spite of our need for bright people.

But a more important reason why the I.Q. is unpopular is that so few people, even teachers, have a clear idea what they mean when they use the term.

The idea behind the I.Q. is that if a quality exists, it exists in some quantity and therefore can be measured. Early in this century the French psychologist Alfred Binet, proceeding on the hypothesis that there was a pervasive, unitary characteristic in each individual, a "general intelligence," constructed a remarkably simple, durable examination to find and measure that supposed characteristic. This test was later adapted for use in America by Lewis M. Terman and others and became the Stanford-Binet intelligence test. It had to be given to one child at a time by a trained examiner. The I.Q., or Intelligence Quotient, was devised as a way of expressing the results of this test. It stood for the relationship between the individual's actual and "mental" ages at the time of the test, and it was derived by dividing the latter by the former and multiplying by one hundred; a given "mental" age represented the average performance by a large number of persons who had been given the test at that age. For example, a child whose age was actually ten and who did as well on the Binet as the average fifteen-year-old who had been sampled for the test was assigned a mental age of fifteen and an I.Q. of $15 \div 10 \times 100$, or 150.

Following on Binet's work, a British psychologist, Charles Spearman, developed a theory that in every intelligence there was a pervasive, "general" factor, and a predominating "special" factor, one of a large number of isolated factors related to specific activities. An American, L. L. Thurstone, carrying this idea farther, recognized the presence of a number of "group" factors, or "primary abilities," narrower than Spearman's "general" but broader than his "special." Among them were the capacities, for instance, to grasp verbal meanings, to use numbers, to see spatial forms and relationships, and to perceive things at a characteristic rate of speed. This tendency, known as "factor analysis," has been carried forward over the years, sometimes to absurd lengths.

Next, a rather large number of multiple-factor intelligence tests were invented which could be given simultaneously to groups of people by untrained examiners. These were the so-called group tests of intelligence, abilities, and aptitudes. Some of these tests were better than others. Some were hurried into widespread use before they had been validated by sufficiently large or sufficiently representative samples of the American student population, and none of them had behind them the many tempering years of school and clinical experience the Stanford-Binet had. It developed that there could be, moreover, a dangerously wide gap between the controlled laboratory use of these tests during their development and the handling of them in ordinary classrooms by teachers untrained in psychology. Since testing takes time and time is precious in school, the group tests were soon abbreviated and truncated. A trained examiner of an individual child can draw the best out of the child and can make allowances for the way the child feels on a given day, or can even decide that a retest is needed; group tests cannot cater to a headache here and a daydream there.

For purposes of reliably identifying students of marked abilities, these group tests have proved to be of little value. "To give every . . . member of the human species full opportunity to achieve his true rating relative to the average in a test," Leta Hollingworth wrote, "it must range in difficulty from what an idiot can do to better than can be done by the most subtle and retentive thinker." The group tests, designed for mass screening and nothing more, do not have enough "top" to differentiate reliably between various degrees of remarkable talent.

A serious drawback to many of the group tests is that in young children the factors of intelligence may not emerge clearly, or may develop at different rates at different ages—one kind of ability moving forward rapidly in a given year, while another seems to rest awhile.

The only kind of I.Q. that is accurate for very young children as well as for older persons, and that has anything like precision and a long-range predictive value, is one derived from an individual intelligence test. Besides the still excellent Stanford-Binet, two more recent individual tests, which are based on the factorial theory and have proved useful and dependable, are the Wechsler tests, one for adults known as the Wechsler-Bellevue Intelligence Scale, and another for the school ages, the Wechsler Intelligence Scale for Children. One of the tragic results of the crudeness and misuse of some of the group tests, the results of *all* of which are called I.Q.s, is that the whole concept of the I.Q. has fallen into disfavor, quite unjustly in the cases of the Binet and Wechsler results, which have value in predicting academic achievement, if not more.

Janet Train has been tested and tested, and examined and tabulated and averaged and classified, and then tested some more, by both the schools of her city and its Youth Development Commission. The latter has been specifically hunting for talent. Yet little is known of the nature and degree of Janet's talent, if she really has one, for the simple reason that she has never been given an individual intelligence test. What emerges from the batteries of group tests she has been given is not a picture of a promising young human being, but a set of variable and unreliable statistics. The one constant has been her talent for communication—about which nothing has been done.

In kindergarten, Janet was given a reading-readiness test that put her in the top five per cent of all pupils her age in the nation. There was no effort, however, to move her ahead into reading any sooner than any other children in the city, for the school administration holds to the widespread view that it is rather sinful for children to begin to read earlier than the "norm." This view flies in the face of the fact that brilliant children often learn to read long before they enter school. Jeremy Bentham became familiar with the shapes of letters before he could talk; at three he read parts of a history of England; at six he read Voltaire's *Life of Charles XII*. Voltaire himself wrote verses almost literally "from his cradle," and Samuel Johnson was "forming verbs when he could not speak plain." Coleridge read a version of the *Arabian Nights* before he was five, and at six he read *Robinson Crusoe* and *Philip Quarles*. At six John Stuart Mill was reading Greek. Tasso began the study of grammar at three. Cavour was taught by his mother to read when he was four.

This is not to suggest that Janet Train is even randomly in a class with the world's great geniuses; it is rather to suggest, if only by a syllogism, that talent, even of a modest sort, may be dampened, retarded, and perhaps stifled by an educational rigidity which decrees that children may begin to read at a certain chronological age, and not one day earlier.

In the first grade Janet took a group test which sought out five supposed factors of intelligence, and because she was presumed to be unable to read, the test was entirely pictorial and instructions were given orally by the teacher—to the whole class at once. On her performance on this test, Janet was assigned an I.Q. of 142.

When Janet was in the fourth grade, she was given another type of multiple-factor group test by the Youth Development Commission, and she was assigned an I.Q. of 130.

At ten and eleven, in the sixth and seventh grades, she was given still another kind of test and was assigned, in successive years, I.Q.s of 144 and 135.

What are we to think? Are we supposed to average Janet's I.Q.s? How rare is her mind?

It might be thought that for operational purposes Janet's I.Q.s of 130 and 144, her lowest and highest, could be considered close enough to each other. But there is far more difference between *true* I.Q.s of 130 and 144 than fourteen points would suggest. The higher the I.Q., the less frequently it appears. Some years ago Lewis M. Terman calculated that on the basis of individual Binet tests, one American child in ten has an I.Q. of 116; one in twenty has an I.Q. of 122; one in fifty has an I.Q. of 128; and one in a hundred has an I.Q. of 130, which Janet was assigned at nine. But only one in ten thousand has an I.Q. of 140, and at ten Janet was assigned an I.Q. of 144. From the point of view of a teacher devising an education to challenge a talent, it would make quite a difference whether a child was one in a hundred or one in more than ten thousand.

Actually, Janet's scores on these group intelligence tests were far more consistent than is often the case. Her I.Q. range was only fourteen points. It is not uncommon to find differences of as much as forty points between the results on two group intelligence tests given at different times to the same child.

But let us look more closely at one of Janet's so-called I.Q.s—the one she was assigned in the fourth grade: 130, her lowest. She was ten years old, and she was given a test designed for children eleven through seventeen years old. The original test of that variety was based on the work of Thurstone and had been carefully constructed at the University of Chicago, and when it had been first published, in 1941, it had represented an important step forward in group intelligence testing, for it was the first comprehensive battery to test the various abilities that were presumed to make up intelligence as a whole. The battery required six full testing periods—at least four hours. But the test was progressively abridged and popularized, and by the time Janet Train came along, it had been cut down so far that the whole battery took only about three-quarters of an hour—less than a fifth of its original length. The abbreviated batteries had been put into widespread use before they were sufficiently refined and validated. There remained some doubt whether the samples on which the norms for the test were based were truly representative of the country; the means of arriving at the I.Q.s and of interpreting them were facile and oversimplified; the test put a disproportionate emphasis on speed; there was not enough evidence that the I.Q. derived from it was stable—that is, remained fairly constant as the child grew older. The battery Janet took at ten contained only one short test for each of five factors: Verbal Meaning (V), Space (S), Reasoning (R), Number (N), and Word Fluency (W). Tests for Perceptual Speed and Associative Memory, which had been in the original battery, had been dropped altogether. Of the abbreviated battery, the Youth Development Commission gave Janet's group, because of the pressure of time, only the tests for V, S, and R.

Many school systems use group intelligence tests as they should be used, as rough screening devices, to be followed by individual tests where needed. But other school systems are not so knowing or so prosperous or so careful. Many a child goes through life labeled with an I.Q. figured not to the nearest five or ten points but to an exact digit, based on a single unnamed group test given at an early age, perhaps on a day when the

child was functioning well but perhaps not, perhaps in a carefully controlled group situation but perhaps not, perhaps by a
skillful teacher but perhaps not, perhaps scored accurately but
perhaps not.

The Youth Development Commission was initiated a few
years ago by a group of professors at a large nearby university, as a long-range project to marshal the school and community resources of an Illinois city of 42,000 people, and to
help the gifted and the maladjusted among an experimental
sample of the city's children to realize their best potentials. The
experimental sample consisted of all the children in the city's
fourth grades in the project's first year, while all the children
in the city's sixth grades that year were considered a control, to
be watched for comparisons. The Commission, made up of
leading citizens and educators, and advised by the university
group, would help the gifted and maladjusted fourth-graders
and not the sixth-graders over a period of years, to see whether
there would be any differences in the ways the children turned
out. Janet Train was in the experimental sample.

The aim of the Commission was to identify and help children in the sample who were gifted intellectually; who had
talent in music, painting, dramatics, dancing, speech, or writing; who were creative; who had the gift of leadership; who
were aggressively maladjusted; or who were withdrawn. The
Commission did its testing in the schools and used, for both
screening and "development," teams of interested and talented
citizens.

The screening for intellectual talent was to discover the children in "the top two or three per cent" on two tests—a group
intelligence test, of which, as we have seen, the Commission
actually had time to give Janet only three shortened sections;
and a "culture-free" test, which based its queries on comic-

book images in order to put children from homes without books on the same footing with more fortunate ones. The Commission staff was far too busy in its vast screening program to take a look at Janet's school records and correlate her remarkable showing on the verbal section of the group intelligence test with her fine work in school in the same area. On her fourth-grade reading achievement tests, for instance, she showed that she was more than four years ahead of her grade. No note was taken of what is probably her real talent.

In the screening for artistic talent, Janet was given low marks. The Commission never got around to screening her at all for ability in dramatics, music, dancing, or speech. She was given some tests for creativity, surely one of the most evanescent and least measurable of all gifts, and these were supposed to be reviewed by a volunteer team of talented citizens; the team never got around to them.

The Youth Development Commission put up a huge identification chart in its offices, and Janet Train's name was finally listed on the chart because of an alleged talent for, of all things, leadership. It was determined that she had this gift on the basis of a questionnaire given her class called a Who-Are-They Test, and because of check marks made against her name on a form called the Youth Development Behaviour Description Instrument. The chart placed her in the 87th percentile in leadership.

We have seen Janet Train as a set of statistics, a profile of test scores. What of the human being?

The fact must be faced at once that Janet Train, who is now eleven years old and in the sixth grade, is fat. Where in all the statistics, in the jungle of percentiles and test results and pseudo-I.Q.s did *that* interesting and possibly significant fact shine through? Eating is Janet's joy and bane. She is a roly-

poly, cheerful, fun-loving girl. "The others all like her," says
Mrs. Hottelet, her teacher. "She never has a quarrel. When she
leaves the room, it's always in a group, and when she comes
back, she's with the same group." Janet does not worry about
her weight, and Mrs. Hottelet has learned to protect her from
teasing by the others, particularly by the boys. Janet is a good
sport; she goes roller-skating nearly every Sunday with two girl
friends at Scotty's Skating Rink, and she takes some bad falls,
but she bounces back up again and rolls away every time. She
tries to make a joke of her awkwardness in gym at school, but
the joke is forced. She spends a lot of time with some people
across the street, the Zimmers, who have a television set, and
the Zimmers have noticed that she squirms and blushes when
a fat person is the butt of humor. Her mother talks about taking her to a specialist but has never really done anything about
Janet's fatness, except to buy her a bottle of reducing pills once,
which Janet refused to carry to school and take with her lunch.
Janet's older sister Mary has gone through life rather sickly and
thin, while Janet has always enjoyed robust health. Janet was
not overweight until she was eight or nine years old, when
suddenly she began to gain. She eats no more than Mary—
recently she gave up bread and potatoes altogether—but she
remains heavy.

The significant thing physically about Janet Train is that she
has energy to squander. She is the most active girl in her class;
she never tires of stirring up fun. Indeed, the Youth Development Commission and the city's school system may have dismissed Janet Train's potential talent from their minds partly
because Janet does not look like their idea of a Brain. Once,
when the popular picture of a talented child, "a pathetic
creature, over-serious and under-sized, sickly, hollow-chested,
stoop-shouldered, clumsy, nervously tense, and bespectacled,"
had been conjured up to Dr. Terman, he commented, "Stereo-
types have almost nothing to do with facts." The connection

between vitality and talent has, of course, long been evident; one of the most enjoyable notices of it came from the pen of Francis Galton, the nineteenth-century English scientist, cousin of Charles Darwin, who, besides interesting his restless mind in such things as meteorology and fingerprints, did pioneer work in the field of heredity. "I think my readers would be surprised," Galton wrote, "at the stature and physical frames of the heroes of history who fill my pages, if they could be assembled together in a hall. I would undertake to pick out of any group of them, even out of that of the Divines, an 'eleven' who could compete in any physical feats whatsoever, against similar selection from groups twice or thrice their numbers from equally well-fed classes.... A collection of living magnates in the various branches of intellectual achievement is always a feast to my eyes; being, as they are, such massive, vigorous, capable-looking animals."

Psychologists are more and more looking for the key to the full expression of talent in that which lies beyond high intelligence: in drive, in irresistible motivation, in the wellsprings of energy and desire. Janet has the energy; it appears she has certain innate capacities. So far no one has tried to help Janet wed the two.

Mrs. Hottelet, Janet's teacher in an elementary school which happens to be named for Woodrow Wilson, is a delicate, white-haired woman in her early sixties. She is kind-hearted, homey, and rather old-fashioned; she seems tired and puzzled by life. She is not badly overloaded in class, as so many teachers are these days: there are twenty-six children in her room, nine boys and seventeen girls. Wilson School was recently integrated with a nearby all-Negro school, and Mrs. Hottelet has four Negro children.

Mrs. Hottelet recognizes that Janet has talent, but the talent seems to her rather passive. Mrs. Hottelet is well satisfied; she is passive herself. Brightness can be bothersome, and Janet is no bother. "If all my pupils were like Jan," Mrs. Hottelet says, "I wouldn't have any trouble. She's not a great hand at speaking out, but she'll wait and take it all in, and when you call on her, she'll have it. She's thoughtful; she waits for the slow ones to have an idea and lets them speak up. She's full of fun, too. She told a story the other day, how she left a note in the refrigerator for her mother—a letter of resignation from making up her bed. . . . Whatever I tell her to do she does quickly and accurately, but she won't have the desire to do anything extra. . . ."

Mrs. Hottelet cannot help being impressed with Janet's accuracy, which seems to have fallen on Janet out of the sky—it is certainly nothing Mrs. Hottelet has cultivated. Not long ago each child in the class wrote a handful of brief portraits of classmates; the group did not know that this was a sociometric device, introduced by the Youth Development Commission, to find out the leaders and the maladjusted. For a supposed leader, Janet did not rate very well, for only two classmates mentioned her; but what was interesting was the absolute correctness of her work, compared with that of her contemporaries. Here is what some of her friends wrote:

I like Sarah Kopp because she dont cuse or she dont act stuck up. She is very good in dodgeball.

Sarah Kopp is good at art and she works hard in her school work she all so plays in the band and she is a patrol gril.

I like Sarah Kopp. She is a good artest and is all ways drawing. She drew my sister and I, a hourse and many other things. She is relly a nice girl.

Here is what Janet wrote:

Sarah Kopp is very nice. She has a good sense of humor. She likes all animals, but she doesn't like school work. Sarah would rather be around horses than be in school. She likes art very much. She likes to skate and ride horseback. She is always friendly except when she is angry. She likes to play dodge-ball and shoot baskets. Sarah gets mad when she doesn't make a basket. She once found a cardinal and has kept him ever since.

Mrs. Hottelet holds to the familiar ways of doing things, and she's a little leery of a lot of the newfangled educational ideas. Sociometrics! And nobody ever says what "enrichment for the gifted" really is! Still, she tries to oblige. For example, one day when Janet finished her work early, Mrs. Hottelet "enriched" Janet's curriculum by sending her down to the school office to straighten out the school's dentistry file. "She did a good job," the teacher says, "better than a lot of us grownups would do, orderly and neat and accurate."

The main form of "enrichment" Mrs. Hottelet uses is to let Janet help the other children with their work. One day in English class—where, if anywhere, Janet's talent needs to be challenged, roused, liberated—the entire period was taken up with discussion of the form of a rudimentary business letter and with copying one from the textbook:

> 1144 Pine Street,
> Oak Park, Illinois
> April 10, 19———

Home Arts Publishing Company
1789 Fulton Street
St. Louis 4, Missouri

Gentlemen:
   Please send me a sample copy of *The Home Decorator,* which you offered over the radio to send free of charge.
> Yours truly,
> (Miss) Nancy J. Holmes

Janet had long been a frequent letter writer. She had written on behalf of the class to the State Agriculture Department in

Springfield for a booklet on soil, and another time to the
Weather Bureau for the records of rainfall in southern Illinois.
She writes, as well, numerous letters to her relatives, and she
loves to answer advertisements. That morning she finished
copying the dull textbook letter accurately and neatly in three
minutes, and she then had the remainder of the period to kill.
At first she reached into her desk and pulled out a novel she
had borrowed from the town library, *College in Crinoline,* by
M. E. Daly, and began to enrich herself in her own way. But
after a while it developed that some of the pupils simply could
not get the hang of blocking the letter into the center of the
page, and Mrs. Hottelet asked Janet if she would move around
and help some of the others—watching particularly for uneven
margins and misspelling. In this way Janet spent the rest of the
period in the course called English, being "enriched"; she did
not get another chance to look at *College in Crinoline* until
midway through Social Studies, in the next period.

It does not occur to Mrs. Hottelet that the schools are failing
a talented child in Janet Train. Mrs. Hottelet sincerely passes
the buck. "She's nowhere near working up to where she could,"
the teacher says. "But I don't know, it seems that there's something in the home situation that isn't challenging her. She
brings these books in, but they're low-quality things, paper-
backs and what I call trash, not literature by any means.
There's something in the home influence. . . ."

Janet's mother grew up in rural villages, Maywood and Pal-
myra, Missouri, and largely to fight the boredom of life on
lonely farms, she early took up reading, both in the papers
and magazines her father bought, *Country Gentleman,* the
Farmer's Journal, the *Kansas City Star,* and in the Victorian novels her mother liked. As a girl in elementary school, she was
the brightest in her class. She dreamed of becoming a surgeon,

and she actually got as far as an osteopathy course at Kirksville, Missouri, State Teachers College, but her father fell sick and could no longer farm, and the Depression came, and because of financial difficulties she never finished her preparation. Later she married a man who had graduated from high school and whose four sisters were all on their way to becoming nurses, and the Trains settled in Illinois, where Mr. Train took work as a machinist for a manufacturing company, and they had three children, Mary, a son Tom, and Janet. They did not prosper, and of late years Mrs. Train has worked as a saleswoman in a dry-goods store to supplement the family income.

In the years before Janet went to school, Mrs. Train used to read to her to settle her down for naps in the afternoon—*The Three Bears, Raggedy Ann, Sixty-Five Bedtime Stories, Black Beauty, Hans Brinker or The Silver Skates,* and though some of the books were much too advanced for the child, Janet paid close attention and on a second reading could always tell where her mother skipped, and would not allow it. As she grew older, Janet never played much with dolls but preferred coloring books and reading. For a long time she was very fond of a toy doctor's kit her mother had bought her.

Mrs. Train is still a reader. One of the reasons her house is so disorderly is that she often reads when she might be cleaning. "I haven't a very broad back for housework," she says. She gets up at five-thirty in the morning, prepares her husband's and children's breakfasts, and then settles down to read until it is time for her to go to work. Somehow life has gone slack for her. She used to like good novels; nowadays she prefers nonfiction. She reads the *Saturday Evening Post, Reader's Digest, Woman's Home Companion, Ladies' Home Journal,* and *McCall's* from cover to cover.

Janet's father, who is mechanically minded and likes to tinker, never reads anything but the sports news in the daily paper. He is firm with the children. He likes bowling and takes the whole family to a casino every Thursday night to league matches, in which he bowls for his company team; Janet's brother Tom used to be a pinboy there until pinspotting machines were installed. Janet is bored by the sport and spends her time either reading or writing short mystery stories, just for fun. Her father built a boat last summer with Franz Zimmer across the street, and they put a fifteen-horse Johnson outboard on it, and in warm weather the two families go boating and swimming in the river at Twin Oaks or Rocky Point.

Janet's sister and brother have limited ambitions. Tom takes after his father; he wants to be a mechanic and will try to get into the Air Force. Mary will be a stenographer or a salesgirl. There is no incentive in the family for any of the children to think about college, because it is assumed that college would be too expensive. Mary brings home movie magazines, and Janet, who sucks in printed matter like a vacuum cleaner, reads them all. If I.Q. tests were culture-loaded in the direction of Hollywood, Janet would score in the near-genius range, for she knows the name, salary, screen record, marital status, and personal foibles of every star.

Janet herself visits the public library, at Fourth and Main, once every week or two, and she carries home five or six books every time. Mrs. Hottelet is right: Janet reads trash, mountains of it. And remembers it all. Nobody has suggested for many years that she read anything else. She hoards, in her cartons in the muddled house, good books she once has loved, such as *Robinson Crusoe, Huckleberry Finn,* and *Little Women;* but just now she is addicted to adolescent-romance series: Janet Lambert, the Parrish family, Betty Cavana, Nancy Drew mysteries.

Once in a while Janet gets a glimmer of aspiration from one of her aunts or from the Zimmers across the street. Her Aunt Sheila, of Seattle, who was formerly an Army nurse and wants Janet to follow her into a medical career, has sent her things from all over the world, perhaps to make her want to get up and out of Illinois: gloves from Italy, a scarf from Scotland, sweaters from Switzerland, and books from England. The Zimmers are gentle, tidy, quiet people, with three children all younger than Janet, and though their income and house are small, they have some pretensions to culture; on their shelves are a *Collier's Encyclopedia* and a set of young people's classics. "We like Jan," they say. "She's a nice open thing—she doesn't whisper behind her hand." Janet is sweet with the young Zimmers and will play games with them by the hour. The Zimmers have a television set, and they have made one rule, for Zimmers and Trains alike—homework first. Janet likes *I Love Lucy,* Ed Sullivan, and *Dragnet*.

The Superintendent of Schools tends to be cautious. He says, "I'm afraid of anything too special for these clever children. I'm afraid of it for our city. We don't like anything that smacks of privilege. But don't worry, we'll reach those children. We'll reach them with enrichment."

Thus the Superintendent articulates the greatest single obstacle to help for talented children in the United States—the widely held feeling that providing such help would be somehow undemocratic.

Among educators, this feeling was brought into the open, as long ago as 1922, by the late William C. Bagley, an influential professor at Teachers College, Columbia. "The development of democracy," Professor Bagley wrote, "has been unquestionably toward the elevation of the common man to a position of supreme collective control," and therefore education in democratic America should be built around the common man. Bagley very much disliked the notion that the education of the common man might be subject to any limitation, of either quantity or quality, by such determinants as the I.Q. Those who advocated the use of these limiting measurements he called "determinists," and insofar as they considered the intellectual capacities of human beings to be hereditary, he called them "fatalists." Bagley believed that in a democracy "'human' qualities, such as sympathy, tact, humor, and sociability, and 'moral' qualities, such as integrity, industry, persistence, courage, and loyalty," were more important than intellectual talents, and this was fair enough, except that he seemed to consider these qualities and talent somehow exclusive and opposed, the human and moral qualities representing common mankind, the intellectual talents representing aristocracy and privilege.

Bagley believed, with an idealism which was not supported by the mounting evidence of clinical psychology, that all human beings were infinitely educable, and he felt that the main job of education in a democracy was not the development of leaders but the training of the common man so that he could tell his leaders "where to get off." All this led him to advocate the concentration by our public schools of their main effort where they were inclined to put it anyhow—upon "average" students. He was even more specific: accepting for the purpose of definition the measurements he criticized, he delineated the common man as having an I.Q. of between 85 and 115. These views of Professor Bagley attracted a wide acceptance among educators, and the predominant policies of American public education for the ensuing years accorded with them; they still have a following.

These ideas have claimed a following because there are wisdom and heart in them—up to a point. A trouble, however, has come from them. The emphasis on common learnings in our schools has led to inadequate provision for those differences between individuals which refresh and renew a society, which provide it with competences, skills, and originalities. The emphasis has not been on what is unique in each young person, but rather on what is shared, on the "norm," the "common."

What makes the notion of an aristocracy of the mind—and

even the recognition of individual differences in our schools—repugnant to Americans is the possibility that heredity may come into the picture. The fact that in our country high I.Q.s appear predominant among the offspring of parents of upper and upper-middle social and economic backgrounds tends to make the I.Q. even more unpopular and to cause programs for high-I.Q. children to be called undemocratic.

It is not at all clear as yet, however, how much of the high I.Q. and the superior scholastic achievement of upper-class children comes from inheritance and how much from the cultural background upper-class families can provide—books, ambitions, intricate vocabularies, artistic entertainments, demands for good schooling, and high goals for achievement.

Evidence has been gathered which makes it fairly clear that certain aptitudes with physiological bases do tend to be inherited—a good example being the sense of musical pitch. Apparently certain physical traits of brain structure, productive of certain basic intellectual aptitudes, can be passed on by heredity. But a chance coming together of most favorable traits, rather than slightly less favorable ones, can produce a heredity of brilliance from a background of modest means just as well as from upper-class backgrounds.

In recent years, thanks to our slowly increasing understanding of the human mind and emotions, and thanks to the mobility and fluidity of our society, psychologists have been coming to believe that the weight assigned to heredity in shaping the statistics of talent may have to be shaded downward, and more weight given to the opportunities and motivations provided by the environment. We have begun to find, at any rate, that potentialities show themselves in places that would seem on the basis of heredity alone to be surprising. This suits us. "The doctrine of equality," James B. Conant has written, "has come to mean in the United States not parity of status for all adults but equality of opportunity for the young."

We cling, and it seems with reason, to the democratic hope

that genius may be discovered among the poor equally as among the children of the cultured upper class. Psychology and psychiatry have brought new understanding of the possibility that talent, intelligence, energy, capacity to do are not fixed, permanent, measurable, wholly innate quantities, but are fluid and variable and depend for their availability on the emotional life of the individual. We seem to be on the threshold of great discoveries about the unlocking of human gifts. This is very pleasant to know, but we have to deal in the meanwhile with a practical situation: *very* far are we from making the latest knowledge of the human brain and emotions available to the ordinary classroom, and in fact even the most primitive and inadequate group tests are not yet universally used by any means. On top of that, many school systems, many parents, many teachers, swayed by a misplaced egalitarianism, fight programs that might bring the promise of equality of opportunity a little closer—that might help realize the potentialities of a Janet Train, who comes from a poor family.

What seems undemocratic is not that special notice should be taken in American schools of special talents, but precisely that Janet Train should not be liberated from her slum home and be given, through education, a chance to grasp the standing in our society that she could easily attain, of a well-trained, useful, productive, comfortably circumstanced, and possibly important professional person.

Harry S. Truman

Before dawn one chilly morning in 1950, I stood in an alley behind Blair House, across Pennsylvania Avenue from the White House, waiting, along with some Secret Service agents, for the President; he had invited me to go along with him on one of his famous early-morning walks. The White House was being renovated then, and the President and his family were living in Blair House for the time being. Because some Puerto Rican Nationalists had, not long before, made an attempt to storm the house and assassinate the President, the Secret Service was no longer allowing him to take casual strolls straight from the executive mansion down past the Ellipse and around the Washington Monument, or out along the Mall, or through Lafayette Square into the heart of town, as he had done all the previous months of his Presidency, walking wherever his whim took him, tipping his hat gravely to other early citizens. Now, in spite of his protests (for he hated precautions on his behalf and spoke sometimes of his honorable station as "this jail I'm in"), the agents were taking him by car to places here and there around the city's edges where he could still stir up his blood but would probably not be accosted, or even encountered, and

"Quite a Head of Steam," *The New Yorker,* April 14, 1951; reprinted in *Aspects of the Presidency,* New Haven: Ticknor & Fields, 1980.

where, because of a daily change of locale, his brisk matutinal presence could not be counted on. We waited, each man hugging and pounding himself to keep warm, while near us the Presidential limousine fogged the air with its rapid breath. Another car, for some of the agents, stood not far away. The agents joshed each other, checked certain weapons with which they were supplied, and now and then looked at their watches. The Boss, as they called Truman when they spoke of him, was due to come out, and they asserted to me that he would appear promptly, at six-forty. The sun was due to rise that morning, and they assumed that *it* would likewise appear on time, at six-forty-nine.

At the turn of six-forty the agents, as if called to order by the blow of a gavel, fell silent. A few seconds later the Blair House door opened, and the President, accompanied by two more agents, came out. He smiled the unforced smile of a man with an already revved-up metabolism, and, looking at us, he said, "Good morning, gentlemen." He was carrying a yellowish walking cane with a rubber tip.

Various agents answered, saying, "Good morning, sir," or "Morning, Mr. President." One of the men opened the rear door of the limousine.

"A little zip in the air this morning!" the President said, and then stepped into the car and sat down on the right side.

"Yes, sir," the agent at the door said. "It's snappy out."

"You hop right in here," the President said to me, patting the seat beside him. The driver and that morning's senior agent, a man named Henry Nicholson, got into the front seat (which was not separated from the back by a glass partition), and the rest of the agents boarded the other car. As I bent over to get into the limousine, I noticed that a small rubber footpad, something like a shower mat, had been waiting for the President's feet on the right side of the floor, and that now his feet were planted tidily side by side in the middle of the mat. The President had settled himself back in the seat. He was wearing a heavy dark-blue double-breasted overcoat, gray suède gloves, and a wide-brimmed, string-banded light-gray felt hat.

Truman turned to me, when I was seated, and said, "Sorry to get you out so early. From what I hear of writers, this must be a strain on you."

I answered, as the cars began to move, that one of the agents had told me the President would make a farmer of me if I stayed around long enough.

"That's right!" the President said. "I've been up since five-thirty. I get up at five-thirty every morning. Most people don't know when the best part of the day is; it's the early morning."

The cars started out on Pennsylvania Avenue. On the far side of the avenue, we could just make out, in the first gray of dawn, that huge architectural cranberry bush, the old State Department Building. The limousine moved slowly.

I asked the President what he had been doing since he got up.

He said, as if he were talking about someone else, "A President has a lot of chores to do."

I said, "Charlie Ross told me that you carry home a briefcase five inches thick every night. Is that what you've been doing—going through your briefcase?"

"That's right," the President said. "I've already read a stack of secret papers. Reports from the military people, from the National Security Council, from Central Intelligence—from Cloak and Dagger, I call them. All kinds of papers that pile up on the desk."

I asked him if he had eaten breakfast.

"Not a bite yet," he said. "I'll go walking, then go to the gym and sweat off a pound or two, then take a swim. After that, I'll eat half the breakfast I want and then go hungry all day long."

"What will half the breakfast you want be?"

"A strip of bacon, a scrambled egg, a piece of toast, and a glass of milk."

"No coffee?"

"I don't crave coffee. It hurts the peculiar talent I have for lying down and dropping right off to sleep in two minutes. Doc Graham [Brigadier General Wallace Graham, the President's physician] won't let me eat the way I'd like to. If it weren't for the Doc, I could eat a whole side of beef for breakfast. I think I could."

The limousine stopped for a red light. We had been going past rows of boxlike government buildings, some of them of the sort that has been called "temporary" for more than thirty years. The day was coming on fast. A few blocks ahead, at the end of the street we were on, we could make out one of the capital's many monuments to heroes of the past. The President called my attention to it. The lights changed, and we started up again.

Having heard that during the earliest morning hours the President takes a surprisingly thorough gallop through the *New York Times* and *Herald Tribune,* the *Washington Post* and *Star,* the *Baltimore Sun,* and occasionally a day-old Missouri paper as well, and having taken a hurried preparatory look at the morning's *Post* myself, only to be rewarded with the gloomy news that the Chinese had the United Nations armies in full rout, I remarked stupidly, "The news was pretty bad again this morning."

Truman turned his head, looked at me rather pityingly, and said, "People who don't know military affairs expect everything to go well all the time. They don't understand. A general can't be a winner every day of the week. The greatest of generals have had to take reverses. I advise you to study the lives of Alexander the Great, Tamerlane, Gustavus Adolphus, Hunyadi—and Robert E. Lee and Stonewall Jackson. You'll find they all won most of the time, but they all had their troubles, too. I'm not upset, like most people, about these reverses MacArthur is taking."

The President went on to make other observations about

that morning's news—about a speech by Acheson, and about some new attacks on the Secretary of State by Republican senators. Then suddenly he broke off and asked Nicholson, "How's your family, Nick?"

Nicholson turned around in the front seat and said, "They're all fine, sir. Nick Junior saved my life this morning. My alarm didn't go off, I guess I forgot to pull the button. He came running in and alerted me. 'You better get up, Pop,' he says. 'It's five minutes to six!'"

"Well, good for him!" Truman said. "He's going to be as smart as his old man. I can see that now."

"He's a fine boy," Nicholson said.

"Oh, he's smart," the President said emphatically.

Now the road swung out beside a body of water and followed its curving shore. The limousine moved at an easy pace. The air was quiet. Below the lightening sky, out over the edges of the city, a low night mist still hovered. The water near us looked like monel metal. On it, not far from us, a cluster of sitting waterfowl black-dotted the slick gray surface.

"Look at those ducks!" the President exclaimed. "Wouldn't you think they'd get cold feet sitting out there? B-r-r-r!"

The limousine began to meet traffic hurrying into the city from the suburbs. Not far beyond the place where we had seen the ducks, a District of Columbia police car pulled out into our path and drove along in front of us. Truman sat forward in his seat and looked rather pleased at having acquired a police escort. "They told me he was going to pick us up along about here," he said. "The regular road is blocked by repairs up ahead. He's going to lead us around a detour."

The President's caravan drove to its destination deviously, as he had predicted. At one point, near some water again, the ground was littered with driftwood and broken branches, which had been washed up there during a windstorm a few days before. As we drove along, the President spoke of that storm and the clutter it had caused. In the distance, while he talked, the roar of a takeoff from one of the city's airports began to build up, like the roll of a huge kettledrum. In the motionless air the noise was insistent and ominous, and all of us in the limousine looked toward its source, hidden in a sullen bank of mist, out of the top of which hangars humped up into the clear air above. Suddenly, startlingly close, there emerged from the low-lying vapor, headed straight our way and slowly rising, a Constellation.

"Look at that thing lift up!" the President said, speaking loudly to be heard above the plane's rumbling. "I don't believe it yet. It's one of the miracles of our age how a big, heavy thing like that will lift up off the ground. I estimate that the machine weighs thirty tons. Think of what it takes to lift thirty tons of machinery off the ground! I can hardly believe my eyes when I see it."

For a moment the plane throbbed directly above our heads, and then very quickly it was gone, and unheard. We looked out from the leisurely moving limousine over the now silent landscape. The bank of mist and the brightening sky above it were reflected in shifting patterns on the nacreous water near us.

I said it was a pretty sight.

The President said, in a voice that seemed very soft after his speech in competition with the plane's noise, "Out here's one place where there's peace." Then, briskly again, he said, "This is a nice morning for walking, isn't it, Nick?"

"Looks fine. Yes, sir," Nicholson said.

After we had driven a little farther the car slowed down and stopped, and the President said, "Well, here's where we get onto shanks' mares."

We stepped out of the limousine and began at once to walk along a concrete pathway that ran more or less parallel to the road. Nicholson and the driver walked close behind us. The

HARRY TRUMAN ON A MORNING WALK

*"Most people don't know when the best part of the day is;
it's the early morning."*

other agents took up various more distant convoy duties. I walked on the President's left. The President carried his cane, swinging it high, in the near—his left—hand.

I remarked on the fact that his pace was lively.

"This is just the regular Army marching speed," he said. "One hundred and twenty paces to the minute, two miles in half an hour. I've always walked at this speed—ever since I was in the Army. Timing is just a knack. I can tell how fast a train is going by counting the telephone poles as they go by."

I asked how long he had been taking morning walks.

"I've been taking these walks for thirty years now," he said. "I got in the habit of getting up and moving around smart in the early mornings on the farm, and then when I got into politics, I couldn't stop. I began to take these walks when I was Judge of the Eastern District of Jackson County, out home, knocking around Independence and Kansas City mornings before breakfast. Then I walked all over Washington when I was in the Senate. You can't think clearly if you don't exercise."

"Apparently you like to keep moving," I said.

"I like being on the road," Truman said. "Fact is, I like roads. My father and I had the road overseer's job in Grandview, where our family is. He had it first and I had it after he died, when I took over the farm. That was before the first war. Back in those times, every man in Missouri had to give either two days' work or six dollars a year toward the roads; some of the overseers took the six dollars and put them in their pockets and let the roads go to pot. We took the work, my father and I did, and we had the best roads in Missouri, in and around Grandview. We didn't get any richer, but we had good roads. My father worked so hard on the roads it killed him.

"When I got to be Presiding Judge, out home [of the Jackson County Court, an archaically misnamed office, which is not judicial at all but executive, corresponding to the county commissioner's office in most places, and having charge of the county's business affairs; Truman was Presiding Judge from 1926 to 1934], I found out that there were some overseers claiming they were putting in thirty-four culverts under the roads at so much per culvert—nearly two thousand dollars apiece, as I remember. I found out they had no idea of installing the culverts; they were just going to pocket the money. It was going to be worth sixty thousand–odd dollars to them in one year to not build culverts. I fired all but fourteen overseers in the county and hired four supervisors, and I began to make them work. I was about as popular as a skunk in the parlor.

"In '28, I went out to build the county some new roads. I had two engineers, Colonel Edward M. Stayton—he's a retired general now—and N. T. Veach—he was and is a Republican. I could then, and I still can, get along with a decent Republican, though Mother never would let one, decent or otherwise, land on the front porch if she could help it—she was such a rabid Democrat. Anyway, I took these two engineers, and we drove over every inch of the three hundred and fifty miles of surfaced roads in Jackson County—only you couldn't call them surfaced roads, really; they were just roads with piecrust on them, water-bound macadam that would scale off in no time. The people voted me ten million dollars to build roads—the first bond issue was six and a half million, then in '31 they voted me three and a half more—and I gave them two hundred and eighteen miles of roads that they're still driving on, as good as the day they were built. They were as fine as the system in Westchester County, New York State."

"I gather you've traveled on roads quite a bit, too," I said.

"Roads are meant to be used," Truman said. "When I was fixing to give Jackson County a new courthouse, I wanted to see some big public buildings with my own eyes before I spent all the money the people voted me for it—nearly four and a half million—so I drove twenty-four thousand miles through Oklahoma and Arkansas, into Texas, to Shreveport, Louisiana, up around to Minnesota and St. Paul, to Denver, Milwaukee, Racine, Chicago, and Brooklyn, looking at the best courthouses and capitols and city halls. I even went and looked at a life-insurance building in Montreal. The man who drove me on that trip was a fellow named Fred Canfil."

I said I had met Canfil on a visit to Kansas City and had found him quite a character.

"Fred's *two* characters!" Truman said. "Fred's a little rough, but Fred's all right; he's as loyal as a bulldog. You know, I took him along to Potsdam with me, as a pro-tem member of the President's Secret Service detail. He was the most vigilant bodyguard a President ever had. While the conferences were going on, he would stand by a window with his arms folded and scowl out the window at everybody who passed in the street, as if he would eat them alive if they bothered the President of the United States. Fred's a federal marshal out home, so one day after a meeting I took him up to Stalin and I said, 'Marshal Stalin, I want you to meet Marshal Canfil.' Well, after *that,* the Russians treated Fred with some respect, I tell you. As I say, Fred and I drove around the country in '34 looking at buildings, and we drove far enough to have gone plumb around the world."

The kind of debris we had seen from the car on the way out occasionally cluttered the path on which we were walking. Here and there we came to a piece of driftwood, or a ridge of tangled marsh grass and twigs, or, as at a point we now reached in our course, a cluster of branches from one of the tremendous willow trees that lined the walk. Crossing this barrier the President lifted his knees sharply, like a drum major, and surefootedly made his way through without breaking his pace for an instant. I dropped behind.

When I had caught up Truman went on, "Then, after the second war began in Europe, I drove another thirty thousand miles across this country, looking at the construction of Army camps and seeing all the waste they were building into them.

Then I came back and set up the Truman Committee. If I hadn't taken that drive, I'd still be just Senator Truman instead of being in all this fix."

I told the President I had heard that he used to have a reputation for being a very fast driver.

"I like to move," he said, "but in all my driving I've never been arrested for speeding. I try to observe the laws of this country. Once, when I was in the Senate, I was driving my family from Independence to Washington, and as I was about to get into Hagerstown, Maryland, I went through a stop sign that I couldn't see because some damn fool had parked his car in front of it. The Madam was in the front with me, and Margaret was in the back with a lot of books we were bringing back East with us. All of a sudden a fellow came along, wasn't looking where he was going, and he swiped me as I came out of the intersection. He hit the left rear fender. It knocked the car cater-cornered. The side where the Madam was sitting hit a lamppost, and part of the post fell down on the roof of the car and gave her an awful jolt; her neck has never been quite right since then. The car was just able to limp under its own power to a repair place, but it was a total wreck; there wasn't enough left of it to save it. We just took our books and things out and put them in a brand-new Pontiac I bought, and went on our way when we were ready. Thank heavens, the insurance company stood in back of the bill. Well, the other driver that hit me had been a local fellow—the authorities knew him—so they'd taken me to the police station and all of that, until they figured out I was a U.S. senator. I wasn't going to get out of it by telling them myself, but they found out, and then they fell all over themselves. They ended up with a formal ceremony giving me the keys to the city. Besides, they had learned that I wasn't at fault. The truth comes out about an innocent man sooner or later, but sometimes it's too late, especially if they've already hanged him."

The President, who was evidently beginning to be warmed

up by his marching, took off his gloves and put them in his overcoat pocket. "In Washington, once," he said, "I went through a stoplight right behind another fellow who'd gone through it, too. An officer stopped both of us. He asked me for my license. He looked at it, and he said, 'Are you the Senator Truman I've been reading about in the papers—the Truman Committee fellow?' I allowed I was. He said, 'You've been doing a good job in there, Senator, you go along now. Just let me get this other fellow out of your road till I give him a ticket, then you can roll along.' I said, 'No, sir, Officer, I'm a citizen like anyone else. You give me a ticket.' I made him give me a summons. But I guess he tore up his end of the thing—the stub. I sent a contribution to the Policeman's Fund for the customary amount. Never heard anything more from it. The truth of the matter is, I had no desire to hear anything! Come to think of it, though, I *did* hear something. I got a nice letter from the secretary of the Policeman's Fund, thanking me for the contribution."

The President walked on a few steps in silence. We were in broad daylight now. The low mist was burning off, and the sky was blue above us. Finally, apparently taking off from a reminder in his previous remarks, the President said, "I'm told that the Truman Committee saved the United States government fifteen billion dollars in waste, delay, and inefficiency. We weren't working for publicity on that job. We never gave anything to the papers until a case was closed, till everything was black-and-white and there wasn't a chance of maligning a citizen in public. All we wanted was to do a good job for our country. I think you'll still find a lot of politicians who feel the same way. You know, people cuss the politicians all the time, but how do you think this country would get along if it weren't for the honest politicians? *Some*body's got to get in there and do the work! Do you know my definition of a politician? 'A politician is the ablest man in government, and after he dies they call him a statesman.'"

Again the President paused. Then he said, "There's no reason why a public servant should want anything for himself. You know, I've noticed that wherever you find a crooked politician, you'll find a crooked businessman behind him. Building the roads in Jackson County and putting up the county courthouse, I learned a thing or two about contracts and contractors; then in the Truman Committee I learned a lot more. Once in a while you run across a contractor that likes to cut corners, and you usually discover that he's got a crooked, pipsqueak politician chasing errands for him. Why are some men so selfish? What do they think they get for themselves? Not happiness—not that. There was a banker out in Missouri I knew— he's dead now—who used to lend money to businesses that were on the way up, and he'd watch the companies, and if he saw one that was sound, he'd wangle this way and that way until he had control of the thing. He wound up with fifteen million dollars in his pocket, but he'd ruined fifteen lives doing it. Now, what good was that?

"And yet sometimes," Truman went on, "I think a liar is worse than a thief. I have in mind all the lying slander you see in public life in this country today, and in the newspapers. You remember what Shakespeare said: 'Who steals my purse steals trash, but he that filches from me my good name makes me poor indeed.'* I think a publisher, or any newspaperman, who doesn't have a sense of responsibility and prints a lot of lies and goes around slandering without any basis in fact—I think that sort of fellow actually can be called a traitor. Truth is one thing.

---

*Truman had taken the liberty of cutting these lines, which are from *Othello,* somewhat, to make a tighter epigram of them, but he had quoted correctly the words he kept. The whole passage reads:

> Who steals my purse steals trash; 'tis something, nothing;
> 'Twas mine, 'tis his, and has been slave to thousands;
> But he that filches from me my good name
> Robs me of that which not enriches him,
> And makes me poor indeed.

A politician can stand a dig now and then if it's the truth. But smears are something else. These fellows talk about being un-American! To my mind, there's nothing as un-American as a lying smear on a man's character. And some of these columnists! When you come down to it, there's just one thing I draw the line at, and that's any kind of attack on my family. I don't care what they say about me. I'm human. I can make mistakes. Any man can make mistakes, even if he's trying with all his heart and mind to do the best thing for his country. But a man's family ought to be sacred. There was one columnist who wrote some lie about my family when I was in the Senate, and instead of writing him a letter I called him on the phone, and I said, 'You so-and-so, if you say another word about my family, I'll come down to your office and shoot you.' He hasn't printed a whisper about them since. I'm saving up four or five good, hard punches on the nose, and when I'm out of this job, I'm going to run around and deliver them personally."

The President unbuttoned his coat and threw it open, without breaking his stride.

"Mr. President," I said, "you spoke of having had books in your car when you had that accident in Hagerstown. What sort of books would they have been?"

"All kinds," he said. "Some legal, some just for pleasure. You see, I was born with flat eyeballs. I had to wear glasses the very first thing when I was a boy. I couldn't get out and play much ball, for fear of busting my glasses, and I was blind as a mole without them. That was when I got in the habit of reading so much. I've always been a heavy reader."

I said someone had told me that for many years he had carried some poetry in his wallet, and I asked him if he still did.

"Yes," the President said, "I still carry it."

He did not seem inclined to say anything more about the poetry in his wallet. Changing the subject, I said that in Kansas

City I had met a Western District Court judge named Albert Ridge, who told me that during the days after the First World War, when he and other ex-artillerymen used to loiter in the Truman & Jacobson haberdashery store, at Seventeenth and Baltimore, Harry Truman, the captain of his old battery, had kept urging him to improve himself. One of the things Truman had done, Ridge said, was give him a list of ten books that any young fellow who wanted to get ahead ought to read.

"That's right," the President said. "I used to drive the boys who hung around the store pretty hard. Especially the Catholics. I used to make them go to Mass. I wasn't going to have any Catholics lay their backsliding at the door of a Protestant! No, really, I'm just joking. Those boys were all very good about getting themselves to church. I'd forgotten about that list for Al. It's true. He'd been a private in my battery, and he came to me during that time after the war—he was studying the law; he wanted to educate himself—and we had a balcony up over the store, and I used to send him up there to work on his books nights, when the other boys were just horsing around, and once he asked me for a list of ten important books to read, to help him get ahead. Al did improve himself, too. He passed his bar exam, made a fine record as a lawyer, and now he's a federal circuit judge out home. I can't remember now what the ten books were."

"Judge Ridge is hazy about them, too, now," I said. "He does remember Plutarch's *Lives, Bunker Bean,* and a book called *Missouri's Struggle for Statehood.*"

"Those sound right, for a starter," the President said.

"If you had to do it over again," I asked, "what ten books would you recommend to an Al Ridge today?"

"Well, first of all, of course, you'd have the Bible. I'd pick the King James Version, if Al would feel like struggling through it—although the Revised Version's practically as good, practically the same thing. Then you'd want some biographies of great men; everybody meets up with difficult decisions, and it's good to know how some big men faced things in the past. Personally, I've always been partial to a book called *Great Men and Famous Women,* edited by C. F. Horne. It was published in 1894, when I was ten years old. Mother gave it to me for my twelfth birthday. There are lots of lessons in that book. You'd want Plutarch's *Lives.* I've been quoting Plutarch all *my* life. You'd want some Plato, especially the parts about the old fellow who took hemlock. You'd have to read Shakespeare—four or five of his plays and all his sonnets. I'd include the complete poems of Robert Burns—there was a fine edition published a few years ago. Then you'd want some Byron, especially *Childe Harold.* Let's see—how many is that?"

We figured out that that was seven books.

"O.K. Then you'd want Creasy's *Fifteen Decisive Battles of the World,* so you could understand a little about military affairs. I'd include Benjamin Franklin's *Autobiography;* you'll find a good deal in there about how to make the best use of every minute of your day, and a lot of horse sense about people. And for a fellow like Al, who was interested in law, and, for that matter, for anyone who wanted to know the basis for the rights we enjoy under law, you'd have to include Blackstone's *Commentaries.* That's ten."

I asked the President if he still found time for such reading.

"Only when I'm off on a vacation," he said, "or sometimes out on the Chesapeake on the boat. Down at Key West last spring we had a lot of fun analyzing poets. Bill Hassett and I spent a whole breakfast on 'The Walrus and the Carpenter.'"

"Is there anything you'd want to add to the list of ten books to prepare a man specifically for life in the Atomic Age?" I asked.

"Nothing but the lives of great men! There's nothing new in human nature; only our names for things change. Read the lives of the Roman emperors from Claudius to Constantine if you want some inside dope on the twentieth century. Read Hammurabi's code of laws. Did you know, by the bye, that those laws were engraved on a column of stone eight feet high? Hammurabi had laws covering murder, stealing, divorce, and protecting helpless people from being gypped and de-frauded—all the same troubles we have with people nowadays. Men don't change."

We were approaching a place where the concrete path we had been following rejoined the roadway. The limousine and the agents' car were waiting at the junction of the path and the drive. The President said over his shoulder to Nicholson, "Well, Nick, I've got up quite a head of steam! How about you?"

"Me, too, Mr. President," Nicholson said.

"Let's call it a walk, Nick," Truman said.

Nicholson told me later that the limousine, which had been brought to this point along the roadway by one of the agents, had come one and eight-tenths miles from the place where we started walking. We boarded it now for the trip back into town. When Truman had settled himself in the car, he reached into a trouser pocket for a handkerchief and wiped away the tears that rolled from his eyes after he stepped from the cold outdoors into the heated car. Then he drew out his wallet, took a piece of letter paper out, unfolded the paper, and held it out to me.

"You were asking about the poetry I carry on my person," he said. "There it is. It's from 'Locksley Hall.' I've been carry-ing that ever since I graduated from high school. I've copied it and recopied it a dozen times."

I took the paper and read, in Harry Truman's bold, slightly slanting hand, in ink, these lines:

For I dipt into the future, far as human eye could see,
Saw the Vision of the world, and all the wonders that would
    be;

Saw the heavens fill with commerce, argosies of magic sails,
Pilots of the purple twilight, dropping down with costly bales;

Heard the heavens fill with shouting, and there rained a
ghastly dew
From the nations' airy navies grappling in the central blue;

Far along the world-wide whisper of the south-wind rushing
warm,
With the standards of the people plunging thro' the thunder
storm;

Till the war-drum throbb'd no longer, and the battle-flags
were furl'd
In the Parliament of Man, the Federation of the World.

There the common sense of most shall hold a fretful realm in
awe,
And the kindly earth shall slumber, lapt in universal law.

When I had finished reading the President said, "Did you
see that part in there giving a forecast on the airplane, and on
air warfare? Don't forget that Tennyson wrote those lines over
a hundred years ago. And notice also that part about universal
law. We're going to have that someday, just as sure as we have
air war now. That's what I'm working for. I guess that's what
I've really been working for ever since I first put that poetry in
my pocket. Do you realize that was half a century ago, less six
months?" He looked thoughtfully out the limousine window.
Suddenly, he exclaimed, "Look at there, Nick! There's a fellow
in summer pants. He's got summer khaki pants on, and white
socks."

"And a green sports shirt," said Nicholson.

"Yes, sir, he's got a green sports shirt on," the President said.
"He must be pretty tough or foolish—one. I reckon he's lost
track of the seasons, Nick."

"I think he has, Mr. President," Nicholson said.

On the way back into town the limousine was slowed almost to a standstill at one place by a press of traffic. The President pulled himself forward on his seat and said, "I've noticed before, there's a bottleneck here for people coming in to work. We're going to have to do something about this place, Nick." Then he said to me, "Do you know, we're going to have a great problem in this country in a few years with traffic? At the rate we're building automobiles and people are buying them, this country's going to have some terrible congestion on its hands— unless it builds more roads and better roads. Roads and bridges. . . . Well, was that a good walk, Nick?"

"Yes, sir," Nicholson said. Then he added, smiling at me, "Frank, here [the driver], says if this fellow is anything like the other reporters as far as physical condition goes, he'll have to go and lie down from now until time for press conference."

The President looked at me and said, "Can't you take a little physical exertion?"

"Maybe it's not the exercise," Nicholson said. "Maybe it's the hour."

"All the same," the President said to me, "you'll find you'll feel better for having taken this walk. A man in my position has a public duty to keep himself in good condition. You can't be mentally fit unless you're physically fit. A walk like this keeps your circulation up to where you can think clearly. That old pump has to keep squirting the juice into your brain, you know."

Eventually, the limousine made its way into the White House grounds through a back entrance, and along a cement-paved driveway to the West Wing, where the President's offices are. When the car had stopped, the President said to me, "Want a swim?"

Mindful of the coldness outside, I was hesitant.

"Come on!" the President said. "You need a little conditioning."

The two agents had got out of the front seat, and Nicholson opened the door for the President, who pulled himself forward and stepped out. I followed. The President walked quickly up a path under a canvas marquee and onto a concrete porch outside his private office. The agents stayed by the limousine.

"Excuse me a minute," the President said, stopping by one of the French windows of his office. "I want to check up on the temperature." He leaned forward and looked closely at a thermometer suspended on a bracket in such a way as to be easily visible from both indoors and outdoors. "Thirty-one," he announced, straightening up.

We walked a few paces farther along the porch, past the Cabinet Room, on our left, to where the passageway turned right and became a colonnade alongside the low-lying structure that linked the West Wing with the main building. At the juncture in the ell, Truman said, "Let's just see what the pressure gauge is doing," and he stepped up to a barometer that hung in the sheltered corner. Again he leaned forward and looked closely.

"Pressure's up again," the President said with some satisfaction; then, straightening up, he turned and began walking slowly along the colonnade. "Thirty point twelve and still going up. Temperature steady. Northwest wind. We'll have good weather for three or four days. It's bound to be fair. You see, our weather forms up away to the northwest, over Bering Strait, then it moves across the country to the eastward; there's also another weather center, down over the Caribbean, and it works on the first one. So if you watch the weather map, you can tell pretty well what's coming along." He stopped in front of a door. "The Weather Bureau sends me a map every morning," he went on. "You'd better not bet on the weather against me! Jim and Nick and Gerry and the other Secret Service agents have tried it, to their regret. Now we've got a good, strong high-pressure area moving in on us, and with conditions the way they are, we can count on at least three days of fair weather. I won't promise that there won't be a single cloud in the sky, but it'll be generally nice. If you have anything important you want to do, any trips or such, you can count on going ahead."

The President turned, opened the door, urged me through it ahead of him, and then stepped inside himself. We were in a long, narrow room, containing a swimming pool. To our right was a door, evidently leading to dressing rooms, and through it now came a young man in khaki trousers and a white T shirt, whom the President introduced to me as Sergeant Gasber. (Master Sergeant Earl Gasber, I learned from him later, was an Army physical-therapy technician who had been keeping the President in training since May, 1949.)

"How're you feeling this morning, Mr. President?" Gasber asked.

"Never felt better in my life," the President said, with obvious conviction. "We've got a guest this morning, Sergeant. Do you think we can fix him up with some bathing trunks?"

"I think so, sir," Gasber said.

Telling Sergeant Gasber and me to come along and see what we could find, the President led the way through the door into a corridor and turned in to a dressing room on the left. I could see that there was a small gymnasium at the end of the corridor, and that there were other dressing rooms opening off it. "Most of these suits are for the fat fellows on my staff," the President said, indicating a number of pairs of trunks on a row of hooks along the wall of the room, "but maybe we can find one that'll fit a skinny fellow like you. Try that one with the zebra stripes. That's a small pair, isn't it, Sergeant?"

"Yes, sir," Gasber said. "That pair ought to work."

The President went into one of the other dressing rooms, and the Sergeant went out to the pool. A couple of minutes later, I heard the clattering of some balance scales, and then the President's voice, in dejected tones: "That's terrible, Sergeant! A hundred seventy-eight and a half!"

"Oh-oh!" Gasber called back. "I'm sorry, sir. Those scales aren't accurate. I've been having a little trouble with General Vaughan and General Landry about their weight. I adjusted the scales so they'd be two pounds too heavy for General Vaughan, then I moved them down to one pound overweight for General Landry. I forgot to turn them back, sir. That should read one seventy-seven and a half."

"That's all right, then," the President replied, relieved. "I was afraid I'd picked up two whole pounds overnight. I guess you gave the Generals a real fright, and that was worth it."

When I was ready I went out to the pool. The Sergeant told me the water was heated to seventy-eight degrees for the President. The President called out that he was going into the gym to do a little exercise, and in a few moments we could hear the squeaks of a rowing machine. "He takes about fifty strokes," Gasber told me. "Then he does setups on a board that's on a forty-five-degree incline; he can touch his toes easy. Then I go in and give him some resisting exercises for his arms and back." While we were waiting, Gasber volunteered the information that the President is extremely punctilious about his appointments with him. "One day last summer," Gasber said, "we had an appointment for four-forty-five in the afternoon. I smoke and he doesn't, so I always go outdoors here to have a cigarette, so the smoke won't bother him when he comes in—I figure he gets enough smoke blowed in his face all day long. So that day I went out for a smoke about four-thirty. There was a Cabinet meeting going on in the Cabinet Room at the time, which I didn't know. I guess they could see me, but I couldn't see them. The first thing I knew one of the doors to the Cabinet Room flew open and there stands the President of the United States. 'Sergeant,' he says, 'these fellows are keeping me overtime today. Looks as if I'm going to run a little late. You'd better go on home. I don't want to keep you late.'" The Sergeant also told me that the President took a lively interest in Gasber's specialty—kinesiology, the science of motion, particularly as it applies to the human muscular system. As for the President's own muscular tone, Gasber said, "Why, for a man pushing sixty-seven, it's remarkable! The way he bounces back from things! I only hope I'm in half as good a shape when I'm his age."

Soon Gasber went into the gym to give the President his resisting exercises, and I took a swim. While I was in the pool, Truman returned to his dressing room and got into an electric sweatbox. He called me into his room, after I had left the pool, to talk.

"The Sergeant keeps me in this thing for ten minutes," the President said. His head protruded from a hole in the top of the box; his glasses were off, and he was turbaned with a towel. "Ten minutes are just enough to lose one pound. Of course I'll get it back during the day, though goodness knows where from—not from making a hog of myself, that's one thing certain. Doc Graham will be in after my swim and sunlamp. He looks me over every day, but I don't know why. He never finds anything. Do you know the Doc?"

I said that I had met General Graham, and that he had told me the President's health was sustained, even through his most trying days, by three health-giving qualities of temperament: cheerfulness, courage, and a mighty stubbornness.

The President said, with a smile, that he was as healthy as a mule. "And a mule," he said, "has an abundance of all three of those things."

I said I understood that Graham came from Kansas City, and asked whether the President had known him out there.

"Never saw him before I went to Potsdam," he said. "I've known his father all my life. Old Dr. Graham is seventy-four now and he'll still get up at three in the morning to visit a sick person; he's one of the most sacrificing men I know. When I got to Potsdam I heard the son was nearby. They told me he'd landed on Omaha Beach with a hospital unit, then he'd been with an airborne outfit in Holland, and got wounded, and then he was the head surgeon of a hospital at Stuttgart. So I asked to have him come up and see me at Potsdam. He came up, and I liked him, and I said, 'How'd you like to go to Washington to take care of somebody?' I thought he'd be pleased, but he said, 'No, thank you.' I asked, 'Why not?' He said he'd had about a dozen years of training in the best colleges and hospitals in the country, he'd taken the Hippocratic oath, he was dedicated to alleviating the suffering of the greatest possible number of people—why should he throw all that away on one human being? But, I said, what if that human being was the President of his country? He said he had a hospital full of men who'd shed blood for his country; he couldn't leave them. So I said, 'Do you realize who you're talking to?' Then he said, 'Yes, sir. I'll obey orders, sir.' So he stayed with the hospital until all his wounded men were discharged or moved home, and then he came to me. He's a bird!"

The President looked at a clock on the wall opposite him. "Doc ought to be here any minute now," he said. "One thing Doc Graham did for me: he got me interested in some of the finer points of botany. That's a hobby he has. You know, I used to have a terrible, unreasonable prejudice against orchids. It wasn't just because they're society flowers, I believed that they were parasites, and I hate parasites of any kind. But Doc Graham convinced me that they're saprophytes, so they don't live off their fellows. I got reconciled to them then. I even went to an orchid show here in town. . . . Sergeant, I think you'd better let me out of here now. I feel a pound lighter."

I went back to the pool, and after the President had taken a shower he came out, wearing a pair of navy-blue trunks and with his glasses on again. He said, "It's a shame this pool can't be put to greater use. You know, schoolchildren all over the country chipped in pennies so this pool could be built for F.D.R. He really needed it. It's just a luxury for me. I wish it could be put to some good use."

The President climbed down a chromium-plated ladder at one end of the pool and struck out for the opposite end with a highly personal stroke, a little more back than side stroke, designed, apparently, to balance progress through the water with the need to keep his glasses dry. "Maybe it's a good thing for Presidents to have a swimming pool, come to think of it," he said as he swam along. "Old J. Q. Adams, when he was President, used to go for early-morning walks, the way I do. He'd walk down by the Potomac and some mornings—of course, Washington was a small town in 1825—some mornings he'd slip off his clothes and take a dip in the river. Well, there was a shrew of a newspaperwoman—Anne Royall was her name—and she'd been trying for a long time to interview old J.Q., and he wouldn't see her. So one day she tracked him on his early-morning walk, and when he took his dip, she sat herself down on his clothes. She wouldn't let him out of the river until he answered her questions. Anne Royall was quite a customer. She was later tried in a court here in Washington, and she caught a big fine as a common scold."

While the President swam on—he did about six lengths of the pool—I went in to dress. By the time I was dressed the President was under a sunlamp in his dressing room and General Graham had arrived. I called out my thanks and took my leave. As I started away, the President's voice called after me, in a tone of kindly derision, "Get a good nap, now!"

Jessica Kelley

On Thursday evening, August 18th, 1955, a delicate little old widow named Jessica Kelley spent three pleasant hours in her apartment, at the rear of the fourth floor of Anna Landi's tenement block, at 375 Main Street, in Winsted, Connecticut, chatting with her nearest neighbor, a middle-aged maiden lady of French-Canadian descent, Yvonne Brochu, who had the fourth-floor front. It was raining very hard, and several times the two women remarked on the pounding of the water on the roof.

"I love that noise," Mrs. Kelley said at one point. "It's so soothing to sleep to. But, gracious, it *is* teeming tonight, isn't it, Yvonne?"

Mrs. Kelley, who was seventy-five years old, had long since made it clear to Miss Brochu that she considered conversation one of the purest joys in her altogether joyful life. She once said to her that she had always loved to talk. Just before her marriage, in October, 1903, her fiancé, a salesman of bars, handles, and trimmings for funeral caskets, told her that the very first things he intended to buy after their wedding were a parrot and a brass bed. On their honeymoon in New York, Mr. Kelley did indeed purchase a fine brass bed; nothing more was

"Over the Mad River," *The New Yorker*, September 17, 1955.

said about the parrot, and some weeks later Mrs. Kelley asked her husband why he had not bought one. "Jessica, dear," he said, "I have you."

The talk with Yvonne Brochu that evening was pleasurable, for Miss Brochu, a tiny person, barely five feet tall, who was a factory worker at Dano Electric, in Winsted, was sweet and patient and a loving listener. Mrs. Kelley had moved into the Landi block only two weeks before. She and Miss Brochu were old friends, however, having shared light-housekeeping privileges in a boardinghouse on Case Avenue several years earlier. For the last three and a half years, Mrs. Kelley had taken room and board in the east end of Winsted, near the Gilbert school, and on this particular rainy evening she told her friend Yvonne how trying things had been there. Mrs. Kelley had been a diabetic for three decades, and so, as it happened, had both her landlady and her late landlord in the east-end home. How prodigally those people had eaten! They had pretended to stay on a diabetic diet, but they thought nothing of gulping down four or five bananas at a clip, a bag of cherries, a box of prunes—between meals, too. *He* had died from it; he did not live to tell of his gourmandizing. And *she* had been so close-fisted! Could Yvonne imagine? Mrs. Kelley had been obliged to keep her perfectly good bedside radio wrapped up in paper and string for three and a half years because *she* hadn't wanted even a tiny dribble of electricity used on her premises. Be saving of hot water! Don't waste a cracker crumb! Mrs. Kelley, the soul of charity, spoke of her former landlady not bitterly but in sadness, with a hesitant, sensitive smile from time to time, as if to ask her friend, "Aren't people a puzzle?"

At about ten-thirty, which was nearly her bedtime, Mrs. Kelley said, "It's so muggy and close, why don't you and I take baths before we turn in?"

So they did. Mrs. Kelley's apartment consisted of a bedroom and a kitchen, each about eight feet by ten and as clean as a

pin, and a tiny bathroom. When Mrs. Kelley took her bath she
was very careful to keep her left foot dry, because while she
was walking to St. James Episcopal Church on the previous
Palm Sunday morning she had stepped off the curb in front
of the First National Store at Park Place, with the stoplight
in her favor, and a lady hit-and-run driver had dropped, it
seemed, out of the carless sky right in front of her and had run
over her foot and knocked her down, and as a consequence she
had spent four months in Litchfield County Hospital and had
had to have her little toe amputated. The foot was still bound
up in bandages; a visiting nurse, who helped her with her insulin shots, kept it dressed for her. The winter before, she had
sprained that same foot when she slipped on an icy sidewalk
on her way to the post office; because she had a will of iron,
and because it was what she had set out to do, she had walked
all the way to the post office and home again on her throbbing
foot. That, too, had cost her some time on her back, though,
thankfully, not in the hospital. It seemed that her left foot
was her Jonah; nothing had ever happened to her right foot.
"That's my kicker!" she once said to Yvonne Brochu, giving
her sound right foot a sharp little swing.

After her bath Mrs. Kelley dressed for bed and then sat on
a small straight chair in front of her dressing table, fixing her
gray hair for the night. She walked out into the hall and called
good night to Yvonne, who had finished bathing in her apartment. Mrs. Kelley returned to her bedroom, pulled down her
tufted bedspread with two bright peacocks on it, got into bed,
read a page or two of her prayer book, and dropped off, under
the soothing influence of the still drumming rain, into deep
slumber.

While Mrs. Kelley slept hundreds of millions of gallons
of rain, part of the fantastic load of water that had been

shipped by the hurricane designated as Diane during its voyage up the Atlantic Ocean, were being bailed out on certain hills of northern Connecticut and were washing down them toward Winsted.

Winsted's Main Street lies along the north bank of the Mad River. For several hundred yards downstream from what Winsted people call "the center"—the point where Elm Street crosses Main and then the river—nearly all the Main Street stores backing on the watercourse were surmounted by rickety wooden tenements, mostly three or four stories high, many of them connected to each other on the river side by continuous wooden porches. These porches were tied together vertically by stairs here and there, which were supposed to serve as fire escapes by way of the stores below. Anna Landi's tenement block, in which Mrs. Kelley slept so soundly that night, was the fourth building below the center bridge; it contained, on the street level, the county agent's office, the Metropolitan Cleaners & Dryers, and Irving's Smart Shop. Directly across the river from the Landi block, and facing Willow Street, was the upper end of a substantial factory building, Capitol Products, where electric toasters and hot plates were made. The backs of the buildings on both sides of the river made a kind of canyon about forty feet wide, with the Mad River in its bed. The river there is normally five or six feet deep.

The Mad River rises in the town of Norfolk, about five miles west of Winsted's center; its watershed lies in rugged foothills of the Green Mountain range, most of which are precipitous on their eastern slopes and are blanketed by forests of birch, ash, basswood, black oak, hemlock, and laurel. Winsted itself lies in an irregular bowl formed by the steep slopes of Street Hill, Platt Hill, Ward's Hill, Second Cobble, and several lesser hills. Southwest of the city and high above it is Highland Lake, which has become a pleasant summer resort not only for inhabitants of Winsted but also for vacationers from far-flung areas of Connecticut. Highland Lake is two miles long and averages a third of a mile in width, and it runs north and south; at its northern end, which is about half a mile from Main Street, it empties into a ravine leading to the Mad River. In 1771, the surface of the lake was raised four feet by a wooden dam and bulkhead. Thirty-five years later a spring freshet and thaw broke the dam, but the weakness had been spotted beforehand, and a working party of men and teams was standing by when the break occurred; they hauled a huge tree trunk into the breach and with spars, planks, straw, swingling tow, and gravel prevented a disaster. The next year a new bulkhead raised the surface of the lake another foot. In 1860 a causeway was built across the northern end, protected by a strong retaining wall and two wide overflow spillways, which raised the surface of the lake five feet higher yet. All this damming was for water power. At one time the waters of Highland Lake turned the wheels of eleven factories scattered down the ravine, which drops a hundred and fifty feet in its half-mile course before it joins the Mad River in Winsted's west end.

Over the years, while Winsted has grown from a cluster of villages to a city of eleven thousand inhabitants, the Mad River, swollen by overflowing water from Highland Lake, has several times risen abruptly and washed out here a bridge and there a house or two. During a spring freshet in 1936, and in the New England hurricane of 1938, the Mad River overflowed into Main Street, and after a flash flood on New Year's Eve of 1947–48, the Mayor of Winsted, P. Francis Hicks, prevailed on Army engineers to spend a quarter of a million dollars dredging the river where it parallels Main Street.

At about one o'clock in the morning a man named Arthur Royer, who lived on the third floor of the Landi block and who had been out visiting friends during the evening, came home. By that time the river had risen enough so that a couple of inches of water was flowing down Main Street, which slopes to the east. Royer, another of Winsted's numerous French-Canadians, tends to be a worrier, and he thought that perhaps before going to bed he should tell the old ladies on the top floor that the river was swollen. He climbed to Miss Brochu's door and knocked. For a very long time there was no answer. "Just anyone banging on your door at one o'clock in the night, would you open?" Yvonne later asked Mrs. Kelley. "And a man's voice! I was glad the door was locked." Royer shouted to Miss Brochu awhile in French, and finally, hearing his words, she roused herself, put on a dressing gown, and answered the door. Royer told her about the water in Main Street and went downstairs.

Yvonne looked out of her window and hurried across the hall into Mrs. Kelley's apartment, and at the door of the bedroom she said, "Jessie! Jessie! Put on the light!"

Mrs. Kelley, awakening, felt concern for her friend. She turned on a bedside lamp. "Yvonne, what is it?" she said. "Don't you feel right? Has something happened to you?"

"The water is coming up," Yvonne said. "You can see it in the street. Come in the front and look out the window."

"Gracious, I don't think I want to do that, Yvonne," Mrs. Kelley said.

Miss Brochu was quite excited, and finally Mrs. Kelley said, "Yvonne, I think we should get dressed."

Miss Brochu went back to her apartment, and both ladies put on their clothes. While they were dressing, at about one-fifteen, they separately heard the sirens of Winsted's Civil Defense alarm system, and Mrs. Kelley relieved her distress at hearing this wailing with the thought that Art Royer, downstairs, had a Civil Defense armband. He would be informed. People would come if there was danger. Later, after she had gone into Miss Brochu's front room and had looked at the glistening, shallow water running down Main Street under the streetlights in the rain, she discussed Royer's C.D. brassard with her friend, and Yvonne agreed that help would come if help was needed.

What neither of them could know was that at that very time policemen, firemen, and Civil Defense volunteers were combing all the tenements along Main Street and telling the occupants to leave the buildings and go to high ground, but that somehow the warners had missed the stairway on which the ladies lived, and that they, together with Art Royer and a woman who was still sleeping like a log on the second floor, Mrs. Peter Placek, had been left stranded in the Landi block.

T he next two hours were anxious ones for Jessica Kelley and Yvonne Brochu. They were together, and that was a comfort, but they were very restless. They went out on the back porch that opened off Mrs. Kelley's rooms, where they peered down at the black river, and then they went to the windows in Yvonne's apartment, at the front, and looked down at the street. The water, which was flowing swiftly along Main Street—from left to right as they viewed it—had crept over the sidewalk across the way. They saw three cabs standing in front of the office of Sox's Taxi, two buildings upstreet on the near side; the water eddied around the wheels of the cars. The street seemed deserted. They expected to see some kind of Civil Defense rescue boat in the flooded street, and they kept talking about it. Where was the boat? When would it come? returned to the porch in the rear, and then went again to Yvonne's window, and so kept uneasily moving back and forth. Finally Mrs. Kelley felt that she must rest her foot, and she took the straight chair from her dressing table and sat in the kitchen.

Then the lights went out. At first both women had an im-

THE LIVING ROOM OF JESSICA KELLEY'S WINSTED HOME

"I like the feel of terra firma under my feet."

pulse to scream for help, but they talked it over in trembling voices and decided that that would be useless in the rain-muffled night. There was no telephone in the building. Yvonne remembered that she had some candles, and, groping her way into her rooms, she found them and lit several. The light was a relief.

Mrs. Kelley began by candlelight to gather about her a small pile of valuables: her black winter coat, her handbag, her prayer book, a few keepsakes, and the dear little green box that contained her insulin packet. In her handbag were her insurance policies, her old-age-assistance papers, and three cloth purses containing her ready money. For more than twenty years she had lived on the nest eggs her prudent husband and father had left her, and now the money was nearly gone. Only a few weeks before, she had applied to the government for old-age assistance, for which she qualified now that her savings were running out. She had just had word that payments of about a hundred dollars a month, plus, she understood, an extra allowance on account of her diabetes, would begin soon. As she sat there in the kitchen she thought, for some reason, of a ten-dollar gold piece that C. L. Maloney, an undertaker friend of her husband's, had given them once as a luck piece, as lightly as if it had been no more than a lucky penny. Then she remembered the meerschaum pipe the Winsted Elks had given her husband just before a trip he and she took to Florida in the twenties; he was fussy about that pipe, but it had led to his giving up cigars, thank goodness. Those were the heydays! They had been caught right in the thick of the Florida boom-and-bust. They had had two thousand dollars in traveler's checks with them, and her husband had literally sunk it in some real estate; the land had turned out to be under water. They had had to wait to come home until another thousand dollars could be wired down from Winsted. There had been a time, in the early years of the century, when the Strong Manufacturing Company, the makers of coffin trimmings for whom her husband worked, met its payroll in gold coins. When she and her husband built a new home, at 23 Wetmore Avenue, they had laid the foundations, waited a year till the crisis of 1907 blew over, then resumed building, and paid in gold the stonemasons who laid the front walk. She forgot how many gold coins that had been, but she clearly remembered handing them out. The men had scarcely been able to believe their eyes. For years she had had stocks and bonds galore. Somehow, Connecticut Light & Power and United States Steel had seemed to last the longest. Now there was almost nothing left, and she was watching every penny. Ten dollars a week to Anna Landi for rent; less than that for food; enough for a while in the three purses; a tiny bit in the bank.

Jessica Kelley could not say she was worth much, but what she was worth was right there in the stiff straight chair in the middle of the kitchen and on the floor around it.

Yvonne Brochu, coming on her surrounded by her little heap of wealth, said, "My goodness, Jessie, where do you think you're going?"

"I don't know, dear," Mrs. Kelley said. "But I'm ready."

At about three-thirty, in a rented room in a building known as the Keywan block, diagonally across and about a hundred yards up the river from the tenement where Mrs. Kelley sat waiting, a young man named Frank Stoklasa was being roused from sleep by the occupant of the next room. Stoklasa was a steeplejack, thirty-two years old. Though slight, he was powerfully built. His hairy arms were covered with tattoos that he himself had applied: a dagger, a snake, the Disney dog called Goofy, a ship, and a death's-head. On the backs of the proximal phalanges of the fingers of his left hand were tattooed the letters L-O-V-E; on those of his right hand H-A-T-E. He was born in Fort Worth, Texas, and his friends called him Tex. He was part Czech, part Polish, part Indian. His mother died when he was twenty-two months old. As a small boy, he had typhoid, diphtheria, and pneumonia. When he was about six, his father took him, his two brothers, and his sister to Oklahoma, and they became Okies—migrant farm workers who moved with the seasons to California, Arizona, Texas, and back to Oklahoma. Stoklasa went to school through the ninth grade, then left his family and wandered all over the Southwest, earning a bare living as a truck driver, gas-station attendant, and common laborer. He fought in a Golden Gloves tournament once in San Francisco. He was taken into the Army in 1942 and, after his training, went to North Africa and Germany as an infantryman. In the Rhineland, he was wounded by shrapnel in his upper right arm, and was shipped home and eventually discharged.

Because he liked to get high up on things, and because the money in crazy climbing was good, Stoklasa went to work for the Brown Steeple-Jacking Company, in Norfolk, Virginia. He did welding and painting on water towers, smokestacks, radio towers, and bridges. Once a man has become a seasoned steeplejack, he hears of every topnotch steeplejacking company in the country, and after two years Stoklasa left Brown's in favor of the Universal Construction Company, in Indianapolis. There he took up, as a hobby, stock-car racing—because it was dangerous—but after some time he dropped it, not because it was *too* dangerous, but because of the expense. From Universal, Stoklasa moved to the Kessler Company, in Fremont, Ohio, and he stayed there nearly six years. In Fremont he married and divorced two young ladies; he was on the road too much to settle down. Several times Stoklasa had seen men "go off," as steeplejacks speak of falling, but it was not until last year that he had his first accident. In Youngstown, while climbing with three other Kessler men over the lip of an empty hundred-thousand-gallon water tower a hundred and fifty feet high, to get inside and paint it, he put his weight on the spider rods that braced the top of the cylinder; the rods had been weakened by rust, and he fell through them fifty feet to the bottom of the tank and broke an ankle. He went back to work as soon as it mended. He was then earning three dollars and twenty cents an hour. For a year or so, Stoklasa had buddied with a native of Winsted named Donald Linkovich, and last spring he decided to move with him to Connecticut. Tex went to work at a dollar-sixty an hour for a tree man named MacBurnie, and worked with him until MacBurnie fell and hurt his back, about a fortnight before Diane; then he took a job with another local tree man, Nickerson, at two dollars and five cents an hour. Nickerson's crew was clearing a forest pathway on Avon Mountain for high-tension wires. Stoklasa had always had a rough time, and he had liked it that way. He was taciturn to the point of rudeness, for he had learned to keep his mouth shut and enjoy himself. He was cynical; there was no room for sentiment in his life. In his view, the average dog's favorite food is living dog meat.

Wakened by his neighbor, Tex put on his dungarees, a T shirt, a canvas jacket, and his working shoes, and went out of the building to move Donnie Linkovich's brand-new Mercury convertible up to high land near the Winsted railroad station, which is across Willow Street from Capitol Products. Then he went into a bar and had a couple of beers. It struck him as being wet as hell out.

At about four in the morning, the whole Landi tenement began to tremble. Apparently the river was running through and around its ground floor and was eating at its underpinnings. At first the motion was barely perceptible, but through the small hours it increased, until it had become a real shaking and heaving, and Jessica Kelley, trying to keep a cheerful front for Miss Brochu's sake, said to her, "Dear me, Yvonne, this is like being on a rocking horse, isn't it?" Mrs. Kelley moved her chair from place to place, thinking that there might be some part of the building that was still. For a while, she sat out in the hallway, on the theory that the center of the tenement might be solid, but she was disappointed. Each time she moved, she fetched along her little clutter of precious things.

Mrs. Kelley held her prayer book in her hand all the time, even though it was impossible to read by the flickering light of candles. She improvised some prayers, particularly requesting the arrival of the Civil Defense rescue boat and, for herself, strength of body and character. She had long thought of herself as physically puny and weak. As an infant, she was plump, she had been told; she was born on Thanksgiving Day, 1879, and, on first seeing her, her father exclaimed, "That's the nicest turkey I ever saw!" By the time she reached high school, however, she had grown thin and jumpy, and for a year or two her family thought she had St. Vitus's dance and put her in a private school on Meadow Street, but she got over the disorder. She had a stillborn baby by Caesarean section in 1905, and from that time on she was never able to have children. Her mission in life, even after her marriage, was to care for her parents, and she eventually came to think she had been too close to them for her own well-being. Three months after her mother's death, in the late twenties, she began to have diabetic symptoms; she had never had a trace of them before. Her husband died two years later. After her father died in 1935, at the age of ninety-three, she shut herself up in the house for several weeks, and pulled down the shades, and would not answer the telephone, and became suspicious of all human beings, and ranged from room to room like a wild creature. But she recovered and began a new life alone.

One thing that helped her in all her tribulations was her

willpower, of which she had enough to dole out to ten strong men. Once, a quarter of a century ago, she read somewhere that tooth infections might have serious consequences for a diabetic, so she called her dentist for an appointment and told the nurse she would tell the dentist what she wanted when she arrived; she seated herself in the dentist's chair a few days later and said, "Take all my teeth out." The dentist said, "Heavens! You have granite teeth. Your teeth are far better then mine, and I wouldn't part with mine for a thousand dollars." It was true that her teeth were sound. Strong and prominent teeth ran in her family. Her father, then pushing ninety, had all his own teeth and could still crack walnuts and untie knots in a clothesline with them. Jessica's teeth had perhaps been too much of a good thing. She had once made the mistake of giving her husband a picture of herself smiling, and every time he looked at it on the bureau he used to say, "Fetch me the toothpaste, Jessie." She told the dentist she had fastened her mind on having the whole set out. He gave her novocain and pulled three teeth, and Mrs. Kelley's jaw began to hurt. By this time the doctor was perspiring and pale. "That's enough," he said. "You can come back another day." "No, sir," Mrs. Kelley said, speaking with difficulty but firmly through the new gap in her mouth. "I said *all*, and I meant *all*." He pulled them all, using nothing but novocain. That was one of the days in Jessica Kelley's life that helped convince her there was nothing even a weakling woman could not do if she made up her mind to it and held fast.

Some of her tenacity had come, she was sure, from her father, William Gilbert Barnes. He was related to the Gilbert Clock people, and after being in the wooden butter-tub and washtub business in New York State for a few years he had come to Winsted and helped make clocks. He had been foreman of Winsted Volunteer Fire Company No. 2 several times and had been an active fireman well into his eighties. He had magnificent white handlebar mustaches, but to his dying day his hair was hardly even gray, and he stood as straight and trig as a fence post. Right up until his ninety-third year he celebrated each birthday by walking the seven miles around Highland Lake.

The building trembled more and more, and Mrs. Kelley began to imagine how pleasant it would be if only she could be whisked somewhere far away—to Meriden, perhaps, or New Britain. If only she could fly! During the three-quarters of a century of her life, aviation had shrunk the earth, but she had never been up in a plane. On their Florida trip her husband had teased her to go up in a barnstormer, but she had refused. He had gone off then without telling her and had taken a flight, and later he had said it was awfully nice and airy up there. He *was* a sly one! She hadn't learned until after his death what a proficient cardplayer and billiards player he had been. She had known, of course, that he spent a great deal of time at the Elks Home and at the Winsted Club, but he had never boasted to her about his skills, and she had come to hear of them only when someone brought his cues around to the house after the funeral. His favorite cue, the handle of which was inlaid with mother-of-pearl, she had given as a keepsake to one of his best friends—Billy Phelps, president of the Hurlbut National Bank. The thing her husband liked best in the world was precisely what she wanted in those anxious hours— to get up and go. He loved to travel. He took two trips a year; he never missed an Elks' convention. The year he was Winsted's Past Exalted Ruler, his lodge sent him as a delegate all the way to Dallas, Texas. He slipped off to New York quite a bit, too, especially during inventory time at the casket-trimmings plant.

Mrs. Kelley reflected that, besides flying, one thing she had neglected and would like now to have done was to learn to swim. Just a couple of years before, a man at the Y.M.C.A. had tried to coax her to take lessons, saying that he succeeded once before in teaching a woman to swim who was over seventy. But she had said then, as she had said to her husband when he tried to get her to fly, "I like the feel of terra firma under my feet." There were times during the early-morning hours in the shaking building when the possibility of drowning in the flood outside forced itself on her, and she reflected that for some hours—perhaps even for some years—she had had sensations like those of a person slowly going down into the darkness of deep water, with the happy scenes of her lifetime flashing through her mind. The sensations had not been too bad. She had had fortunate years; she considered herself ready for whatever might be her lot.

It was beginning to get light, and Yvonne Brochu came running in from time to time with alarming bits of news. It was still pouring. The water was almost up to the awnings on the stores across Main Street, and it was going down the street awfully fast—maybe thirty miles an hour. Two of Sox's taxis had simply disappeared. The water was coming down in great surges—could it be that the causeway at Highland Lake was giving way? There was something floating down Main Street that looked like a refrigerator. And there was a brand-new car—just being rolled along! There went Sox's other cab! A chair from the hairdresser's was going down the street! There was a whole roof out there floating down!

Worst of all was when, after peering out from the back porch awhile, Yvonne came in crying, "The bridge has gone, Jessie! That bridge has gone!"

Mrs. Kelley spoke in as careful a voice as she could command. The bridge at the Winsted center had been built of steel. "I think you must be mistaken, dear," she said. "It must be that the water's over it and covers it, because it's rising so fast."

"No! No! I saw the bridge go," Yvonne said. "It's gone."

After a good long wait, so as not to be rushing hysterically to check up on a piece of calamitous information, Mrs. Kelley went out on the porch and looked upriver and saw for herself. The bridge was washed away, no mistake. Mrs. Kelley returned to her chair and prayed some more. She wept, too, but she managed to hide her tears from Yvonne.

Not long afterward there was a terrifying crash out back, and bricks and glass and something very heavy fell. Mrs. Kelley and Miss Brochu went to the back window and saw that a whole corner of the brick Capitol Products building was sagging and gaping, and a cement floor was hanging down like bent cardboard. Huge machines had slid about, and the fall had probably been that of one or more of them into the river.

Art Royer came running upstairs, and rather wildly he suggested that the ladies leave the building with him. They would go out the front door into Main Street. He would go in the center, he said, and hold the two ladies by the hand. Yvonne Brochu pointed out that automobiles and refrigerators were bobbing downstreet like corks; people wouldn't last thirty seconds in that water. All during the morning, Mr. Royer kept renewing his mad, chivalrous offer.

Some time later Mrs. Placek, a solid, phlegmatic woman of sixty-nine, whose husband was away in Waterbury, said she had been sleeping until a few minutes before. "The water woke me up," she said. "It told me, 'Get up, you lazy head.'"

In a calm voice, Mrs. Kelley welcomed Mrs. Placek to her apartment and said, "Things seem to be giving way outside."

"This whole building's going," Mrs. Placek said gloomily.

"Oh, dear, no, I doubt *that*," Mrs. Kelley said.

In just a few minutes, this doubt of Mrs. Kelley's was badly shaken. In full sight of Yvonne and Art Royer and Mrs. Placek—she herself, thank heavens, was not watching—a building across and up the river, the first one this side of the washed-out bridge, slowly twisted and went limp and simply fell into a thousand pieces into the river.

The building that had fallen was the Keywan block, in which Tex Stoklasa had had his room.

It was six o'clock, and the flood had reached its crest, which it was to hold for nearly six hours. The rain continued. Highland Lake was running over its spillways and tearing out threatening gullies right across the macadam road on the causeway on either side of them and causing terrible damage in factories and homes between the lake and the river below. All the way from Norfolk, the Mad River was brimming. Along Main Street it was fifteen feet above its normal level, and the water was ten feet deep in the street itself. It was literally ripping up Main Street. The pavement and sidewalks were being sliced away and gutted six feet deep. The water had broken the plate-glass windows of most of the stores along the street and had ruined their stocks. Winsted Motors, a Buick showroom and service station that had straddled the river high up on the street, had been completely demolished, and its new and used cars were rolling all the way downtown, and its roof had lodged itself in midstreet right in front of the Town Hall. On the second floor of the Town Hall, forty-one policemen and Civil Defense workers and the chairlady of the Winsted Red Cross were marooned. All but two of the town's twelve bridges had collapsed or were about to. A four-story hotel at the foot of the street, the Clifton, had floated off its foundation and into the river and downstream three-quarters of a mile, and had settled on the town ball field, more or less erect but with its two lower floors worn away. The water was doing damage to private property that the town estimated at nearly twenty-eight million dollars—more than the entire grand list of assessed taxable property, for assessments in Winsted, as generally in Connecticut, are considerably under real values.

After Tex had had his drinks, he had returned to the Keywan block and sat up talking with several other men there. From time to time they had gone outdoors to pick up news and watch the river level. After the bridge went it appeared to them that the foundations of the Keywan block were threatened, and they had gone up to get the landladies, two elderly maiden sisters known in town as the Garrity girls, to evacuate. But the Garrity girls had long considered the building their home, and to them home had always meant safety, and they had refused to leave. After quite an argument Tex and a friend had bodily removed the ladies, and within minutes the building had fallen. Tex had not had time to go back for his things, and into the river had gone his climbing equipment: his shield, sleeves, pants, boots, belt—nearly six hundred dollars' worth of gear.

A few minutes after the collapse of the Keywan block, the next building downriver, a fifty-year-old brick structure called the Bannon block, turned half around on its base, partly crumbled at the bottom, and leaned over at a crazy angle away from its downriver neighbor, the Capitol Products building, and toward the Keywan foundations.

Tex joined a crowd of about two hundred people on the higher ground near the railroad station and, through the gap where the Keywan block had been, watched what was now happening on the far—the Main Street—side of the river. It was quite a show.

Mrs. Kelley and her companions were subjected to a series of horrifying wrenches, and the Landi tenement perceptibly heeled toward the river. A large piece of plaster fell from Mrs. Kelley's bedroom ceiling. Mrs. Kelley, who was sitting in the kitchen, wanted then to get that room out of sight, but she could not close the door, because the frame had been twisted and the floor was all out of kilter.

The four people in the Landi tenement had no way of knowing that the three buildings upriver from theirs, undermined by the water and battered by descending debris, were crumbling and falling, one by one. First went the four-story Petrunti block, containing Riiska's Taxi Stand, Rocky's Garage, and Luben's Cleaners; then the two-story building with Pelkey & Simpson's hardware store; then, next door to the Landi block, the two-story building that housed Jimmy's Restaurant.

Terrified by the cataclysmic shaking in Mrs. Kelley's apartment, and seeing the crowd across the way by the railroad station, Art Royer went out on the balcony at the back and waved to the people there and beckoned and held up four fingers, indicating that there were four people in the building to be somehow saved.

Tex Stoklasa saw Royer. He ran into the Capitol Products building and crept out onto the very edge of the sagging concrete floor of the plant's press room and looked the situation over. He was about ten feet above the surface of the Mad River, down which all sorts of heavy debris were swiftly floating. The Landi building was straight across from him. The river was several feet up the wall of the ground floor of the Landi block, and of the buildings below it. At first, Stoklasa thought he might be able to throw a rope across to a balcony, if one of the people could climb down to catch it. Then he saw a double clothesline stretched on pulleys between an upper floor of the fifth building downriver from the Landi block and a wooden building belonging to Capitol Products, adjacent to the one he was in. He ran around into the wooden building and found that the pulley at the near end of the clothesline was attached to its outer wall, right next to a window.

Then, in a tenement two buildings down from the Landi block, over Pete's Barber Shop, he saw a thin young man and a plump young woman standing at a third-floor window and apparently calling for help, though over the rushing of the river, the grinding of lumber in it, the pounding of the rain, and the whistling of the strong wind he could not hear their words. He tried to signal to them to make their way, if possible, down to the building with the clothesline—the Lentini block—but they evidently did not understand.

There were others around Stoklasa now, and someone suggested writing a message on a piece of cardboard and displaying it. Soon Tex was holding up a big card on which was written, "COME DOWN HERE," and he pointed across at the Lentini block. The man disappeared from the window.

Tex told the people around him to try to find a length of half-inch rope and a climbing belt.

The young man and woman in the tenement over Pete's Barber Shop were Billy Fields, a twenty-seven-year-old employee at Hickey's Fur Shop, and his wife. When Fields read the sign, he at once started working his way downriver. On a stair landing of his building he found a long-unused, locked door connecting with the next building, the Serafini block; he broke it down with his shoulder. He went out onto a back porch of the Serafini block and saw that the next building downriver, the Orsi block, was only one story high, with a roof sloping back from Main Street. He ran down the fire escape to the second-story balcony of the Serafini block and there discovered that he could climb around the end wall of the balcony and drop a few feet to the Orsi roof, and he did. At the far end of the Orsi roof, he had a six-foot climb up a wooden wall to a sort of lean-to roof over the back rooms on the second floor of the Lentini block. Once he was on this roof he was able to make his way up to the balcony from which the clothesline ran.

By this time someone had produced a rope from the New England Knitting Company factory, across the street and upriver from the former site of Keywan's, and someone else had miraculously procured a belt with a pulley on it. Tex saw that the rope, while far from new, was a sturdy half-inch line—regular nine-hundred-pound-test rope, of the sort steeplejacks are commonly satisfied to use. He tied one end of it to the upper strand of the clothesline and pulled it across the river. Fields untied the rope from the clothesline. Tex held up a new cardboard sign: "TIE ROPE TO POST. KEEP AHOLT OF END." Fields did as directed. Tex strung the belt pulley onto his end of the line and took turns of the rope around two stanchions inside the wooden Capitol Products building and directed men to hold the free end and keep the whole line taut. He took everything off but his dungarees. He slung the belt outside the window, backed into it, so that he sat in the loose loop of the belt facing the Capitol Products window, and pulled himself hand over hand across above the river in the pouring rain.

Stoklasa and Fields dropped to the Orsi roof, swung around the end wall of the Serafini balcony, then ran along the connected porches. Fields stopped off for his wife; Stoklasa went on to the Landi block and up the fire escapes to Mrs. Kelley and her companions. Curtly, Stoklasa directed them to follow him. Mrs. Kelley put on her winter coat and picked up her pocketbook and went out on the porch after the young man. The others came behind.

Stoklasa on one side and Fields on the other pushed and supported the women past the one dangerous point—out around the end of the Serafini porch and down onto the Orsi roof. Mrs. Kelley felt all out of breath, but she trusted the strong, half-naked young man. At the far end of the Orsi roof, Tex above and Fields and Royer below raised the women to the lean-to roof of Lentini's block, and from there to the Lentini balcony. When they were all assembled Tex began to explain how to ride the belt across. The rope sloped downward to Capitol Products. At its lowest point it was about fifteen feet above the water. The lean-to roof provided a good launching platform. Whoever was going over, Tex said, should sit in the belt facing Capitol Products, cross his feet over the rope ahead of the belt pulley, and grasp the rope with his hands and feed himself down the incline. Mrs. Kelley gasped. She hadn't the strength for such work. An argument followed as to who should go first. Tex urged Mrs. Fields to go. She refused. Fields tried to persuade her. She wept, and finally said she would never go.

Then Tex turned to Mrs. Kelley and said, "Come on, lady, I'm taking you over."

"Gracious!" Mrs. Kelley said. "I'm not certain I *want* to go over on that little rope."

"There's no time to lose," Stoklasa disgustedly said to the whole group. "All these buildings may go down."

Mrs. Kelley was surprised to hear herself say, "Tell me what to do. I'll go."

The next thing Mrs. Kelley knew, Stoklasa had lifted her like a doll off the porch and out onto the slanting roof. He was strong!

"What've you got that for, for Christ's sake?" he said, pointing to her pocketbook. "We may go in the river."

"I've got valuables in there, young man," she said. "If I go in the river, that goes with me."

"Throw it on the roof," he said.

"It goes where I go," she said.

"God damn it, throw it on the roof," Stoklasa said. "I'll bring it over. Take that heavy coat off."

"Excuse me, I'm staying dry," Mrs. Kelley said with considerable spirit. But she did put down her bag, with a great deal of reluctance. She had already let herself be separated from her insulin packet, for the first time in many years. And now her money. She kept her coat on.

"O.K., come on," Stoklasa said roughly. "Let's get going."

Stoklasa sat in the belt at the edge of the lean-to roof, put his hands and feet up, and directed Mrs. Kelley to lie supine on him, tucking both legs through the loop of the belt. She found herself with her bad foot lying on the young man's legs and the other up over the rope above his feet. Tex told her to hold the rope with both hands, and keep them moving constantly, hand over hand, feeding out rope as they moved.

"Let's go," he said.

"Oh, dear," she said. "I'm so nervous."

"Don't worry, lady, I'll get you over," he said. "Whatever you do, don't look down."

They swung out over the river. They moved terribly slowly. The rope rubbed Mrs. Kelley's right leg. The line swayed in the wind. It was raining.

From the Capitol Products side the sight of Stoklasa with the little old lady in the black coat on his belly, slowly easing down the swaying line, was so fearful that many people felt ill and some had to look away. The proprietor of the factory had to leave the building and stand on the railroad-station side.

Now someone in Capitol Products spotted an old, old man in a window of one of the buildings upstream from the rope. He had a white stubble on his chin and was wearing a hat in the house. He was watching Stoklasa and Mrs. Kelley and smiling and nodding, apparently oblivious of all peril.

About halfway across Stoklasa grunted and said, "I got to take a breather. Hold up." He stopped. "This is rough," he said. "We ought to have a block and fall."

Mrs. Kelley, looking steadfastly up at the leaking heavens,

felt so agitated that she wondered whether she was going to be able to keep hold of the rope. At last the young man told her to start moving again. The rope began to burn her leg. They seemed to make steady progress, but about ten feet from the far side Stoklasa stopped for another rest.

"I'm getting out of breath," Mrs. Kelley said. "I feel as if my breathing is going to be shut off."

"Hang on," Stoklasa said. "It's only going to be another minute."

He started again.

At last the hands of two men named DeLutrie and Shakar grasped Mrs. Kelley, and she heard one of them say, "It's all right. I have you. You're safe now."

"I know it! I believe you!" she said feelingly.

Then she was cradled like a child in a man's arms in the window. "I couldn't have stood much more," she said between gasps for air, and she tried to smile.

Someone drew up a wooden crate and sat her on it. How good it felt to have her feet on a solid floor! Terra firma! She still felt out of breath, and she asked if she could have a sip of water. Someone said there was no water; after a few moments she was handed a bottle of cream soda. Then an office chair with a spring on it was produced, and she was tilted back in it, and someone fanned her with the top of a carton. She began to feel more composed, and she sat up straight. She noticed that a pocket had been sheared off her coat. "Well!" she said cheerfully. "Thank goodness for my coat. I'm dry as a chip, anyway." A woman handed her a cup of hot coffee, and she drank every drop. "That *is* bracing!" she said. Then all at once she grew terribly disturbed, for she had thought of Yvonne. "Can you tell me whether someone is about to come over on the rope?" she asked a woman nearby.

By that time Stoklasa had gone back and both Fields and his wife had crossed safely on the belt, without Stoklasa's help.

Fields had gone first, to show his heavy wife how to manage, and she had relented from her determination never to ride that rope. Mrs. Kelley had not seen them lifted into Capitol Products.

Yvonne Brochu was on her way across, solo, when Mrs. Kelley asked about her, and in a few moments Mrs. Kelley saw her friend being helped into the window. The seventy-five-year-old woman stood up and tottered to her young friend and took her in her arms. "I'm so glad to see you, my dear," she said.

On the other side, Tex helped first Art Royer and then Mrs. Placek onto the rope. Then he scrambled along the buildings to find the old man in the window. This was a seventy-seven-year-old town character named Sam Lane.

"Come on," Stoklasa said. He was getting tired, and he was impatient. The buildings were shaking badly.

"What do you think I am?" Lane said in a cracking voice. "A tightrope walker?" He chuckled.

"You coming or not?" Stoklasa asked.

"I can't leave Queenie," Lane said, shaking his head. Lane has a squat, miscellaneous dog he calls Queenie; he tells Winsteders she's a spitz—she chaws tobacco and spits, he says.

Tex climbed back and rode the rope from Capitol Products, carrying Mrs. Kelley's pocketbook and the one belonging to Mrs. Placek. He dropped the pocketbooks on the floor and walked out of the building. Someone tried to shake his hand, but he wouldn't be grabbed. There was a Navy helicopter landing near the parking lot of the Pontiac place downriver, and Tex ran down to it. The pilot asked for a volunteer to be lifted on a harness to rescue a woman from the Burke & Navin building, which was all twisted in the current at the foot of Main Street. Tex said he'd go. The copter carried him over and dropped him on the roof. He climbed down and broke a window to speak to the woman. She came at him half-crazed and asked him what he meant by breaking in the windows of a woman's home. He said he was the fellow who had come to save her. She said he wasn't the right person; someone else was coming for her.

"All right, you dumb jerk," Tex said. "Stay there and drown." He waved for the helicopter to come and pick him up.

In the next twelve hours the flood abated, almost as quickly as it had come up. The building in which Lane had decided to stay with Queenie remained standing; he eventually walked out onto dry land on the arm of a policeman. The Burke & Navin building, where Stoklasa had left the woman who was expecting someone else to come and save her, was frightfully battered, but it did not fall, and she, too, walked away from the wreckage. The Landi block, in which Mrs. Kelley and her friends had lived, sagged further, but it did not collapse. Perhaps she and the others might have safely stayed in it—but who could have foreseen that?

Mrs. Kelley and Mrs. Placek were taken into the home of the man named DeLutrie, who had helped them into the window of Capitol Products. In the next few days they and friends who visited them talked of little but the flood. Yvonne Brochu, who had been given shelter in the home of some people who lived not far from the DeLutries, went back into the Landi block and fetched, among other things, Mrs. Kelley's green box containing her insulin packet. Often the ladies talked of Tex. Once Mrs. Kelley spoke of how muscular he had been. "A fine young specimen," she said. "I've never seen a more fearless man." Then, with her hesitant, puzzled smile, she said, "I wonder why he did it. I don't think it was exactly out of the kindness of his heart. He was really quite impatient with us, and, gracious, he used rough language. I guess he did it just to dare the Devil."

A fortnight after the flood Mrs. Kelley had what seemed to be a mild upset connected with her diabetes—something that had happened to her several times in recent years. She lost her appetite, became nauseated, and could take nothing to drink. She went to the hospital, and the doctors soon put her straight. She was, as always, cheerful and talkative. Then, on a Sunday, sixteen days after her deliverance from the violent floodwaters, she suffered a cerebral hemorrhage and died quietly in bed.

Varsell Pleas

One April morning in 1964, seventeen Negroes, country people, crossed the courthouse square in Athens, Mississippi, footing stiffly along, conscious of eyes on them, and approached the north door of the county seat, a brooding building of dark-red brick with spiked turrets at its corners and a golden-domed cupola with a four-faced clock, which said it was half past nine. These were cotton-and-soybean farmers from the vicinity of Noonday, thirteen men and four women.

Out in front were Randoman Tort, known to Negroes in the county as "a broad-speaking man"—or, as the local rednecks would vehemently put it, a right uppity nigger—and Reverend O. O. Burring, with a straight, cautious carriage, and taciturn Albert Parrisot, who belonged to the N.A.A.C.P., and bear-bodied James Drake, president of the P.-T.A. at the Noonday rural school near where the seventeen lived. Empria Meeks

---

"A Life for a Vote," *Saturday Evening Post*, September 26, 1964. At the time this article was published, the blacks I wrote about were taking great risks and were in great danger. (Whenever "Varsell Pleas" drove me anywhere in his car, during the time I was staying with him, we were followed by a pickup driven by whites with a shotgun prominently displayed.) For this reason, I changed most of the names of people and places. It is safe now to print the real names of Varsell and Mrs. Pleas: Norman and Rosebud Clark.

had her two-year-old, Erma Jean, in her arms, because all her other eleven children were in school or gone and there was no one to leave the girl with. Mrs. Tulip Caesar, a settled-aged lady, was with the group, and Meshak Lewis, and Billy Head and Elzoda Lee.

And with them, among the others, was Varsell Pleas, a solidly built forty-four-year-old farmer, a rather aloof man who walked with his head canted slightly back. His brown cheeks seemed festooned up into pronounced bulges, perhaps partly because of a habit he had of pursing his lips in thought before every utterance of speech; the whites of his eyes were yellowed from years of blown loess and bright sun, and the right eye had a disconcerting outward look, ever so slight, a minor cast. Pleas was not among the first, but as the group moved up the concrete path to the courthouse he found himself bunched with those who had been. He slowed his pace. He knew the gravity of what he and his friends were doing. They were putting their lives on the line. They were colored, and they wanted to qualify to vote in one of the roughest corners in all the South—in Ittabala County, Mississippi.

Varsell Pleas had learned through many hard years that the vote is the real issue in Mississippi. School integration, job opportunities, cotton allotments, social mixing, mongrelization— all other problems, all slogans, all shibboleths give way to the issue of the vote, which is the means to power. In a few counties like Ittabala the vote is in truth a life-and-death matter, and the reason is twofold. In Ittabala County, as elsewhere in the South ever since the seventeenth century, Negro labor has made possible a way of life the whites do not wish to give up. And in Ittabala County, Negroes outnumber whites 19,100 to 8,200. In all the time since the Mississippi Constitution of 1890 was promulgated, only twenty-six Negroes have had their names entered in the book of qualified voters in the red courthouse in Athens: about forty-five hundred whites are registered today. The whites of Ittabala County mean to keep it that way; the Negroes intend to register.

The seventeen had slowed down on the path for good cause. On the steps before them, in uniform, armed with a pistol and a billy, stood Sheriff Haralson R. Lee, who is the soul of the county's law and is not given to budging.

Pleas heard one of the Negroes at the front say, "Move on forward, folks."

"Hold on there," Pleas then heard the sheriff call out. "None of that goddamned forward stuff around here. What do you people want?"

Randoman Tort, whom the sheriff knew, now spoke up. "Mr. Lee, we only come to register."

"Register for what, Tort?"

"Register to vote."

"Who you fixing to vote for?"

"We might could vote for you, Mr. Lee, if you was running." Tort smiled as he said this, perhaps to signal deference, perhaps sensing the irony of the offer.

"No use to vote for me. I already been elected." The sheriff gave back the smile of the man who always has the last word. "All right, Tort," he then said, snapping off the good humor, "you all disperse yourselves and go around to the south side of the courthouse and stop under that shade tree. Don't go in no big crowd, go in twos."

So the seventeen did that, and they stood in hushed pairs and threes under the elm tree at the northwest corner of the courthouse yard for a good while, waiting for something to happen. Silent in the sunlight near them, at the head of a slender shaft of stone, a stone man stood, a beautiful young soldier of the War Between the States, at whose unveiling, on December 4, 1905, Miss Annabell Tull, of the C. R. Rankin Chapter of the United Daughters of the Confederacy, spoke these words in dedication: ". . . From his hands came down to you a wealth

of priceless heirlooms: patriotism passed down from his fore-
fathers who fought for rights in 1776, the same true patriotism
that shone in 'Sixty-one to 'Sixty-five, heroism that did not fade
in all the many changes from wealth to poverty, nobility that
rose above defeat, faith in the right, generosity, courage, every
trait of a people that make a nation great."

At length the latter-day vessel of those valued heirlooms,
Sheriff Haralson R. Lee, came out to the tree, put his hands on
his hips, and in what seemed to Pleas a very loud voice said,
"All right, now, who wants to go first?"

The Negroes exchanged looks. At first no one seemed to
want to volunteer.

Then Tort stepped forward and said he would be first. The
sheriff directed him to the office on the right just inside the
south door of the courthouse, and Tort walked away.

For two hours nothing happened, and Pleas wondered what
the officials inside could be doing with Tort. Pleas knew that
the actual process of registration should only take about fifteen
minutes, long enough to fill out a form with twenty-one questions. This form was the Mississippi white man's means of
keeping the Negro from voting. The black man had been
fundamentally disfranchised in Mississippi under the state
constitution that was adopted in 1890, at a time when most
Mississippi Negroes were illiterate, by a clause requiring that
every voter should be able to read any section of the state constitution *or* "be able to understand the same when read to him"
or "give a reasonable interpretation thereof." In 1955, in the
angry aftermath of the Supreme Court decision on school
desegregation, the state legislature, taking into account the
spreading literacy of Southern Negroes, passed a bill requiring
a written test for registration, on which the applicant must
demonstrate that he could read *and* write a clause of the constitution *and* understand it. Whether the clause had been
rightly understood was entirely up to the subjective judgment

of the registrar, who in Ittabala County was Circuit Clerk
James Z. Williams.

At about noon Tort came out and said he had not yet seen
the circuit clerk. The lady in the office had said Mr. Williams
was busy in court; Tort could sit and wait. Just now, two hours
later, the lady had said, "Well, I'm going to dinner now. You
can come back after." And he had said, "Yes, Ma'am, I'll be
back after dinner." So the seventeen scattered. Pleas went down
with some others to a place kept by a Chinese man on Chick-
asaw Street to get something to eat.

By the time the circuit clerk's office reopened, the candidates
had reassembled under the tree. During the dinner hour policemen had been brought in from other parts of the county;
there were now some ten or fifteen uniformed and armed men
standing in the shade of the courthouse near the tree, among
them the familiar Noonday officer, Town Marshal L. O. Trent.
Again there was a long wait; finally Sheriff Lee beckoned to
James Drake to go in, and he did.

Standing under the tree, waiting again, Varsell Pleas could
not help seeing that the group was causing a sensation in the
town. People had come to watch all around one side of the
square. Though court was supposed to be standing, white faces
appeared in the courthouse windows; Pleas counted nine heads
in one window. He wondered, Could Mr. Williams really be so
busy? Pleas hated this building. He had lived just outside Athens for three years, from 1944 through 1946, and he remembered two cases that had come to trial here that last year. In
the spring a Negro boy named Henry Larkin, crossing a street
on a bicycle in Bula, nearby, had bumped into a white man,
who had shot him dead; in court the defendant said that the
boy had ridden the bike at him after he had bawled the boy
out, and the accused had been acquitted by a jury in less than
half an hour. Later that summer four white men had been
charged with whipping a Negro man, Brutus Simpson, to

death, because he had allegedly stolen some whiskey, and with putting his body in a lake down in the next county; the men had admitted having flogged Simpson but had denied having hurt him enough to kill him, and a jury had acquitted them in ten minutes.

In midafternoon the Negroes under the tree saw Drake leave the courthouse, but he was not allowed by the policemen to rejoin the group. About an hour later Tort was admitted to take the test; he was out again rather quickly, and he, too, was kept from the others. At four-thirty, Sheriff Lee told those who remained that the office was closed, there wouldn't be any more tests that day.

It took three days to test seventeen people. The second and third days, the police were out in even stronger force than on the first day—at times there were nearly twenty law-enforcement men on hand. Pleas wondered, Who were they protecting, and from what? The cops were given chairs against the building. The Negroes were kept waiting under the tree.

Midway through the third morning, Varsell Pleas' turn came, and he entered the building. At first the circuit clerk's office, with a long counter thrown athwart the entranceway, seemed dark as a crow's throat after the brightness out-of-doors. The circuit clerk was in, but Pleas was told to take a seat. After a few minutes Williams came out and said to the lady in the office, "I have to step across here a minute, be back directly." He was gone an hour. Pleas sat tranquilly; it had long since become obvious to the Negroes that a stretch-out was on, and Pleas knew there was no use getting upset.

Finally the clerk returned, and he beckoned Pleas to the counter and asked him his name. Calling Pleas by his given name from then on, the circuit clerk asked: Why did Varsell want to register? Had he been advised? Had anybody been teaching him? Had he been going to meetings? Were other Negroes from Noonday going to try to register?

A lifetime of practice went into Pleas' noncommittal answers.

Williams took Pleas into a very small room across the hall, scarcely more than a closet, with a single dim bulb hanging from the high ceiling, and handed him the registration form and assigned him Section 76 of the constitution to copy and explain: "In all elections by the legislature the members shall vote viva voce, and the vote shall be entered on the journals." Pleas had been studying the constitution for several weeks, and he knew several of the twenty-eight sections of Article 3, the state's bill of rights, by heart, but there were 285 clauses in the whole document, and he had never happened to find out the meaning of the phrase "viva voce." Since then he has often wondered how many of the county's registered whites know its meaning.

When Pleas handed in the test, the lady in the office told him to come back in thirty days and find out whether he had passed or not.

A policeman at the courthouse door told him to move on away, stay clear of them niggers under the tree.

Pleas said he had to take some of them home in his pickup.

The constable said, "That don't make no difference. Stay clear, hear?"

So Pleas waited on the other side of the square the rest of the day to take his friends home.

Now the sense of danger came strongly out. The *Athens Courier* proclaimed to all the county the names of the seventeen Negroes who had attempted to register. The day after the paper appeared, the white owner of the land east of Pleas', an electrical-equipment dealer from Joshua City, named Rainsford, who did not live on the land but rented it out, and who had long before told Pleas he could fence a small plot for a table garden, drove to Pleas' house, which is in open country six miles northeast of Noonday center.

"Varsell, take that fence down."

"You fixing to sell that land, Mr. Rainsford?"

"Sold it. Sold it to the government."

"You sold that little old piece to the government, Mr. Rainsford?"

"Never mind, you just take that fence down."

"Mr. Rainsford, me and my whole family's right busy chopping cotton"—the Negroes' expression for hoeing—"but if you could give me two, three days, I could get that done."

"That'd be all right, Varsell. Just see you do it."

That was the beginning. Two days later Marshal Trent came up from Noonday and said, "Varsell, if you should happen to need me for anything, you just call on me. Anytime."

Pleas recognized this as the time-honored offer of protection that served, by underlining the danger, to intimidate.

At the regular citizenship meeting at the Baptist church called Shore of Peace the next Wednesday night, one of the men, in the spirit of the Mississippi state motto, *Virtute et Armis,* "By Virtue and Arms," urged all those who had tried to register to get up on their praying and to have their guns clean and ready.

When Pleas got home, he checked over his three shotguns and his rifle—weapons with which, for years, he and his three older sons had hunted small game in fall and winter months, to supplement the family larder.

One evening about nine o'clock, in the next week, a car drove in by Pleas' house and a white man with a beer can in his hand walked across the headlights. Varsell jumped out one of the back windows and looped around in the dark through his pasture to try to see the car. At the side door the man asked Mrs. Pleas if Varsell was home.

"He was here a minute ago," said Mrs. Pleas, who didn't like the way the man waved his beer can around. "He ain't in the house. Meshak Lewis, he was here a few minutes ago. Varsell was right out here talking to him. Children"—Mrs. Pleas called out at large to any of her eleven children (Varsell Jr., 19, Orsmond, 18, Robert, 17, Cleontha, 15, Pomp, 14 Ervin, 13, James, 12, Edward, 11, Icie, 9, Sussie, 7, and Larnie, 5) who might be within earshot—"where'd your daddy go?" Silence from the children. Actually Varsell Jr. and Orsmond had also gone out a far window, each with a shotgun; Orsmond said later that "if they'd have jumped Daddy," he himself would have aimed at tires first.

"He must have gone up to Noonday."

"How long's he been gone?"

"Must've just left."

"What time'll he be back?"

"I really couldn't tell. He could be gone to Athens." Mrs. Pleas peered out at the car. "Won't you all come in and wait? Ask your friends in." This was a formality, and both parties knew it. Mrs. Pleas was trying to find out all she could. But the man drove off. Varsell said he'd seen three others in the car.

A few days later—about two weeks after the registration attempt—word came from the domestic-help grapevine in Noonday that "they were planning something" for eight of the people who had tried to register, and Randoman Tort, whose house was near the main highway, Route 57, was first on the list; it was not known exactly what "they" had in mind.

The very next night after these warnings Tort got his. At about three in the morning a fire bomb was thrown in his house, which caught fire. He ran out with a Remington automatic .22 and, seeing two figures, fired at them, and they fired back. The attackers, apparently not having expected gunfire, ran off after having discharged several shots at Tort and into the house. With buckets of water from the hand pump in the yard, the Torts put out the fire.

The following day Tort called the F.B.I. and the sheriff; both came and inspected the damage. That evening Sheriff Lee returned and arrested Tort for arson—for setting fire to his own house. He was in jail for two days and then was released on a three-hundred-dollar bond. The charges against him were dropped when the case reached Jackson and the Justice Department took a strong hand in it. The involvement of out-of-state F.B.I. in the Tort case apparently caused "them" to call off, at least for the time being, the other attacks they were rumored to have planned.

After Tort was cleared, Varsell Pleas went up to Athens and asked—knowing what the answer would be—whether he had been passed for registration. The lady in the office got out his application and she said, "No, Varsell, you didn't pass."

"Can you tell me, Ma'am, just where I didn't pass?"

The lady gave both sides of the sheet a quick look, and she said, "No, it just says, 'Failed.' It doesn't say why. You just failed, that's all."

"Yes, Ma'am," said Varsell Pleas, and went home. Not one of the seventeen had passed.

After these events, "getting the box," as he and his friends called qualifying to vote, became, more than ever, the central goal of Varsell Pleas' life. He was now forty-four years old, he owned his own farm, his older children were leaving home, and he had irrevocably put everything he was and had in jeopardy for this single cause. He felt himself prepared, by the education and experiences he had had, to vote—fully as competent, in his own estimation, as many whites he knew.

He was born on July 16, 1920, near Indianola, Sunflower County, in the rich Delta, seventh child in a family of nine, son of a sharecropper who had made ten crops for a planter named Spurlack. On that place, as Pleas tells it, the bell rang at fore-

day, and the boss sat in a chair at the gear house with a leather
strop in his hand for the blacks who turned up late. The crop-
pers got six bits a day, and the owner furnished fifteen dollars'
worth of food and clothing a month at his planting commissary. A family with numerous children to work in the fields
might clear three hundred dollars when the crop was in; this
had to get them through to the following spring.

When Varsell was eight his father, having raked his shin on
a barbed-wire fence, contracted blood poisoning; a doctor cut
off his leg to try to save him, but he died. Varsell's mother took
her family to Joshua City to live with her father, an industrious
man who rented a few acres "for the fourth dollar"—a quarter
of what he cleared—from a white named Ratliff, a Freemason
and a kind man. In younger years Granddaddy Archer had
saved some money to buy mules by making bricks in dry kilns
and "getting out" boards for covering houses. Varsell adored
him. He taught his grandsons to fish for catfish and grunters
and gars in the Delta lakes, and he told stories that his father
had told him about slavery. In those Joshua City years Varsell
was an everyday companion with a white boy, Jimmy Ratliff,
with whom he milked cows and gathered eggs and went fishing, and Mrs. Ratliff helped Varsell with his lessons. He went
to school through the seventh grade. He walked five miles to
school and five miles back, and he remembers not the weari-
ness but the roadsides fringed with dusty wildflowers—eye-
bright and pleurisy-root, maypop and spatterdock.

But then "things went out tough and hard"—the Depression of the early thirties brought ferocious times for Granddaddy Archer, crowded on a small tenancy with his daughter's
family, and in winter croker sacks did for shoes, and the diet
was cornbread and sorghum syrup, over and over. In 1934 Varsell left this hardship and went to Jackson, where he found
urban hardship even more squalid. He got a job at a white
hotel, for one meal a day and six dollars a week and rare nickel

tips, running errands on a bicycle, sweeping out the parlors, carrying out trash. He could live. He was fourteen, and salt fatmeat only cost a nickel a pound in those days, and you could get a twenty-four-pound sack of flour for forty cents. He even saved a few dollars. But it was not a life—not the kind of life his grandfather had showed him how to live.

In 1936 his mother wrote him from Leflore County to say that Granddaddy Archer had died, and she had married again, and that he should come up and help out on his stepfather's farm. And so at sixteen Varsell entered a career of cotton farming. He worked hard, sun to sun, and he learned what a man had to do.

Two years later, at eighteen, he married in haste and soon became a father; his stepfather loaned him a hundred dollars to buy a mule, and he found some land he could rent in the vicinity of Noonday, in Ittabala County. He has lived in Ittabala ever since.

Created in 1827, Ittabala County has always been a violent place. It has 795 square miles of good land on the border between the rich Delta and the loam-and-loess hills, land worth fighting for—and Choctaws, Chickasaws, and Yazoos fought for it as it was stolen from them. The county has long had a large proportion of Negroes who own land; today sixty-nine per cent of the cultivated land is in Negro hands.

After his first crop Pleas cleared $250, and he bought a second mule. By 1941 he had saved enough to put the first installment down on a six-year-old Ford truck, and he began hauling stave blocks and pulpwood, and he was soon earning as much as forty dollars a week. Then his marriage went bad, and he moved west of Athens, where he rented, alone, a small farm in the hills. He was classified 1-A in the draft, but, for some reason that he never understood, the draft board just didn't get to him.

In Athens, in his twenty-third year, he met Holly Bell

Chronister, a beautiful light-brown-skinned girl from outside of Joshua City, the daughter of capable people, a carpenter and a practical nurse, and herself better educated than most— "promoted to twelfth." She was spirited, emotional, hard-working, and bitter-edged. Varsell married her, and the next year, while the announcers were talking on the radio about the invasion of Normandy, Varsell Jr. was born, and the next year Orsmond was born, and the next year Robert was born. Pleas needed a bigger place, and he found one he could rent near Noonday. Landing there changed his life.

Four years earlier, under authority of the Bankhead-Jones Farm Tenant Act of 1937, the New Deal's Resettlement Administration had bought a number of failing plantations in that area—Cincinnatus, Intention, Harper's, Yazoo, The Bogue, Persimmon Tree—and had set up a series of projects for Negroes, men just like Varsell Pleas, who had spent their lives as frequently moving tenants and sharecroppers in a restless search for a stable living. At first the projects were cooperatives and rentals; then, a year after Pleas began renting up nearer Noonday, the Farm Security Administration took them over and made long-term loans to the Negroes to enable them to buy plots of land of about fifty acres each. Pleas soon heard that the rednecks had nicknamed the federal projects Nigger Paradise, and that made him think they must be all right; he went to the F.S.A. office and applied for a unit. But so many had already filed applications that the plots were all gone.

As time passed, "the projects," as the Negroes continued to call them, looked better and better, and Pleas decided to wait out a turn to join one. He worked hard and lived frugally, putting all he could save into building a small herd of Guernsey-Jersey cows. As the years went by, he saw the farmers on the projects begin to work with tractors; he was still mule farming.

Eight years and five more children after his first application,

Pleas got his chance. He heard of a farmer in The Bogue who had fallen behind in his payments, and Pleas arranged with the man and with the Farmers Home Administration, which had taken over the projects, to assume the farmer's indebtedness, $728, and to buy the farm, on a federal forty-year, five-per-cent mortgage (the white man's banks in Athens charged Negroes eight per cent and ten per cent) for $6,104. To pay off the other man's delinquency, he borrowed $460 from Holly Bell's family and sold three cows. The F.H.A. made him a five-per-cent operating loan, with his chattels as securities, for equipment, seed, fertilizer, and pesticides, and he put up five more cows as down payment on a small Ford tractor.

After these deals his herd—his show for years of sweat—had dwindled, but for the first time in his life he was his own man. He now had fifty-nine acres of good, high loam-and-sand earth, with no low swags or ditches with standing water, and no clayey "buckshot" soil, and he had an industrious wife, and a tractor, and a feeling, new and strange, that some white man or men in Washington, D.C., were aware of him as a human entity.

Now came a time of building up. Since even the most industrious Mississippi Negro could not live on terms of equality with the Mississippi white, the project farmer turned to a prestige of things. There was an approved order of purchases. Pressure cooker first. Then, before the first summer was out, refrigerator—forty dollars down, with three years to pay. Then, after the first cotton-and-soybean crop had been sold and the F.H.A. interest of a little more than three hundred dollars had been paid in, a clothes-washing machine. (Water for the washer came from a hand pump in buckets and was heated in caldrons over a wood fire in the yard.) And the next year—emblem of, and contributor to, prosperity—a freezer, in which, after slaughter, cuts of hogs, fowl, and beef cattle could repose till needed for the table. More and more, Varsell

Pleas was building a life insulated from the whites, whom he saw only in stores. The F.H.A. even had a Negro supervisor. By his third year in the project he had a total income of $10,000 and he paid off all his debts on appliances, and he bought eight cows—money in the bank.

Varsell Pleas, a Mississippi Negro, could not believe in the long duration of good times, and sure enough, a turn for the worse soon came. After the Supreme Court decision in *Brown* v. *Board of Education,* May, 1954, the white men in the state, who had long had a saying, "The way to keep a coon from climbing is to trim his claws," got out their shears and went to work.

At first the curbs were legalistic and economic. The new voter-qualification forms were introduced, closing down the Negro's chances of registering. Credit in the stores and for farm goods became tighter. The dirt roads in Negro areas were "pulled" less often than earlier by the road scrapers. A great blow to Pleas came in 1957, when the federal government, whence in the past had come beneficence, introduced crop allotments. Pleas was told that he could plant no more than eleven of his fifty-nine acres in cotton—hardly enough to make tractor farming worthwhile. From then on he began to feel a pinch; he started taking three-per-cent emergency loans from the F.H.A. each summer to pay for "poisoning" his cotton, as the farmers called spraying for armyworms, boll weevil, and spider rust.

Then, with the sixties, came violence and outright cheats. Pleas began to hear of the White Citizens Councils and, later, of a resuscitated Ku Klux Klan and of a group that called itself Americans for the Preservation of the White Race. Ugly threats were passed in the towns, and Pleas heard of beatings. Negroes disappeared; bodies were found in lakes. Pleas saw, close at hand, a struggle for the land as the whites began to use every possible means to drive off Negro landowners. In five years eight families lost their land in The Bogue, and one of them lived next to Pleas.

In this case the farmer, named Cheer, had borrowed $325 from Mr. Rainsford, the merchant, when Cheer's wife had had to go to a hospital for a goiter. Rainsford seemed openhanded, and said there was no hurry about repayments; he later gave Cheer credit to buy a tractor. Two years later, after Cheer had borrowed money a third time, Rainsford agreeably said he could ease the terms and times of repayment on all these loans if Cheer would like to take out a second mortgage on his house; Cheer signed, and Rainsford had "cotched" him. On Cheer's first tardiness in payment of interest, Rainsford's former easygoing manner vanished as with a clap of hands, and the mortgage was foreclosed. Cheer moved his family onto a nearby "good" plantation, Mr. Pine's, where he and his wife and children worked for three dollars a day apiece; he lasted one year there, then drifted to the notorious Sutter plantation, where the hands got two dollars a day; and the next year he left for Chicago. To Ittabala County Negroes, Chicago has always been the symbol of the outside world, and Pleas had noticed that two kinds of Negroes went there—young ones on the way up, and older ones, like Cheer, on the way down.

Not an excitable man, but one in whom there is an inner firmness like a metal armature, Pleas began in the early sixties to talk around with other intelligent Negroes in the projects, "to seek up in," as he puts it, "and see what we could do to eliminate these problems." They agreed on the need to be well informed. Pleas, like most of his neighbors, had a television set, and he listened intently not only to local news but to public-service programs on the race question, to *Meet the Press,* to United Nations debates.

One day in the summer of 1961 Pleas received a notice from

the county office of the Agricultural Stabilization and Conservation Service saying he was over-planted in cotton by four and four-tenths acres. He drove to the A.S.C.S. office and said he was not satisfied with the measurements; his oldest two sons, who had studied agricultural surveying in high school, had measured his land, ten square chains to the acre, and their figures did not agree with the county surveyor's. An official told him that he could put up fifteen dollars to have his land remeasured; if he was right, he'd get his fifteen dollars back. Pleas decided to risk the money. The surveyor returned, and Pleas and Varsell Jr. and Orsmond followed him as he made the new measurements. Pleas went to the office a few days later and learned that his sons' measurements had been correct, and he got his money back. That saved acreage made eight hundred dollars' difference in Pleas' income that year, and confirmed Pleas' suspicion that the county office of A.S.C.S. dealt carelessly, to say the least of it, with Negroes. Ever since then he has been saying to his neighbors, "It's better for the one who stands up for his rights than for the one who keeps it cool."

By now Pleas and his friends realized that their essential helplessness stemmed from their want of the vote, and when, in the early spring of 1963, they heard that the Movement— as the Mississippi Negroes refer to any and all civil-rights efforts—had begun work on voter registration in Leflore County, they drove the more than fifty miles to Greenwood and were directed by Negroes to the office of the Council of Federated Organizations, an amalgam of the leading civil-rights groups working in Mississippi, and there they asked for help. C.O.F.O. sent a young teacher, Joe Merriam, from the Student Nonviolent Coordinating Committee, down to Noonday for citizenship classes, and suddenly everything began to fall into place for Varsell Pleas and his friends. They were "going into the Movement."

Joe Merriam found the Noonday Negroes extraordinarily

sophisticated about local politics. Pleas could tell him the specific duties of the county sheriff, treasurer, assessor, surveyor, school trustees, and road supervisor, and he knew all the incumbents' names, and which were fairly decent, and which were vicious; he knew that his taxes helped pay for white schools that were far away from, and far better than, his own children's schools, and that he was taxed for a public library to which he was not admissible, and that no one was doing anything about the fact that airplane "poisoning" of cotton was killing the fish in Ittabala Lake, and that school only ran eight months in Noonday. Merriam concentrated on preparing the Noonday people to register. He unfolded to them the intricacies of Mississippi laws on the franchise, and he explained that even if one has registered, he must have paid a poll tax for two years before he can vote in state and local elections. He told of the investigative and protective powers of the Justice Department. He began teaching the state constitution; the first clause Pleas memorized was Section 14: "No person shall be deprived of life, liberty, or property except by due process of law."

In April, 1964, the seventeen went to Athens and stood under the tree.

The rest of that season Pleas worked unusually hard at his farming, because he had arranged to rent nine acres of cotton land from a Negro widow who lived nearby in The Bogue.

One day in the fall, when he was out picking cotton with his whole family and a number of hired hands—he could have rented a cotton-picking machine but preferred to hire Noonday Negroes to pick by hand, in order to give them work—a boy drove up in a pickup and ran into the field to tell Varsell that some of the rednecks down in Jade County, the border of which lay about ten miles south of Pleas' farm, had gathered together to kill the Movement's citizenship teacher down there—would he please call the F.B.I. in Greenwood? Pleas went to the nearest phone but could not get through. He drove to Greenwood to the C.O.F.O. office, which was able to reach the F.B.I. Its agents drove down and rescued the man from his mother's barn-loft, where he had been hiding.

In the weeks that followed Pleas harvested forty-four bales of cotton, which brought him $5,500, and almost exactly two tons of soybeans, for which he got $2,325. From this crop cash he had to pay back an F.H.A. short-term operating loan of $1,800, plus five-per-cent interest, and an emergency loan of $200 he had taken out, because during a wet spell he had had to have his cotton sprayed by airplane, plus three-per-cent interest. He had had these expenses during the year:

F.H.A. payments	$400
Fertilizer and seed	550
"Poisoning"	300
Gasoline	500
Rent for widow's land	625
Food	400
Payment on a soybean combine (owned with two others)	350
Clothes (for 2 parents, 11 children)	400
Health	100
Insurance	150
Electricity	125
Cooking gas	75
Labor, cotton picking	300
Maintenance of farm equipment	100
Miscellaneous	200
Total	$4,575

Since Pleas' fiscal year is based on crops rather than on the calendar, a part of his cash surplus had to keep the family going until the spring, when he could get his next year's operating loan. He had also sent Varsell Jr. off to Alcorn Agricultural and Mechanical College in the fall, and the boy's year in the trade school would cost $500. It was a fairly favorable year, thanks to the widow's fields.

Every bit of Pleas' spare time was now devoted to the Movement. He attended citizenship meetings regularly, called on others to persuade them to go to the courthouse to register, studied further on the constitution, and went himself a second and a third time to take the test. He did not pass either time, nor had he expected to; he thought he should keep trying. In January he went to Athens to pay his poll tax, against the day when he might pass. He went to the A.S.C.S. office in Athens and asked that Negroes be represented on the county committee that sets crop allotments; he was told that the matter would have to go to the committee for consideration, and, of course, nothing came of it.

One day on an errand in Joshua City he ran into James Ratliff, his childhood friend, the son of kindly white parents. He had seen Ratliff occasionally over the years, and recently he had heard that his old companion was now a Citizens Council man.

"How do, Mr. Ratliff." Pleas had called him "Jimmy" before their voices had changed.

"What's wrong with you fellows down there?" Ratliff asked.

"What do you mean?"

"You-all trying to get up something?"

"What do you mean, Mr. Ratliff?"

"I seen in the paper that you was up to register. You niggers ain't qualified to vote. You don't know what you're doing. I'd stay out of that mess if I was you."

After that Pleas was not so sure that the race problem could be solved simply by having children grow up together in integrated schools. He had heard a note of threat in the voice of his childhood companion.

In the spring reports came that the Movement was going to mount a big Summer Project, for which many Northern students, both colored and white, would come to Mississippi. As the time for the project approached, tension grew, especially as it became known that whites—even white girls—were going to live in Negro homes. Then one day a C.O.F.O. man asked Varsell Pleas if he himself would take a couple of the students into his house; the C.O.F.O. staff man spelled it out that this would be a dangerous hospitality. Pleas said he'd like to think it over.

Varsell Pleas made a reckoning of what was at stake— besides his life, to the risk of which he was almost inured by now.

With all of the years' humiliations and strains, there was a priceless tranquillity in the dusty white six-room house on the curving road in The Bogue. Voices were never raised there. The children knew their chores, and at dawn they fanned sleepily out without having to be told—Orsmond to milk the cow, Robert to sweep the house, Ervin to make the beds, Pomp to fill up the hot-water caldrons in the yard and light the wood fire under them, Cleontha to help Mama cook, Edward to churn, Icie and Sussie to clean up Mama's room. James, the seventh, was off in the hills living with Pleas' mother, and caring for his father's herd of sixteen cows and calves, the family bank account; Grandma got fifty dollars a month from Social Security.

In the muddy hog pasture around the barn were four fat full-grown swine and five shoats; a milk cow was in the meadow; chickens, guineas, and turkeys quarreled under an ancient cottonwood; twenty fruit trees walked out across the table-vegetable field; wax drippings made a sanitary coating on the concrete floor of the outhouse, which the family spoke of as "the lavatory"; the clanking hand pump by the toolhouse gave plenty of cool, iron-tasting water.

Mama had always had a green thumb—though of late years she had had scant time for the borders by the front path, and they had grown ragged; she kept a stand of tropicals on the porch beside the two rocking chairs, one home-caned with intertwined store string, where she and Daddy sat at sunset and talked, screened from the dusty road by a mimosa, a chinaberry, a castor-bean tree, and three sightly varieties of smoke tree. A foxtail pine gave thick afternoon shade across from the back door, for shelling or peeling or sewing.

One son was at Alcorn, a college of sorts; the second would go next fall to Mississippi Valley College, which was not accredited but was better than no school at all.

Now in the spring evenings the whole family gathered in the living room, on whose pale blue wood walls, among framed and cornucopiaed "arrangements" of imitation roses and grapes and poinsettias and calla lilies, hung three separate pictures of John F. Kennedy, one with Jackie and one with John Jr., and photographs of Varsell Jr. and his girl in the academic caps and gowns of Noonday Attendance Center; beside the television set was an open gas space heater, and on it were souvenirs—china animals, a miniature wooden churn, a cute little iron model of a coal cooking range. On the linoleum-covered floor was a linoleum scatter rug, with black, white, and red checks. The children disposed themselves on the heavy sofas and couches of the living-room "suite" and watched the programs—as the images flickered, Icie combed out and braided Cleontha's hair—until heads began to nod, one by one, and Mama quietly said, "Sussie, go wash your feet and get in bed. Ervin, put Larnie to bed; put him in with Pomp tonight." It was considered a treat to have the youngest for the night. By ten all were down, the children in twos and threes.

At a citizenship meeting the next Wednesday night Varsell Pleas raised his hand and said he would take two students, if he could borrow a bed. The widow from whom he rented his extra acres did soon lend him a double bed, which, by knocking down two built-in storage closets, he was able to fit in the back room along with the freezer and the washer, and he shifted from the side room, where there were two beds, the four children who had been sleeping there, and distributed them around. The beds in the house would be crowded through the hot summer—except for the guests, who would each have one to himself.

Before the students arrived in Noonday, there came on television one evening the foreboding announcement of the disappearance of three civil-rights workers in Philadelphia, over in Neshoba County. It seemed that the worst fears for the summer were going to be realized. Down the domestic-servant grapevine trickled word, a few days later, that the whites were saying those "mixers" had scooted off to Chicago, where they were drinking beer and enjoying the publicity. But Varsell Pleas thought of Henry Larkin and Brutus Simpson and the citizenship teacher hiding in his mother's loft; he had no doubt the three civil-rights workers were dead in a lake or a swamp.

A week later the Summer Project came to Noonday, and two young men were assigned to Pleas: Tim Shattuck, who was white, a doctor's son from Roslyn, Long Island, a Yale student, quick-witted and intense; and Bud Samson, a light-skinned Negro, a lawyer's son from Michigan who had been through the civil-rights wars as campus chairman of CORE at a Midwestern university—he had a hundred-day jail sentence on appeal at home, as a subsequence of some sit-ins he had led. Elsewhere around Noonday were deposited two sophisticated Negro girls from Baltimore, who had demonstrated in Cambridge, Maryland; two California students; three white girls from various Eastern colleges; a white Indiana boy; and two more white Yale students. The leader of the project in the area was a C.O.F.O. veteran who had spent several weeks in the state prison farm at Parchman for disturbing the peace of Mississippi the previous summer.

Because the Mississippi police were following the Philadelphia pattern of arresting Project volunteers for trivial or trumped-up traffic charges, and because the maximum danger seemed to be upon release from jail after these arrests, the students wanted to follow state driving regulations meticulously. One of the rules was that they would have to replace their out-of-state license plates, on the three cars they had, with Mississippi plates, if they were going to stay in the state more than a month, and a few days after they arrived, Varsell Pleas drove up to Athens with some of the boys to help them with this transaction. When they left the capital, they were followed for some distance, but nothing happened.

The next day, in a grocery store in Athens, Pleas got notice that the whites, too, had a grapevine. The proprietor sauntered over to Pleas and said, "Varsell, it true what they say, you got some of these agitators staying with you?"

"I got me couple of students, yes, sir."

"You ought not to let them stay with you. If they had no place to stay, they'd have to go back where they belong."

But Pleas was long since hardened to white intimidations. He sent all his children to the freedom school that the students set up in the Baptist church and in an abandoned house not far down the road from it. The children's regular public school had never excited them. It had an enrollment for 1963 of 510 but an average daily attendance of only 405.2, since many children, especially on the plantations, stayed out to work in the fields. It was housed in a twenty-year-old firetrap, with an oil-burning stove in each classroom, and it ran for only eight months of the year. Per-pupil expenditure was less than fifty dollars a year; many first-graders were eight and ten years old; the Negro principal, who had six children, was paid $4,800 a year; and the poorly trained Negro teachers, who got as little as $3,000, were afraid to try to register to vote for fear of being fired. At the freedom school the children got the first taste they had ever had of unstinting kindness and solicitude from whites as Yale and Smith students started in with the younger ones on fundamentals of the three R's. Robert, the third boy, a teenager, told his mother that he'd learned more Negro history in two days than he had in eleven years of public school.

Robert Pleas had been apt and keen as a small boy, but he had chugged nearly to a stop in school in recent years. He was a good farm worker, particularly on the tractor, poisoning cotton while the plants were low, but now he talked halfheartedly of finishing high school and of trying to get into the Air Force. He had driven a school bus the previous year for clothing money; had found chemistry and history tolerable but had failed English—he had despised his English teacher, who could not speak as grammatically as his mother and father. What he liked best was hunting. When the muscadines began to ripen, and corn was solid in the ear, and the persimmons were right, then the raccoons would come out, and Robert sometimes winged three or four in an evening. He was a sweet shot—a squirrel would run up a tree to get away from the family Winchester in his hands, but if that squirrel poked two inches of his head around to see if the coast was clear, Robert would decap him at fifty feet. Now, however, the freedom school was getting Robert interested, and at meals the two students, Tim and Bud, would fire him up to work for the race. Pretty soon he was saying he thought he'd bone next year, and get to college if he could, and work in the Movement anyway.

Bud and Tim came in excited to the Pleases one night, reporting that at one of the houses over near the highway a white man had been seen fumbling around in the back yard with a flashlight. The owner of the house, with a shotgun on his arm, accosted the man. It turned out to be Bubba Goodheart, a local farmer who had just been made a deputy sheriff in order, it was said, to keep an eye on the invaders. Brought into the cone of a large battery light, Deputy Goodheart shouted that he had had instructions from "higher up" to "protect" a student named Peter Marston. Where was this boy?

One of the Project workers asked Deputy Goodheart why he hadn't just come straight to the front door, if that was his errand.

The deputy said he'd got lost.

There was in fact a Harvard student named Peter Marston in the Noonday contingent, and it came out later that there had indeed been orders from Jackson to look out for him. Pete was the son of a wealthy Boston corporation lawyer, a Harvard graduate, one of whose former college classmates was now a big shot in the White Citizens Council down in Jackson. Pete's father, who disapproved of his being in Mississippi at all, had asked the Citizens Council friend to "keep an eye" on Pete, and an official friend of the friend had obligingly ordered a tail put on the boy. Bubba Goodheart had come blundering forth to carry out this command. Pleas and all his friends believed that the reason he was in the back yard was to try to spy out the sleeping arrangements of white girls in colored homes.

Now a wild man came one night to the Noonday citizenship meeting: Isaac ("Zingo") Ostrowski, a fifty-two-year-old contractor from Oregon, who told the Noonday farmers that he was going to build them the nicest meeting hall they'd ever seen. Six feet tall, built like a pro football tackle, Zingo had got a bee in his bonnet the previous winter, had visited Mississippi in the spring and had talked with C.O.F.O. leaders, then had gone back to Oregon and had raised, singlehanded, ten thousand dollars. With a carpenter friend whom he had enlisted, and with a station wagon full of building tools, he'd taken off for the Mississippi Delta and had wound up in Noonday.

Mrs. Pleas was elected secretary of the new community center that he was to build, and one of the neighbors leased an acre not far from the main road. Zingo ordered lumber from a Jackson firm, but there followed mysterious delays in delivery; so Zingo made a phone call to Tennessee, and a few days later a big shiny trailer truck from that state drove in and unloaded a heap of things. The farmers at citizenship meetings arranged to procure volunteer labor to help Zingo. Pleas put in a day; workmen began arriving in parties from all over the county as word went around that a Negro hall was being built where movies would be shown and meetings would be held, and that there was going to be a free library of seven thousand volumes, and a kitchen, and a room for kids, and running water and two flush toilets. When the floor was laid down, everyone turned out with hammers and worked, colored residents and white students together; Randoman Tort said it was the first Integrated Nailing ever held in Mississippi.

R obert was soon head over heels in the Movement; a factor in his sudden dedication may have been the attractiveness of one of the Negro girls from Baltimore, Charlotte Bunson, a student at the University of Maryland, daughter of a high-school vice-principal. Robert spent much time around the Freedom House, a second abandoned farmhouse, across from the freedom school, where Charlotte and other staff workers lived. There he became interested in what he overheard about the voter-registration canvassing that Tim Shattuck and Bud Samson and others were doing, and soon he got himself excused from freedom school to go out on the voter drive.

The first day he went with Pete Marston to The Bogue. At each house Pete would talk for about fifteen minutes about the vote, and about going to the courthouse. His being white was both an advantage and a disadvantage, for though he had to overcome a reflexive suspicion and dislike, he also commanded, even from Negroes three and four times his unripe age, a certain passive respect and obedience, no matter how grudging, that had been bred and drilled into them from birth and from long before birth. Having Robert with him, a local Negro farm boy whom most of The Bogue people knew as the son of Varsell Pleas, was a help.

They took notes:

Mr. Aurelius. Says he backed down but thinks he will go if he has some support. Mr. and Mrs. Aurelius Jr. Both are scared. Should return.

Mrs. Cunninger. Has tried three times.

Mary and T. C. Hampton. Uncertain and fearful. He is reported to be informer to Mr. Pine, white planter. Wife, however, might come around. Man is 85, wife 62. Don't like it here but afraid to vote. Mrs. Shucker. Has tried once. She is 72. Will go down if she feels the energy. She is coming to citizenship meetings.

Mr. Joe Perry Chesnut. Wife works for school. Intimidated through the school system.

Mr. Whitsett. "May have to go to hospital soon."

Mr. and Mrs. Rankin. He works for white builder in town, both scared. Eddy, the son, is very sharp, says he will go in a full car.

Mr. Sam Harbison. Uncle Tom. Will vote when all Negroes are allowed to vote.

For Varsell Pleas and others of the older generation, citizenship meetings continued in the rickety church next to where the studs of the new meeting hall were already being framed. This church, with a slightly tilted steeple, contained five rows of crude benches, and its walls were decorated with offering

banners and a calendar with a picture of Jesus protecting a
lamb and a C.O.F.O. poster of a Mississippi highway patrol-
man out of whose eyebeam jumped the question IS HE PRO-
TECTING YOU? Here the Noonday farmers debated whether to
try to found a new cooperative store. The farmers felt at the
mercy of the white merchants in Athens, and they wanted the
economic independence of a low-price supermarket that would
belong to Negroes throughout the county. They sought legal
advice on this idea from the Movement in Jackson. A miniature power struggle was developing in citizenship meetings between the firebrands and the more cautious heads; Pleas,
always an aloof man, was not in either faction. "I'll just try to
splice in and get you folks to quit arguing," he said once.

Toward the end of June a large shipment of used clothes,
collected in Northern drives, came to Noonday, and Pleas volunteered to distribute it. He picked out a few pieces to fill gaps
in the wardrobe in his own family—little Larnie was soon
sporting a pair of too large and somewhat frayed sailing shorts,
safety-pinned with an overlap at his waist, so that down the
sturdy dark thighs ran strings of yacht-club burgees—and
then undertook the dangerous work of hauling bundles to the
miserable shacks of plantation sharecroppers. The white planters had made bluntly clear their hostility to the Summer Project, and to the Movement as a whole. The threat: "If you want
to get in that mess, you'll have to move off my land." Pleas was
a Baptist, and he attended, as had numerous plantation Negroes, Fair Heaven Church, which had recently hired an itin-
erant preacher from downstate named Burroughs, a registered
voter who preached voting. When word reached the planters,
Mr. Pine and Mr. Sutter, that Reverend Burroughs would get
his flock worked up with the spirit to where he could do almost anything with them and then would switch off to registering, the planters refused to let their Negroes go to that
church anymore. The half-naked children of these depressed

and hopeless people flocked around Pleas like sparrows when he drove up with cartons of clothes.

On the first of July, Robert had an accident with his father's tractor; he collided with a carload of Negroes who had clearly been drinking. The others were let off, but Robert, the son of a Negro who had tried to register, was booked for reckless driving, failure to yield, and drunken driving. Pleas went to court with his son and he told the judge that he wouldn't argue with the first two charges, but that Robert never drank.

"I didn't make these charges," the judge said. "Mr. Good-heart made them."

"I didn't think that was fair," Pleas said. "As far as I know, Robert never has taken a drink."

"All right," the judge said, "we won't charge him with that this time."

This was another confirmation, for Pleas, of the importance of standing up to the white man, in cases where he felt he was right. Even so, the fine was fifty-five dollars.

Now the solid summer heat came, with temperatures in the nineties and the air as still as a shameful secret, day after day after day. Mrs. Pleas sat in the shade of the foxtail pine trying to cool herself with a cardboard fan with an ad on it for Strowder's Funeral Home and Burial Society. Summer nuisances hummed and crawled—sand flies and mud daubers, robber flies and stinkbugs. The men worked hard poisoning the cotton, and nerves wore thin.

As the meeting hall arose, a massive affront of raw lumber visible to all eyes from Route 57, so also did tension rise in the area. Rednecks drove their pickups and cars slowly along the dirt road past the building, looking it over.

At four in the morning, on Sunday, July 26th, a Negro named T. O. Lacey, who lived not far down the road from the construction, was wakened by a flickering light, and, running out, he saw a student's car, which had been parked in front of the house opposite, in flames. He wakened the people across the road, hosts and students, and they tried vainly to put out the fire with water from a hand pump. At daylight nothing was left of the car but a shell. A shattered gallon jug, which had evidently contained kerosene, was found on the front seat.

After that three Negro families, Pittman, Jones, and Tort, who lived along the road, set up an armed night watch, some sleeping during the first part of the night, some staying up till late. In early July the Movement supplied three shortwave radios for these three families, so when an unknown vehicle drove in the head of the road the word could be passed along. One night Bunell Jones set out in his pickup to patrol, and a Negro student staying in his house jokingly asked him, "You going out in that dark night all alone?"

"No," Jones said, "I got thirty-two brothers with me, and six cousins"—two 16-gauge shotguns and a revolver.

Pleas, who lived three miles from the new building and was not involved in the watches, was putting himself more and more deeply in danger, however, by repeatedly taking people to the courthouse in Athens, on gas furnished by collections at citizenship meetings, to try to register. Because no applicants ever passed, taking people to register came to be called "making a water haul"—or, getting no place. But the whites noticed. "Here comes old Varsell," Pleas heard a deputy sheriff say once. "He sure is up to his ears in it."

One of Pleas' guns was old, and he decided to replace it. (Section 12 of the constitution affirmed "the right of every citizen to keep and bear arms in defense of his home, person, or property," and no license was needed.) But in the hardware store in Noonday the dealer refused to sell him one. "Guns is put up now," he said. Pleas drove to Jackson and bought a new gun, no questions asked, at Hunt & Whitaker's. He took to retiring early, so he would be easy to wake from two o'clock on—when most of the violence against Negroes in the state had been taking place. A shotgun stood at the head of his bed, another by Orsmond's, and one by Robert's. Every night four thin dogs and two thin cats lay down in the dust at Pleas' back door, and the racket they raised when anything moved in the neighborhood quickly wakened the house.

One evening late in July, Tim Shattuck, who had been trying to make friends with white-shy Larnie, the five-year-old, and had once heard Larnie muttering about "the wheet," asked his host to tell him honestly what he thought about the white students' having come down from the North for the summer.

Pleas, after the usual pause for thought, said in an unemotional voice, "It's the best thing that's happened since there ever was a Mississippi. I just love the students like I love to eat. Listen, they showed they're willing to *die* for us—two of those three at Philadelphia. If more come down here, I'd get out of my bed for them and sleep on a pallet in the toolshed. They're doing things we couldn't do for ourselves in years on end. They've taken away a lot of fear of the courthouse, and people ain't so scared to come to citizenship meetings anymore. They're giving some of our older kids subjects they should have had in school all along—French and typing. And they're so natural—like brothers and sisters. Another thing: the governor is going to have to be more careful what he says now, because a lot of bad smells are getting to the outside world that never did before. And we got out-of-state F.B.I in here, and federal lawsuits. It's all changing, it is sure enough changing, right this summer. I hope you can come back another season. If you can't, send somebody else in your place."

Tim asked, "What about the whites? Are we making it worse for you with them?"

"No," Pleas said. "About the whites, there's bad ones and right decent ones. The bad ones been shooting colored people all along and throwing them in lakes, a bunch of students don't change that. The all-right ones, they're kind of gagged up. But we're going to set them good ones free—ourselves and them. These white folks have ridiculous fears. I tell you, we don't want nothing from them but stop. The Negro people ain't going up after them. We country Negroes don't do people that way. I think we got more real religion in our blood than the white people; we been told since weaning, 'Don't throw stone for stone.' But they better not come messing in our homes, setting fire and getting up a big killing scrape. That won't *never* scare us. That ain't *never* going to keep me from taking folks up to the courthouse. Because I tell you something, Tim, we're going to get the vote in three to five years, and when we do, the Negro man's vote is going to count just as hard as the white man's vote. I'm paying my poll tax to keep ready."

A few days later Tim had a story to tell the Pleases; it was a story which, against the background of the three killed at Philadelphia, made a big impression on Robert Pleas.

Tim had just got out of one civil-rights car in Athens, that morning, and was waiting to be picked up by another to go canvassing in Meeks, when a man of about forty, in a blue sport shirt and khaki work pants, stepped out of a knot of men, pointed at Tim's nose, and then touched it repeatedly with a forefinger, and said, "You ain't shit. You ain't even shit. You ain't as good as shit." Tim, who had been trained in passive responses to abuse and violence, stood absolutely still and looked straight in the man's blue-gray eyes. The man began hitting Tim in the face, forehand and backhand, and then, as others began closing in with glistening eyes, Tim suddenly assumed "the nonviolent crouch"—dropped to his knees and formed a ball of his body, folding his hands over the nape of his neck, so that as many vital places as possible were protected. The man, who seemed startled by this bizarre defense, kicked him halfheartedly a couple of times and then walked away; the others also drew back.

At about this time the emphasis of the voter-registration drive changed. The student canvassers began registering Negroes for the Freedom Democratic Party, which planned to challenge the seating of the regular Mississippi Democratic Party delegation at the Democratic National Convention. Robert Pleas began working hard on freedom registrations, and this work took him closer to danger and clinched his commitment to the Movement.

One day he was canvassing in Meeks, a mean town on the eastern border of the county, with Bud Samson, the Negro CORE student. They were standing on the front porch of a house, signing up a Negro woman, when a white deliveryman arrived. He asked the boys what they were doing. Bud explained. The man asked a question.

Bud answered, "Yeah."

The man said, "You mean, 'Yes, sir.'"

Bud said, "Where I live we don't talk that way."

"You're where I live now, boy."

"O.K., if it'll make you happy. Yes, sir."

The man asked for identification. Bud gave him a clipping from a Chicago paper, showing his picture and identifying him as a leader of a sit-in.

"This you?"

"Yes." Omission of "sir."

"You got a hard head, ain't you, you color-blind little bastard? I might have to soften it up for you."

The man moved toward Bud, and Robert, to his own astonishment, found himself making a definite move. He reached his draft I.D. card out toward the deliveryman as he moved on Bud, and this served to distract the man. With further abuse and warnings, he left.

The next week, Varsell Pleas was told his son Robert would not be given back his school-bus driver's job in the fall.

Now came two pieces of news that lifted all the Noonday Negroes' spirits. The Mississippi State Democratic Convention, mindful of the challenge to be offered at the national convention by the Freedom Democratic Party, postponed until after the national convention at Atlantic City the question of how to handle the ballot in November, whether the party's electors should be designated for Johnson or for Goldwater—so that for the first time since Reconstruction days Negroes had been able to influence directly the course of Mississippi politics. And then the bodies of the three dead civil-rights workers were found—that showed the F.B.I. really meant business in Mississippi, and maybe the roughest of the whites would think twice before they hurt anyone.

In the hottest weather, in August, came revival time. For a week Varsell Pleas was somewhat turned aside from work for the Movement as he went to revival meetings at Fair Heaven Church every evening at eight. On Saturday night, after meeting, he and Holly Bell sat up late into the night reading the Bible aloud to each other and talking about what they had read. The next morning Varsell went to clean the leaves and scare the water moccasins out of the edge of Mrs. Hodgkins' pond, and at noontime Preacher Burroughs, with Pleas' help for the immersions, reaped fourteen souls. The temperature of the air was over a hundred, and when Pleas got home, he kept his wet clothes on till dinnertime.

A white tablecloth was set on the kitchen table that noon, and before dinner a quiet young man from Lockfire, rather scholarly-looking, with steel-rimmed glasses, named Louis Weems, drove in with Pleas' seventy-nine-year-old mother. All sat down to eat. Pleas said blessing. Then Pleas' mother said, "Louis here just spent five months in Parchman."

"Whatever for?" asked Holly Bell. "You ain't that kind of boy, Louis."

And then, over a baptism-day dinner of chicken and dressing, sweet-potato pie, rutabaga and greens, black-eyed peas, fried tomato, and hot biscuit, Louis Weems, speaking in genteel tones, told the pillar of Fair Heaven Church and his wife, fresh from the week of hymns and conversions, how, having run into debt on his hill-farm wages of three dollars a day, and needing fifty dollars in a matter of hours, he had gone out with two others and stolen three hogs, which they'd sold in Athens for eighty-five dollars. Then he told about life at Parchman, how he'd worked like a slave under a driver in the cotton fields, how he'd become a "walker," counting sleepers inside the wire at Camp 8, and how he'd been cut on the arm one night by a real bad boy.

When the story and the meal were done, and everyone sat sweating at the table, it had come round to seem to Varsell Pleas, and he said so, that the crime was not in the hog-rassling but in the pay the man had gotten and the credit squeeze that had driven him to the theft.

"That's right," Holly Bell said. "You ain't never been that kind of boy, Louis."

"I did the wrong thing," Weems said, "and I paid off with my five months."

T he roof was on the meeting hall. None of the insurance agents in Athens would write a policy for the building. The sightseers were coming in droves, white men moseying past at five miles an hour. Tort was talking about holding an Integration Ball after the place was opened. Everyone expected a bomb.

On Saturday night, August 8th, a Negro man named Stanley Chunn was walking along near the meeting hall, headed out Route 57 for a beer, when a car drove by and dropped something on the ground not far from him. He thought it was just some trash, and he walked on. Three or four minutes later—he had nearly reached the highway—there was a sharp explosion back on the road. Negroes gathered from all around—nothing but a hole in the dirt road. Everyone guessed that the white men, intending to bomb the meeting hall, had lit their long fuse in their car, had been startled to see a Negro walking in the road in an area known to be heavily armed, and had dropped the device in the road and skinned out.

The next morning, F.B.I. men came to investigate—and word was passed that they were men with out-of-state accents. Within two days, the Negro grapevine had told the Noonday people exactly which white man had bungled the bombing— a certain deliveryman from near Athens. He had done a poor job; they'd no doubt be back.

In a farm-equipment store in Joshua City one day, the proprietor, Mr. Scott, said, "What are you all going to do when those white people leave you and go back on home?"

Pleas said, "What do you mean?"

"You're going to be coming up here to your old white friends in Joshua City after they've gone, asking for our help. The help just might not be here anymore."

Pleas understood the implied threat. Everyone had been speculating about new outbreaks of violence when the Summer Project pulled out, but Pleas knew that there would not be a sudden break. Three white students planned to stay on for good in Noonday; what had started as a summer drive was turning into a permanent program. So successful had the summer effort been that the C.O.F.O. people were talking of expanding their project into at least two adjacent states, Alabama and Arkansas.

So Pleas answered with a certain confidence. "It ain't going be any different, Mr. Scott. I always figured we helped each other: you give me credit, I buy your cultivator and harrow and poisoner and all like that."

This answer, delivered in gentle tones, left Mr. Scott thinking about an implied threat, too. Pleas could buy elsewhere.

The great sky cooled as autumn came on. Pleas began picking cotton, the combines moved through the soybeans.

The two oldest left for college, but the younger ones could pick till school began at the end of September. Integration, just beginning in first grade in Jackson, Biloxi, and Leake County, was far off for them, but it was rumored that they might be involved in a school boycott in November to protest the conditions of their schooling.

Robert and a local girl, Dearie Mae Jones, of one of the night-watch families, went off in a bus with student friends of the summer to the National Democratic Convention, and Robert, who had never before been farther from home than Jackson, demonstrated on the Atlantic City boardwalk while the politicians seated two Negroes as delegates from Mississippi. Varsell Pleas arranged a twenty-three-hundred dollar F.H.A. housing loan, for thirty-three years at four per cent, to install running water in his house, add a bathroom, put on a new roof, and build a new front porch. He kept going to citizenship meetings; he was working on the new co-op store, but voting came first with him, as always.

The Justice Department had brought a suit against the circuit clerk in a nearby county, charging discrimination against Negroes in voter registration, under the 1964 Civil Rights Act; and as soon as that case was won, as Pleas confidently expected it to be, he planned to go up and try again to register in the Ittabala Courthouse. They'd find new gimmicks to prevent him, for a while, he supposed, and they might try to hurt and even kill some Negroes, and he supposed he might be on their list for all he'd been doing, but he was not afraid; someday it would not be a water haul.

This year Election Day would pass him by, but with prayer

and hard work, keeping guns clean and not venturing away from the house at night, going to the courthouse again and again, he thought that he would, at last, get what he wanted. He expected things to grow worse in Mississippi before they grew better, but he had made his personal reckoning and had long since decided that a vote was worth a life—without a vote a life was not one's own.

Erskine Caldwell

Erskine Caldwell was born poor on December 17, 1903, in a tiny three-room manse at a mere crossroads in cotton country in Coweta County, Georgia. His father, Ira Sylvester Caldwell, was an Associate Reformed Presbyterian minister, whose salary was three hundred and fifty dollars a year. His mother, Caroline Bell Caldwell, had been a teacher of English and Latin in seminaries and colleges for girls and young women in the Carolinas and Virginia. His grandfathers were a cotton farmer and a railroad telegrapher.

Reverend Caldwell was frequently moved from parish to parish, in Georgia, the Carolinas, Tennessee, and Virginia. Erskine's mother taught him at home; he begged to be allowed to go to public schools, but she was convinced that she was better qualified than the teachers Erskine would have drawn in rural schools. Through his childhood, she dressed him in bizarre homemade clothes—a long white linen blouse with a loose leather belt, and bloomerlike trousers. She kept him in curly ringlets until her older sister, a registered nurse, on a visit, gave her a sedative to put her to sleep and took Erskine

Commemorative tribute, American Academy of Arts and Letters, December 4, 1987; *Proceedings,* Second Series, No. 38, American Academy and Institute of Arts and Letters, New York, 1987.

out to have a haircut. When he was thirteen, he showed his parents a twenty-two-page "novel" he had written, and they were so shocked by his spelling that they finally decided to send him to school.

In those young years Erskine saw with his own eyes both the degradation and the inner riches of the very poor, both white and black, in the cotton and tobacco South. His most cherished playmate, for whom he yearned, in a way, all his life, was a black friend named Bisco. After Erskine was sixty, he wrote a nostalgic book, *In Search of Bisco*. While he was still a boy his father, riding his circuits, took Erskine with him as he made pastoral calls in tenant shacks and hovels. The son would never forget witnessing foot-washing services, a clay-eating communion ritual, a coming-through orgy, a snake-handling performance, and emotion-charged glossolalia and unknown-tongue spectacles.

From his youngest years, he fought being poor. As a small boy, he peddled bluing to black washerwomen for ten cents a packet. He scavenged and sold scrap rubber. He substituted illegally for a village postmaster. At thirteen he took a job as driver of a Y.M.C.A. auto at an Army base in Tennessee. At fifteen, he got a night job shoveling cottonseed in an oil mill in Georgia, alongside young blacks who by day were houseboys or yardmen for whites, and whose tales made the job, as he would later write, "a seminar devoted to the theory and practice of male and female aberrant relationships in an American small town." In later years he would be—intermittently with his writing and obviously enriching it—a stockman in a Kresge store, a cotton picker, a cook, a waiter, a taxi driver, a soda jerk, a stonemason, a professional football player, a bodyguard, a stagehand in a burlesque theater, and a hand on a boat running guns to a Central American country in revolt.

When he was sixteen, while his family was living in Wrens, Georgia, he got a job turning the hand press of the local weekly newspaper, the *Jefferson Reporter;* he was soon allowed to set type by hand, and then to write short news items. And suddenly, with so little to go on, he knew who and what he was. It was no time before he was sending reports of local semi-pro baseball games to the *Augusta Chronicle,* and then sending general news pieces to that paper and to the *Atlanta Constitution,* the *Savannah News,* and the *Macon Telegraph.*

Caldwell's higher education consisted of entering and dropping out of two colleges. The first was called Erskine College—named, as he himself was, for the founder of his father's sect, one Ebenezer Erskine—in the town of Due West, South Carolina. Later, having run off to Louisiana and having landed in jail for vagrancy, and having dabbled at various jobs, including journalism, he discovered the existence of a long-forgotten scholarship at the University of Virginia for lineal descendants of soldiers in the Confederate Army. Having somehow established a claim to it, he was admitted in spite of his abysmal academic record. There, in the college library, he helped himself to the only true education he thought he needed, first in little magazines, *transition, This Quarter,* the *Prairie Schooner;* then in novels, *Sister Carrie, In Our Time, Winesburg, Ohio.*

When he thought he had learned enough to make a start, he married a graduate student named Helen Lannigan, dropped out again, took a job as a reporter for the *Atlanta Journal,* and wrote short stories in his "spare" time. Three years later, in 1928, he moved with Helen and their two baby sons to a small house in Maine, where he planted vegetables, chopped firewood, and wrote short stories. Winter came and they had almost nothing to live on. He had arranged to review books for the *Charlotte Observer* and the *Houston Post.* The person who had set this up for him sent scores and scores of review copies, which he sold to a bookstore in Portland for twenty-five cents each. The family nearly starved; they ate potatoes and rutabagas he had grown the previous summer, and scant groceries bought with the money from reviews and the sale of the books. He wrote in an unheated upstairs room wearing a Navy watch cap pulled down over his ears, a sweater, a leather jerkin, and a padded storm coat, and with a woolen blanket wrapped around his legs.

He had collected several shoe boxes full of rejection slips when, at last, *transition* accepted "Midsummer Passion," a story which has since had many lives in anthologies. Alas, *transition* paid nothing. But Maxwell Perkins, then editing *Scribner's Magazine,* saw the story and wrote him. Caldwell sent Perkins a story a day for a week. Perkins rejected them all, so Caldwell slowed down and sent him two stories a week until, finally, Perkins accepted two. He told Caldwell he would pay "two-fifty" for both of them. Caldwell said, "Two-fifty? I don't know. I thought I'd receive a little more than that." Perkins offered three-fifty. "I guess that'll be all right," Caldwell said. "I'd thought I'd get a little more than three dollars and a half, though, for both of them." "Oh, no!" Perkins said. "I must have given you the wrong impression, Caldwell. I meant three hundred and fifty dollars."

That marked a turning point. Caldwell would never be desperately hard up again. With a boost from Alfred Kreymborg, who with Lewis Mumford and Paul Rosenfeld edited the *New American Caravan,* and who had liked a story of his, he found a publisher for a short novel he had written, entitled *The Bastard.* No sooner was it out than it was attacked as obscene; it was ordered shipped out of Maine within forty-eight hours.

Three years and three books later came *Tobacco Road,* which was even more violently attacked. At first it sold only a few thousand copies, and Caldwell, discouraged, wrote a book with a Maine setting, called *A Lamp for Midnight,* which wasn't published for twenty years. He had just finished writing *God's Little Acre* when he was invited by M-G-M to Hollywood, at what seemed to him the astounding salary of two hundred and

ERSKINE CALDWELL ON TOBACCO ROAD, 1936

"I was only trying to tell a story."

fifty dollars a week—the first of several stints as a screenwriter that he, like Faulkner, Fitzgerald, West, and others, would undertake over the years. Then Jack Kirkland's stage adaptation of *Tobacco Road* opened on Broadway and put Caldwell on easy street. It ran seven and a half years and brought him two thousand dollars every week.

And so he was free to do whatever he wanted, and what he wanted was to roam and to write. The peripatetic life of his childhood had imprinted him with vagabondage. I have counted twenty-eight homes in which he lived, and there were probably others. He had four wives and many secretaries. After his first nine books (published in six years), his restlessness took him on the road to do a picture-and-text book about American types with the photographer Margaret Bourke-White. He left Helen to marry Bourke-White and work with her, but she turned out to be even more a wanderer than he, and they parted. Soon afterward he met an undergraduate at the University of Arizona named June Johnson, and married her, but it turned out that she *hated* to travel; they divorced. On New Year's Eve, 1958, he married his then secretary and editorial assistant, Virginia Fletcher, and with her he would live, in truth, happily ever after. She was perfectly attuned to his metronomic life: six months each year of writing, six to see the world. She embedded a paradox of serenity in his restlessness.

He roved for the sake of his writing, keeping journals wherever he went. "The need to write fiction," he would report, "had become as demanding as the craving for food when hungry. . . . I had never known a time . . . when I was unable to write a short story or a novel for lack of an idea and suitable material." And indeed it came about that in the years between the publication of his fourth book, *Tobacco Road,* in 1933, and the publication of his fifty-fifth book, *With All My Might,* in 1987, Erskine Caldwell became the most widely read living author on earth. Up to the time of his death this year, eighty million copies of his books had been sold, in forty languages.

How do we account for such an extraordinary outcome? The easy answer, most frequently given: what he wrote was sexy; it was salacious, pornographic. But that won't wash. In terms of explicit sex, *Tobacco Road,* read today in comparison, let's say, with John Updike's *Couples,* is as mild as a Sunday-school picnic. It is true that much of Caldwell's writing has a hot erotic power, but it is delicately delivered, and even in the relatively puritanical thirties, among all the charges of obscenity and pornography brought against his early books in New York, Boston, Philadelphia, Cleveland, Detroit, Chicago, and elsewhere, only twice were permanent legal bans imposed. The mayor of Chicago succeeded in banning the play of *Tobacco Road,* and Boston's Watch and Ward Society achieved a ban against *God's Little Acre.* "I didn't consider that I was doing something that I shouldn't," Caldwell said in a rare interview four years ago. "I just thought it was natural to make a story as compelling as possible."

Was it because of his compassion for the downtrodden of this world—because he was a proletarian novelist, in the best sense, in times of great suffering and change? It is true that when he went to the Soviet Union with Margaret Bourke-White, he was given so many rubles for his Russian royalties that he could afford a luxurious suite at the National Hotel, in the astonishing oval parlor of which there was a grand piano, a bearskin rug, and amorous cupids on the ceiling. But Caldwell disavowed this role and was steadfastly apolitical all his life. "I was not trying to prove anything," he was to say. "I was only trying to tell a story."

He chose the right word to account for his success: his best work *is* compelling. Its surface is very plain, but, reading it, one has a sensation of diving deep into a vivid dream. At the edge of terror, sweet wishes come close to fulfillment, and then drift tantalizingly away. This is very often the case in his short stories, some of which—such as "Kneel to the Rising Sun," "Candyman Beechum," "Country Full of Swedes"—are clas-

sics of narrative power. "By an astounding trick of oversimpli-
fication," Kenneth Burke wrote, "Caldwell puts people into
complex situations while making them act with the scant,
crude tropisms of an insect—and the result is cunning." Crafty,
that is to say, balanced on a razor's edge between hilarity and
horror. And all is told in a quiet conversational voice, which
speaks in the rhythms of truth.

Caldwell kept himself apart, striving for these effects. "The
fewer writers you know," he said once, "the easier it is to avoid
being caught up in that mishmash of literaryism which to me
is a very deadly kind of existence." Faulkner once named him
as one of the five best contemporary writers, along with Hemingway, Dos Passos, Wolfe, and himself. An interviewer asked
Caldwell if that high ranking pleased him. "I never think in
those terms," he said. "I'm just an ordinary writer, I'm nothing
special; so I don't have to have that kind of appreciation. I can
do without it. All I'm interested in are the books that I've
written. I'm just the writer. The books speak for themselves."

Children of
Holocaust Survivors

Shimon and Yael

Now we are in the family room. One whole wall is covered
with books—angular Hebrew characters on their spines.
The hero sits with his back to the books—sits bolt upright in
front of the printed record—in a straight, wide wooden chair.
He is, like the chair, solid; his big arms lie on the chair's arms.
His feet are planted wide apart on an Oriental rug, which
takes the chill off part of the gray terrazzo floor. His wife sits
on a daybed against the wall across from him. The guest is to
his left, in front of an open window, through which comes a
wild whistling of birds declaring their territories. There are
few other sounds from outdoors. The kibbutz is at rest. It is
Saturday, the Sabbath.

"Something to drink?" the hero asks the guest. "Coffee?
Tea? Whiskey?"

It is ten-thirty in the morning. The guest laughs at the idea
of whiskey at ten-thirty in the morning.

But the hero's face is serious—broad, bold, slightly puffy
around the eyes; it is said that he has had several heart attacks.

The guest asks for tea. The hero's wife—herself a legendary

From "Successors," *The New Yorker,* December 16, 1974.

leader of the ghetto fighters in the remembered time—gets up
(her back is slightly bent, her eyelids hang in sleep-loosened
folds over eyes that seem to be dark wells into which all the
family's valuables have been lowered for safekeeping until the
danger—what *is* the danger?—has passed), and she goes to
the small cookstove in the work space of the next room to set
water to boil. Water drums from a faucet on the kettle bottom.
The kettle clatters on the frame of the burners.

The door slams, and the son, Shimon, a twenty-six-year-old
reservist, shuffles in on sandals. He makes it obvious that he
has just got up, makes it obvious that he has been told to come
here at this time. He is handsome—a more delicate face than
his father's. He is wearing a T shirt and parti-colored denim
slacks, brown and tan, flared out from the knees downward.
He is clean-shaven, his hair is neatly combed, his expression is
sullen. He sits down on the end of the daybed. His mother
speaks to him; he murmurs something offhand.

"The Jewish home in Poland before the war was at the end
of a straight line," the hero is saying. "The furniture was static,
it was heavy. You see," he says, "there was a certain stability. No
one had a wristwatch then; there wasn't an alarm clock at each
person's bedside. The whole family told time by a huge
wooden chime clock, which no living member of the family
had gone out to buy; it had been handed down from generation to generation."

The mother returns with a tray, on which are cups of coffee
and tea, already poured, and a pint of Black and White, and
glasses. She passes a cup of tea to the guest. At the same time,
the hero leans forward and puts a glass beside the teacup and
splashes into it a dollop of Scotch. The guest raises an arresting
hand. The hero pours himself a man-sized slug.

"To life!"

"To life!"

"It has been so long," the hero says, with what must be a

stinging throat. "The idea of this country," he says, "for a Jewish boy in Europe then, was based on the Bible; he knew it only through the Bible—its history, geography." He sets fire to a cigarette with a lighter made in the shape of a hand grenade, and smoke rides out on the casual words he speaks about his generation of rebels. "The old straight line was broken. . . ."

Slam. It is Yael, the daughter, a student of psychology and sociology at Hebrew University. She is twenty-four, shorter than the rest of the family, with cropped straight blond hair and a wise, serious face and a stocky frame. She, too, sits down on the daybed. Murmurs to the mother.

The hero, speaking of the stages of his growth into Zionism, says, "When I was sixteen, I kissed girls in Yiddish; when I was eighteen, I kissed them in Hebrew." He says that he and his comrades studied everything: pogroms in 1881, 1907; the location of every single factory in Palestine; the literature of the dream of the return to Eretz Yisrael.

Somebody bangs hard and repeatedly on the glass of the louvered windows; alarmed, the guest turns around to see who is intruding on the family's privacy so rudely and with such bad temper. But no one is there, and gradually it sinks in that there has been a quick series of sonic booms. We are in the far north, near the sea. The uncertain Golan Heights—supersonic seconds away. The guest thinks of that wooden clock in Poland. . . .

"What we had to learn emotionally," the hero says, *"they"*—his eyes, which, embedded in their bruiselike settings, seem the eyes less of a fighter than of a poet, flicker toward the downturned faces of Shimon and Yael—*"they* take for granted. They didn't need any ideological training to arrive where they arrived. They were just born. They only had to live life here to know everything. They speak eloquent prose without even knowing they do."

The hand grenade goes off again; the cardiac case draws,

inhales, and enjoys; smoke comes out through his nose. "Before the Yom Kippur War," he says, "everything seemed natural
to my son and daughter—natural and organic. But *after* the
war they came to realize that they are links in a chain. My
generation moved from theory to life, and they now have had
to move from life to theory. But it's an illusion," he says, "to
think that the Messiah will come in my lifetime—or in theirs.
A mistake people make is to believe that history turns on a
single day, in a single hour. Everything is a process. . . ."

The guest has known about this hero and heroine for more
than a quarter of a century. Pictures still sear in his imagination
of this man and woman crawling through the Warsaw sewers,
escaping the ghetto after the doomed uprising. He first saw
Shimon and Yael twenty-three years ago, right here, when they
were three and one, golden-haired babies coming from the
children's house for the evening time in the family room—the
kibbutz then just a cluster of huts around a dusty patch of
grass. The hero has devoted his lifetime to building on the
kibbutz grounds an imposing museum, to which schoolchildren and soldiers come in busloads from all over the country
to learn about the Holocaust. The museum has a model of the
whole Warsaw ghetto, street by street, house by house, with
little lights showing where the Judenrat was, where the Pawiak
Prison, the bridge, the bunkers, the sewer manholes, the Um-
schlagplatz and the fateful selections; and glass cases enclosing
unspeakable artifacts—brassards with the Star of David, insignia of the S.S., tools of torture and genocide, a cake of Jew
soap—and rooms full of photographs, scenes from the ghetto,
glimpses of the process, many of the pictures slightly blurred,
as if to look at the faces and faces and faces of those who were
lost caused the camera itself to quake and tear its lens away
before the shutter was even closed.

"But let him speak for himself," the hero suddenly says, wav-
ing a hand toward his son. And to show that he means it he

gets up out of his chair and moves back into a shadowy corner of the room, and Shimon, with graceful arrogance, crosses the room and takes his father's chair.

He says, "Five months."

"In the south," he says. "The Egyptian front."

From the shadows, the hero, unable to restrain himself, says, "Shimon was the first male child born in the kibbutz."

Shimon is a sometime third-year student at the Technion, in Haifa—the country's foremost technological college. Sometime because there are interruptions. "I've been called up again," he says.

He says, "Northern front."

He says, "I've been out just six weeks this time."

Shimon does not make the mass in the wooden chair that his father did, but he is every bit as impressive in it as the hero was—coiled energy, chary words in a tight voice, a disdainful and condescending expression.

He says, "Armored reconnaissance."

The hero intervenes again. "They had so many losses in the Yom Kippur War that the Army had to change their tactics," he says. "They pressed forward too boldly."

Shimon says, "I have one more year at the Technion."

He says, "I'll work in our factory here at the kibbutz."

"Electronic equipment," he says. "Condensers."

"We have one engineer," he says. "An older person."

He says, "Basketball. Chess."

The hero breaks in once more, saying, "He's trying to learn to drink, but he's not very good at it yet."

Shimon's face shows nothing. "Kibbutz parents," he says, perhaps picking up the image of the links, "had a choice—to come here or not to come. But we were faced with being born here." He shrugs. "This is my home," he says.

He says, "Their generation had to build a society. Now that it's built, we're thinking about other problems."

He leans forward and holds his head in his hands and is silent for quite a while. Then he says, "I don't think I have any goal in life. I live here. There are problems that need to be solved, but I can't see myself going into politics. I don't know what I want in the long run. . . . Of course, peace."

Then Shimon is abruptly as voluble as his father was a few minutes ago. He says, "What I think is that we should believe the Arabs when they say they want to destroy us. They said it in '56, '67, '73. I took a trip to Spain last year, and I met a young Arab boy there. He told me his parents used to live in Zichron Ya'akov, down the coast here. He thinks the solution should be a simple one: his return and my departure. He doesn't believe in compensation. If you ask me, young Arabs are more extreme than their parents. Sure, my parents wanted to return to where their ancestors had lived; and now *he* wants to return, and he wants *me* to leave. Since I also have a case, I don't agree to that. Both sides are right. But he won't meet me halfway."

He says, "Nothing. There's nothing I can do about it."

Then he says, "Defend myself."

He says, "I just live from reserves to reserves." He does not use the natural phrase: from day to day.

He says, "Peace seems very far away. I expect another war in a few years, maybe months. I don't know if I'm more pessimistic than my parents; I do know that I'm more realistic. To them, everything is ideological—whether to have a new storage room in the kibbutz. To me a storage room is just a fact of life."

"The Yom Kippur War started people talking about political change," he says. "What change?" Shimon's voice is edged with scorn. "We have the oldest government in the world. They haven't let a younger generation develop."

The hero mildly says, "There is no empty space in nature. When Moses died, Joshua took over."

Yael speaks for the first time, uttering for the guest's benefit, with a glint of mischief in her eye, the question that has been hanging in the air all along: "How does it feel, Shimon, to be the son of heroes?"

Shimon's expression does not change at all. He says, "Wonderful. Every morning when I get up I feel full of pride."

The mother says, "That sarcasm—*that's* the difference between our generations."

The father says, "When first he holds his son's hand in his, the sarcasm will disappear."

Perhaps to appease or dispel the image of the links, now startlingly reinvoked, Shimon says, in an abrupt, terse dismissal of all the talk of generations, "We are sexually freer than our parents, but"—his voice is slightly grudging—"the basic concepts haven't changed."

After a while the family takes the guest to lunch in the kibbutz dining hall. As the group moves to one of the many tables, a round-faced, fair-haired girl sitting at the next table beyond sees Shimon, and her face suddenly seems to come out from under a cloud. Her skin glows, she laughs loudly. Shimon reacts but plays it cool. While Yael and the guest discuss Israeli novelists over lunch, there is much byplay between Shimon, who eats very little, and the girl behind him. Does she have a cigarette? She doesn't, but she gets up and goes somewhere to find one for him. She tosses it to him. He needs a match. Once again she goes and fetches, and tosses. Soon, the cigarette half smoked, Shimon moves away from the family and joins her, standing in the aisle between the rows of tables. But when the family leave the dining hall he walks out with them. Outside in the sunlight he turns his back on them, says something over his shoulder about a chess match he wants to watch, and starts away. He has not looked at the guest. As he walks, and without turning his head, he gives a casual backhanded wave to no one in particular.

His mother asks if he will come back to the room before the guest leaves. He says he will.

But he doesn't.

Now we are in Yael's room at the Hebrew University, in Jerusalem. Rows and rows of long, one-story student dorm-huts cling to the western hip of the hill on the crest of which soar the gross white monumentalities of the Givat Ram campus. Yael lives in Row 3, Building 8, Room 5: a humble box-within-box, with a room-wide shelf for a desk at the window end, some bookcases, two beds. One bed has a bare mattress; Yael lives alone for the time being. She is in a sweater, slacks, sandals. Her skin is shiny. She speaks in a very low voice, not about her studies but about being a soldier.

"I was in the tank corps," she says. "The last year of my tour I enjoyed. By then I was a second lieutenant, and I had to take care of fifty girls. In the Yom Kippur War, I was called up again, like everyone else; my job was to get wounded men's families in touch with them."

Soon she is explaining what must seem to her the natural superiority of kibbutzniks, who crowd the élite defense forces—as tankists, parachutists, commandos, armored scouts—and who, though comprising less than a twenty-fifth of the population, have numbered, in the country's wars, more than a quarter of the casualties, and in hazardous units a far higher proportion. "It is easy for kibbutzniks to adjust to the Army, because conditions there aren't too different from those in the kibbutz. Kibbutzniks have had a harder life than city people; they're used to communal living. The kibbutz expects you to be an officer, to volunteer, be in a dangerous place; if you're just a clerk, they don't like it. There's something else, too. In a kibbutz competition isn't stressed at all—the group is what is important—and in the Army you have your first chance to show that you may be better than anyone else.

"In the country in general," she says, "and in the kibbutz, the importance of the Army has diminished a bit. Dayan said it will be dangerous when our youth will not want to volunteer and will not want to fight. It's a shock to me to read in the papers criticism of our Army higher-ups. Up till now, I've had complete faith in all these people, but apparently even at very high levels they can make mistakes. If they can make mistakes at the top, that's dangerous, too. I still believe in the Army. I believe it's a good Army. People come and people go, but the Army remains. It may be one of the last things you can believe in. It is less corrupt than the government and the other public services. And it is strange—it's not militaristic.

"In the Palmach, in the generation of those who fought in the War of Independence, they had an ideal of a new Jew: a tough guy. Father talked about links in a chain. We don't like such big words; they're too pompous. And we don't have big ideas, either. Of course, peace, and a strong economy. But we don't think the way to handle things is through the tough-guy manner. You saw Shimon—cynicism and assumed in-difference.

"When I was young," Yael says, "there were fewer cynical jokes than there are now about volunteering and about the possibility of being killed. The younger people are even more cynical than we, but they still wind up in the same units. In the seventh or eighth grade, I was a little girl; now they're little women and little men down there. Things come at these young people much faster than they used to come at us. We had a hard time tracking down a radio for our class in school. Now everyone has a transistor. Who ever used to dream about own-ing a record-player?"

Auritte and Moshe

The philosopher is short in stature, tall in talk. His favorite pastime, it seems, is to dazzle. He indulges it now in the

living room of his modest apartment at the edge of Rehavia,
one of the more desirable residential quarters of Jerusalem.
The little room teems with his ideas. His listeners: two foreign
guests, man and wife; an assistant professor of literature from
the Hebrew University and her shy husband, who has lost a
hand in one of the country's wars; and the philosopher's own
wife, who by no means lacks opinions but defers, for the moment, to his. And also, from time to time, drifting in and out,
his daughter Auritte, who is fourteen; his son Moshe, who is
twelve; the guests' daughter; two neighbor girls who have
dropped in to play; the literature professor's adorable, though
whiny, baby girl; and a small white dog with a slangy American name, something like Slats or Dopey.

The philosopher's features, which seem to have been im-
provisationally crowded together behind a pair of glasses, are
swarthy; he is Ashkenazic but, rather, looks Sephardic. From
the next room, his study, comes a sweet odor of book learning.
In another time and place—in the world re-created by the
Hebrew novelist S. Y. Agnon, for instance (the philosopher has
touched briefly on Agnon's work, not failing to mention the
Nobel Prize in 1966)—he would surely have been a rabbi
steeped in Mishnah, Gemara, Cabala; at the rate he is talking
now, perhaps a Gaon, perhaps even a Wonder Rabbi. As it is,
in this country of wars and sorrows, he is an agnostic and a
philosopher, conversant with all branches: moral philosophy,
theory of knowledge, symbolic logic, linguistics, and so on, not
to mention garden-variety secular wisdom. Having behind him
not only the Europe of his young manhood but also post-
doctoral work at Yale and a year of teaching at St. Andrews,
in Scotland, he is a man of the wide world. On a coffee table
is a glistening golden globe of the earth, about six inches in
diameter. The philosopher's wife reaches forward. Apparently
in answer to a small trigger, the northern hemisphere rises
with an alarming clang away from the southern, and up from

the hollow interior, quickly opening out, like a chrysanthe-
mum blooming in stop-action photography, comes an elaborate
flower whose petals are cigarettes, ready to be picked, one by
one, by smokers—of which there are several in this room.
Soon mantled in pale smoke, the listeners are given a brief
disquisition on a certain heaviness of kibbutz life. Disapproval
of the mode of *clinging to* the Holocaust. Bad, for example, to
live in a kibbutz the very name of which, translated, is Ghetto
Fighters. "It is so gloomy," the philosopher gloomily says. In
his own life, he has made every outward effort to mute the
memories of that time. Undeniable that in the forests of the
imagination partisans forever lurk. He was one. Was born
in Warsaw; grew up in the left Zionist movement Hashomer
Hatza'ir—the great Mordekhai Anilewitz, later commander
of the Warsaw uprising, a childhood friend. When the Germans entered Poland, analysis of conditions dictated removal
to Lithuania, where one could more or less disappear into a
Jewish community in a very small town. After the Germans
invaded Russia, partly by way of Lithuania, analysis of conditions dictated removal to a large city; the Kovno ghetto was
convenient. In 1944, at twenty-four, he escaped to the woods
and swamps and fought there as a Jewish partisan until the
end of the war. But those forest memories are deep and distant,
and he has neither thrust them upon his children nor shielded
his children from them. Imagine his surprise, last year, on finding Moshe, then only eleven, reading about those days in the
book of which he himself, the father, is co-author, *The Story of
an Underground*!

The scene has not changed, but the characters have. Auritte
and Moshe are now chatting in the living room with the
foreign man. The other adults have gone to the kitchen; the
other children are playing a variant of jacks in Auritte's room.

Auritte and Moshe are small and tall, in the same sense in which their father is. Like him, they are Ashkenazic in being, Sephardic in seeming. Like him, English-speaking. Diction: crisp. Fluency: excellent. Grammar: very good to excellent. Pronunciation: Scottish-American. Unlike the father, they are beautiful—immaculate in knitted clothing, yellows and browns, not quite matching. They are indeed the little woman and little man of Yael's description. Auritte, delicate-looking, with plastic-rimmed glasses, sits up more demurely than her mother. Moshe leans back, slouches more than his father; a cowlick droops over his olive-skinned forehead toward his huge, burning eyes.

AURITTE: We're very different with our parents than they were with theirs. Things there were then and aren't now. The games they played and how they studied. My father made his studies on a little table surrounded by beds in a crowded room—very poor. He was a Jew surrounded by goyim. Here I am in my own country—and you see how we live.

MOSHE (*pointing at the large television set in the corner behind Auritte*): We can watch any evening, Saturday mornings.

AURITTE: During the Yom Kippur War, they started showing films on Saturday mornings, because the fathers that were in the Army didn't want their kids running around in the streets—and after the war they didn't stop the programs. Last Saturday, let's see, we watched an Israeli picture—

MOSHE: It was Gary Cooper.

AURITTE: Not last Saturday.

MOSHE: Gary Cooper. It was.

AURITTE (*embarrassed, going back to the earlier subject*): My parents' parents had a very strict attitude. Now we're much freer. My parents respected their parents more than we do. Now we can have arguments. We have the courage to say what we think. When our parents talk about cleaning up our rooms, or practicing—I play the piano, Moshe plays the violin—

MOSHE: I don't practice even an hour a day.

AURITTE:—we feel we can talk back. Or, for example, we say we don't like the food. It starts with mumbling and comes to shouting. So Mother finally says, "What's right for me to do is not right for you to say."

MOSHE (*evidently thinking of his father amongst the goyim*): Even when we were in Scotland, we weren't dirty Jews.

AURITTE: The first day there, one of the children called Moshe a Pakistani! It was because his skin is a little dark. It was the first impact of racism—the first time we even thought about anti-Semitism.

MOSHE (*beginning to speak as if reciting something he has memorized*): In the other war—Father's war—the Jewish people couldn't defend themselves, they had no country, they didn't have any hope at all. Now we have our country and our Army and our people, and we can defend ourselves.

AURITTE: The Arabs are fighting us because they think we are in their country, not because we are Jews and only because we are Jews.

MOSHE (*himself again*): I heard there are some Nazis that came and are helping the Egyptians.

AURITTE (*embarrassed for him again*): We have a stronger sense of the past since the Yom Kippur War. We felt our country and the need to defend it and how valuable it is. If you speak of losing a war, you don't know how the Arabs would treat us, and you might have to go back to the Galuth—the Diaspora.

MOSHE: We know more about the Holocaust than the other students. Their parents are younger than ours and were born here.

AURITTE: I don't see why we have to have all these wars. The Arabs and the Israelis—we're both people. We have inherited this problem. The parents give it to the sons, and the sons to theirs. Like in Ireland—the people don't even know what they're fighting for. The Arabs say this is their home. I can't say whether we lived here before them or they first. We didn't really talk together or sit together to try to understand each other—how can we know each other?

MOSHE: I am more pessimistic than she is. Look, all the youngsters have to go in the Army, and they fight the Arabs, and when they see the Arabs try to kill them and see them kill their friends—

AURITTE (*arguing with him*): But you saw the program from the southern front, after the pullback, when our soldiers were talking with the Arab boys, and they were exchanging gifts, and laughing. They were *people*.

MOSHE (*curtly*): Those were Egyptian boys, not *Arabs*.

Ora and Yitzhak

This apartment, on Cheshin Street, in the northern reaches of Tel Aviv, is tiny, and its well-worn furnishings suggest years of scrimping for the sake of children. On a shelf, reminding of a brave past, is a brass-trimmed toy cannon, which has lost one of its wheels. The administrator's wife serves coffee, tea, cake. The children are not here. We will drive out later, the administrator explains, to Ramat Hasharon, a suburb north of the city, to call on Ora and her husband at their apartment; it is only fifteen minutes away. Yitzhak, "my little boy," is out of town, on a Passover vacation trip to Eilat with friends.

Memory of the Holocaust is a large part of what the administrator administers, and he begins at once talking of the shadow of the great tragedy which lies over the country. The month of May, 1967, just before the Six-Day War, he says, was the period when every citizen was obliged, for the first and worst time, to face his feelings about another possible round of genocide—Arab destruction, this time, of Jewry.

What a wiry bantam he is! He has doubtless been too busy to trim his odd little mustache, which twinkles as he talks. Its gray hairs droop straight downward, forming a ragged fringe over his lower lip and seeming to filter the meaning of all that he says, so that what must have been profound in his larynx sounds rather thin by the time it gets out into the open air.

He has, to be sure, plenty to keep him busy. He is chairman of the Organization of Partisans and Ghetto Fighters; president of the World Federation of Jewish Fighters, Partisans, and Camp Inmates; chairman of the Federation of Polish Jews; member of the executive committee of Yad Vashem, the national monument and museum of the Holocaust. He is, besides, full-time director of the Health Insurance Institution of Histadrut, the national labor organization. He seems always to have been in charge of whatever he worked at: in Poland, after the war, he headed the organization for the emigration of Jews to Palestine and, later, to Israel; he himself was one of the last to leave before the Polish door was slammed, in 1949.

He speaks with an executive deliberation that seems to make his big, strong wife fidget. Into the large spaces between his sentences she drops ideas. "Before the Six-Day War," she says in a low, modest murmur, "the fear was greater even than the fear in Europe, because this time we had the children. Ora was in the Army then."

As they go on to speak about the two children, the administrator's wife gradually makes it evident that she is one entity of which her husband has not taken full command: her voice grows louder and more distinct, and before long she is doing much of the talking.

The first difference that Ora and Yitzhak noticed between themselves, as children of the Holocaust, and most of their Israeli friends was that a valuable generation was lacking. The father says, "They would ask us, 'Why don't we have grandfathers and grandmothers like the others?'" There is, besides, a marked difference between the two children themselves. Almost a decade separates them. Ora is twenty-five now, and Yitzhak sixteen; it is as if *they* came from two generations. While

Ora was growing up, the parents told her a lot about the past, and she, deeply influenced, would never go to a German film or buy anything made in Germany; whereas Yitzhak has been resistant—asks why German children should be held to account for what their parents did. When the principal of Yitzhak's school asked the administrator to come and speak about the Holocaust, Yitzhak objected, and the father had to go to another school. "Yitzhak," the father says, "has had some kind of reaction." "He says he has had enough of the subject," the mother says. "It is hard for us to understand why."

Now it is time to leave. It is agreed that the parents and the guest will go in separate cars; the guest will follow the administrator. The latter's leadership qualities assert themselves when he gets behind the wheel of his automobile. He sits up very straight, and his car shoots away into the trafficky night. In a nation of mad, headlong drivers, he is indeed one to show the way—to anyone who can keep up with him. He knows where he is going, and *whoosh*—he goes. Twelve minutes of chase (he had said it would take fifteen) to the suburb of Ramat Hasharon.

The guest feels pale as he enters Ora's apartment. Ora, it turns out, *is* pale. She is just settling her eight-month-old daughter, Yael, down in a little reclining box on the floor. Her husband is introduced—an economist for a large business firm; he has the handsome, knowledgeable look of a comer. The administrator asks if he may pick up his grandchild. What answer can there be? Ora, her husband, and the guest sit down in the living room; Ora's mother and father—he jiggling Yael on his shoulder—go to the kitchen.

The living room is large, bright, and stylish; it has a look of potential affluence. A record-player on a shelf; several feet of L.P. albums. Contemporary prints on the walls. A tall white paper-lantern lamp.

Ora sits near the record-player. She looks as if she could be easily hurt. Her dark, shoulder-length hair has a slight wave, and whenever she stops to think she bows her head, and her hair falls forward and partly hides her pale face.

She says, "But I felt strong during the war. I didn't want to go to the shelter. Mother was afraid, but I had no fear. I felt no fear. And yet when I think of what my parents went through I'm not sure I could have stood it. I'm not used to suffering. My generation was born without troubles. We just live. My parents gave me everything I wanted. I never needed *anything*."

In the kitchen, the inevitable has happened; the baby has been jiggled too much and begins to bawl. Ora looks up but doesn't move. Her mother comes into the living room and gets the reclining box and goes back, and presently the crying tapers off into caught breaths.

"A woman was captured in Egypt who'd been spying for us," Ora says, "and I thought how lucky it was she didn't have a baby...."

Ora says, "Father forgets. I wouldn't let him go to *my* school, either. He always asked me to take him to my school, and I never would let him go. A young person doesn't want to feel different. I did feel different, because Father was famous, and his name was in the papers. Because he had *done* things. I was lucky, in a way, because I was a girl—I didn't feel a pressure to do things. It's different for men."

And she says, "I don't like to hear stories about the Holocaust. Father is a rather closed person, but Mother always wanted to tell those stories. But I'd say, 'Yes, yes, we know, we know, we know.'"

She says, "They took me to Warsaw when I was twelve. They showed me where the ghetto had been, and where they got out of the sewers. I tried to picture all the things I'd heard, the stories I'd read...."

Ora's mother brings some snacks in from the kitchen—chicken and pickle on thin slices of bread. Ora eats nothing.

"I think we could have avoided the last war," she says. "Why were we so proud after the Six-Day War? We should have been more giving. We should have drawn back. Our biggest problem is how to survive. I know that we have to have our country, but I also know we're doing a misdeed to others. Others who have lost their homes. I feel for the Arab, who wants his home back. People need to have room. I don't want the Arabs to suffer. I've felt this all along—since even before the Six-Day War."

Now Ora's white face looks quite desperate and seems to swell, and the facial veins stand out, as if some inner solvent had begun liquefying all her dissatisfaction and doubts, pressing them up into her face, toward her eyes.

"I do nothing! Nothing! I've just read a collection of stories by Amos Oz. I didn't *choose* the book. It was just lying around. I'd read it before. I came on it, and I read it. I picked it up because it was lying there, and read it. Time is passing, and I want to do things. I want to live. For eight months, ever since the baby came, I've just been sitting and doing nothing. I'm getting older. My time has gone by very fast. Until now, I've felt that the whole history of the Jewish people started just twenty-five years ago, when I was born. Everything was set for me in that history: six years of childhood, twelve years of school, two years of Army, four years of university. Then? Then the child, and then—just sitting and thinking, 'What will happen? What will happen?' We're under pressure. We have no time. You can only make your way—maybe only a few degrees—when there's a catastrophe. And then you do it badly, because you're so rushed. I used to have daydreams. I saw myself in them. I was afraid. I kept telling myself, 'This is going to turn out all right. This is going to have a happy ending.' I was always helpless. I knew that someone would come to help me. . . ."

Yitzhak is back from Eilat. He is a sixteen-year-old weed. He can't keep his long, thin hands off his long, narrow face. It is evening, but he looks as if he had just waked up. He also looks as if he were about to burst into laughter. His face is red.

"Yes," he says, "I got a bit burned. We slept in tents on the beach. There was a bit of wind, but it was O.K. There were thirteen of us. I've been with these boys since first grade; we've always gone to shows together, you know—played soccer, watched basketball games. My favorite team is Hapoel Tel Aviv. There's this one guy—two meters seventeen centimeters tall. Over two meters, they're mostly Americans. My favorite Israeli player is this Barry Lebovitz, only he's gone to study in Holland. But he'll be back. Anyway, on this trip, you see, the point was we didn't have any teacher or anyone supervising us. Just on our own. One of my friends"—suddenly Yitzhak does break into laughter, and he cannot stop for a long time—"he couldn't go with us because his parents wouldn't let him go. He had to go with his *family*"—he laughs some more—"for this tour in the Sinai! With a whole group of adults! In a bus! They just left today! Anyway, we slept on the sand. We bought canned food in a supermarket, heated it up, fixed eggs and coffee—you know. Most of the time, we just hung around and talked. About anything, you know—the chief of staff resigned. Girls. Alistair Maclean, Ian Fleming. James Bond movies. *Ironside*—that's my favorite TV series. Singers—Cat Stevens, Leonard Cohen. And, you know, the things we want. Me, peace and a motorcycle—only I know my father won't let me have a motorcycle. You know, and about going in the Army, getting away from the house at last, having some independence. And jokes. If a member of the Cabinet comes to your house, don't ask him to sit down—he might stick to the chair.

And then the one about the three important people who go back to the Tel Aviv hotel. They live on the sixtieth floor, and the elevator's just broken down. The clerk suggests they sleep on the lobby floor, but they decide to walk up, and they make a deal—that for the first twenty floors, one will entertain the others by singing songs; the second twenty floors, another one will tell jokes; and the final twenty, the third man will tell sad stories. So the first twenty—singing, fine. The second twenty—jokes, fine. Then, between the fortieth and forty-first floors, it's the third fellow's turn, and he says, 'Now I'll tell you the first sad story: I left the key to the room on the desk down in the lobby.'"

Esther

The psychoanalyst speaks East European–flavored English. "Here there has been a certain mythologization of the role of the hero," he says. The doctor's voice has a nasal resonance, and is soothing.

We are at dinner. The doctor's wife, a slim woman wearing metal-rimmed glasses, brings dishes in from the kitchen and puts them on the low table. The doctor married her in Sweden after the war; now she is a teacher at the Hadassah Medical and Dental School, here in Jerusalem.

"There are two images," the analyst is saying. "To be a fighter—this is idealized. The leaders of the country give us also this ideal—to be tough, not sentimental. The state of the mere survivor, on the other hand, has had a negative image. It was weak—how to go without resistance. It carried a symbol, what we call *sabon*—soap. You know which soap. This is bad. This is not an identity of one who could hate, or take revenge. It was passive."

The host is seated on a love seat next to the guest and talks warmly to him. The three young people at the table are somewhat restless. The analyst's son-in-law—the soldier Sraya, in uniform, at the guest's left—smokes a great deal. He has an astonishing way of putting a cigarette into his mouth. He taps an end up from the pack, pulls the cigarette out with thumb and forefinger, and then, holding it out in front of him at waist level for a second, tosses it up into the air in an arching curve toward his mouth, end over end, and miraculously it comes to rest between his lips, with the filter tip rightly in place, all ready to be lit. He will do this, as if it were the most natural act in the world, in midsentence, during conversation. His wife, Esther, the doctor's daughter, has begun talking about their dog. "He snores," she says, "and wants to be near Yaya"— that is Sraya's nickname—"so all three of us have to sleep together. And he stinks." Esther, who was in the States as a teenager for two years while her father did post-doctoral work at Yale, speaks fluent American-student English.

Yaya, who understands English but is unwilling to speak it, tells a story in Hebrew, and everyone but the guest laughs.

Esther translates for the guest. "Yaya says his colonel has this dog, and the other night the colonel got up and went outside to take a peepee, and while he was out there the dog climbed into his warm bed. And the men in the unit said the next morning, 'So now we have a *real* dog for a colonel.'"

The host's manner of a healer does not flag. "Many people who came through the Holocaust did not wish to transmit to their children their value scale," he says to the guest. "They gave double-bind messages. They said, certainly with pride, 'We do not wish to speak of it.' But on the nonverbal level, another message—a matter of shame. It was a *shameful* secret."

The guest is aware of a certain authority the doctor brings to his comments, for he has told the guest that his own psychoanalysis, undertaken in the course of his training, was "a working-through of the issues of my survival" in Europe: first in a series of labor camps; then for six months underground,

passing as a Gentile; then in the Kraków ghetto; then in the
concentration camp at Theresienstadt. Over the years, he has
made numerous psychological studies of Holocaust survivors
and their families.

Esther gets up to help her mother bring on the main course.
She is twenty years old, and she is five months pregnant. She
is wearing a short, expandable print blouse, and though she
had some difficulty early in her term, she is a picture of health
now. She has a round face, a full neck; her glowing skin seems
crammed to bursting with potentiality and energy.

The analyst leans toward the guest and says in a confidential,
though to all quite audible, voice, "Yaya's brother was killed in
the Yom Kippur War, and he and Esther felt a great need at
once to have a child—rebirth, the continuation of life."

Another daughter, a schoolgirl of sixteen, Micki, is sitting
next to Yaya and cannot tear her eyes away from him. He is a
big-chested man of twenty-three. On his shoulder straps are
looped a pair of the three-banded cloth insignia of a captain.
He sits with arms akimbo, hands on knees. His shirt is open
at his throat, showing a T shirt and, above it, matted hair.
Occasionally he reaches inside and vigorously scratches. He has
the beginnings of jowls. His eyes are dark, and he frowns even
when joking. He does not like being cut out of the conversation, and it seems to the guest that he does not much like what
his father-in-law is saying, and that he likes even less whatever
the foreign guest says.

"During the Eichmann trial the attitude began to change,"
the host says. "People became more aware of the role of those
who stayed alive—what difficulties there had been, that it was
not so easy to resist. But then, during the last war, we identified
much more with the problem of survival. We saw that it can
have many positive values that we can identify with."

Yaya flips a cigarette into his mouth. Esther calls down the
table to him that he is smoking too much. Belligerently—

though obviously in good humor—he counts the butts in his ashtray in Hebrew. He reaches the number eight. He lights the one between his lips.

"The older officers," the psychiatrist says, "were saddened by the young soldiers in the Yom Kippur War—the first war in which eighteen- and twenty-year-olds were exposed—because these young men modeled themselves on the Palmach ideal and on the ghetto-fighter ideal, as they saw it. They rushed into battle—too far. Now we are mourning. Not just for the two thousand five hundred who were lost. We feel sadness, distrust, and somehow also there is hopelessness. A feeling of massive mourning—a delayed mourning for the six million. The rage at Dayan—he was a symbol of the harsh, strong, active man without sentiment. A false prophet! He didn't allow us to feel our losses—that death is something possible. We have to stress the positive values of survival; to live to fight another day, to get food, to learn, to memorize a poem."

Then the doctor points out that this apartment, perched on a steep hillside in southwest Jerusalem, is on a street that is named for a poet, Saul Tchernichowsky—after Bialik the most important poet of the Hebrew Renaissance at the turn of the century. From the love seat the doctor and the guest can see a breathtaking view of lights flung in random necklaces on the shoulders of the opposite hills.

Yaya speaks. Esther has appointed herself his translator. With sparkling eyes, she renders not only his words but also his sullen manner into something exuberant, aggressive, and her own: "He says that the criticism of military men has been very demoralizing to the soldiers in the field. All those demonstrations—people like Moti Ashkenazi and other former officers standing outside the Knesset and shouting about mistakes up the line. If soldiers criticize soldiers in Jerusalem, pretty soon they'll be doing it in the field, and you can't run an Army that way."

Micki and Esther help their mother clear the dishes. Micki retires to do her homework. Esther, moving to the chair next to Yaya, takes out some knitting. She stands up and shows everyone a yellow sleep suit she has finished except for joining the seams—hangs it down her front and laughs, as if she were measuring it against the fetus within. Then she sits and goes to work on what seems to be a sweater, also yellow. Between cigarettes, Yaya reaches out his left hand and fingers her hair or strokes her shoulder or, when she rests, holds her hand. They kiss once. She knits and translates, her eyes lifted from the work and flashing at the guest and at her father.

Yaya and the doctor have a few brief exchanges, and then Yaya lets loose.

Esther puts her knitting down on her knees. Her head is canted back, her face is radiant. She lets him speak a long time, and then she says, in English, "He says that they ought to stop calling the Yom Kippur War *Michdal*—the Failure. He says that the men in the field don't like to hear civilians criticize the Army. He says there was this colonel who got up in public and said that his children were ashamed of his being in uniform. And another officer went home after the war, and he was going into his apartment, and he met this neighbor of his—a male, he wasn't even a reservist—who had sat the whole thing out, and he said to the officer, 'You fellows certainly screwed it up for all of us in *this* war.'"

While Esther talks, Yaya loudly cracks the shells of pistachios between his teeth, picks out the meats, and eats them. Esther is more and more carried away as she speaks. She leans forward, her face still tilted upward, and she is in a rapture. She goes very fast, not seeming to have to recall what Yaya has said, and the guest soon gets the impression that she is adding things—indeed, that she has begun saying in her own way things she has heard Yaya repeat often. She no longer attributes the speeches to him, and she seems to be aiming her passion both at the guest and at her father.

"This was a victory," she says. "Even greater than the Six-Day War. We were taken by surprise because of some errors of intelligence, O.K., but once we got going we won greater victories than in the other war. There were mistakes made in the Six-Day War, too, you better believe it. There was the battle, right here near Jerusalem, for what they called Munition Hill; there were blunders, and terrible casualties. But this time—in Syria there were tank battles like none in human history. Greater than El Alamein or Stalingrad or—Father, what was that battle in Europe?"

"The Bulge."

"The Bulge. Afterward there were six hundred wrecked Syrian tanks. And in the south they were running away so fast that one tank would climb up on another, and sometimes you would have three layers of wrecked tanks. And our fliers—Yaya's older brother was killed, he was a Skyhawk pilot—I mean, this is what *I* am saying, Yaya doesn't talk about this—but he wasn't *shot down*. None of our fliers was shot down by enemy pilots. They had Russian missiles—a new type. Our pilots could see the missiles coming up at them—ten, twelve, many at a time, like rain coming upward from the ground. Look, there have never been better pilots than ours. Not English, not American, not German, not Russian, not Japanese, not Chinese—none! The Russians sold pilots to the Egyptians; our pilots shot them down. Every man in our Army was a hero. There was one tankist who ran out of ammunition, so he took grenades and jumped out of his tank, and he climbed up on the Syrian tanks, opened the lids, and dropped hand grenades in, and destroyed seventeen tanks. You know what stopped us? The major powers stopped us. It was political. We could easily have taken Damascus, but the politicians listened to the two big powers, and it was the politicians who said no, and we actually had to retreat. If the major powers hadn't stopped us, we would have had total victory—for all time."

The doorbell rings. Two new guests arrive. When they are

settled, Yaya says, in perfect English, "To summarize our conversation, we were saying that if the Russians and the Americans would just stop meddling in the Middle East, we could take care of the Arabs."

He puts a pistachio between his teeth. His lips curl. Is that a smile? *Crack!*

Nohi

Nohi, the teacher's son, seems to live in a delicately balanced universe of opposites. His father died when he was six; he is now twenty-one, a lieutenant in the Army. His mother, the teacher, has a disconcerting habit: she looks directly into one's eyes with an expression of absolute candor, as if about to spill everything—and then she *waits*. The guest, bathed two or three times in that blazing confessional look and that long, expectant silence, has quickly grown cautious, and he already empathizes with the extreme wariness of the son.

This lady is a powerful force. As a very young girl and woman, in Warsaw, she risked her life, month after month, on what was called "the Aryan side," caring for Jews who were living in hiding outside the ghetto. Her husband died here fifteen years ago. She has managed very well—has worked as a teacher in Givat Hashalom, a Tel Aviv intermediate public school, giving instruction in everything but shop, gym, and art; keeps a tidy, small apartment with a pretty garden in a quiet suburb; and has given Nohi everything in her power, doubtless including, many times every day, that look.

Nohi, on a weekend pass and out of uniform, fresh from a shower after playing some early-afternoon basketball with friends, pours out one contradiction after another. When he entered the school where his mother teaches he hid from the other teachers the fact that he was his mother's son. She did not teach him herself, but on the other hand, he says—a phrase that seems to be stored close to his tongue—although he doesn't want to pay her too many compliments, he has to say that he got a very good education from her. He grew up in an atmosphere in which the Holocaust was present—he turns his eyes toward a photograph on the wall of his mother's sister and colleague in Poalei-Zion Left in Warsaw, who did not survive, alas—and this probably strengthened his character. However, probably other things—his father's early death, for example—had more influence on his character.

While Nohi sits offering his thoughts and taking them back, the teacher brings from the kitchen copious dishes of gigantic native strawberries, upon which towers of whipped cream have been erected, and she sits down and begins shelling pecans and standing their meats up in the firm white shapes.

On first thought, Nohi is saying, the Arab guerrillas' massacre of men, women, and children in Qiryat Shemona the other day brings to mind the assassination of the Olympic athletes, but on second thought, if you take time to think about it more closely, it is more like the Holocaust—murder without mercy. However, this is a lot closer to home for him, a lot more vividly conceptualized in his mind, than things that happened in the past. . . .

He wavers from topic to topic, and within each: the pros and cons of various political figures—Yitzhak Rabin, Pinhas Sapir, and Golda (she should have retired sooner; on the other hand, she was the only real man in the party). The pros and cons of various careers—whether, after the Army, to get a job as a security man for El Al or study aeronautics at the Technion or think about the whole question some more and decide whether there are more interesting possibilities. He gets a laugh from the guest with a humorous line but immediately says, "I don't want you to think I'm a joker."

The white towers bristle with golden nut meats. The teacher's eyes are mercifully downcast as she listens.

Then Nohi says, "I make a much less sharp distinction between the generations than most people my age do. However, I do sometimes see a clear distinction, and that tends to throw me back toward those who say there *are* differences. Those who were born and raised here are a lot freer than those who were born in Europe; they have a feeling of belonging, of not being merely annexed. This is dangerous, though, because it may bring on the argument of the differences between being a good Jew and being a good Israeli. I don't want to go into the definitions of Jew and Israeli, but in general, personally, I feel more Israeli than Jewish. I am a Sabra, and I don't think Sabras should be ashamed of me. On the other hand, on certain occasions, on Yom Hasho'a—the Day of the Holocaust—or at Yom Kippur, when I hear the Kol Nidre, I feel I am a Jew. But in general I feel I am an Israeli. This feeling of young people, of being first of all Israelis and then Jews, is very difficult for parents—Zionists—to accept; it may disturb relations between parents and children."

Later, Nohi says, "Personally, I don't believe there will be peace. I think the aim of the Arabs is very clear—not peace but the opposite. It is very naïve to think there won't be another war."

The guest waits again for the other hand. This time, it does not come.

The teacher pushes the dishes of strawberries toward the two men. There is also cake.

The guest murmurs something about the caloric hazards of dropping in on anyone in this country, no matter at what time of day or night.

"No one, " Nohi says, once more without qualification, "will feed you better than my mother."

The teacher's large, honest, direct gaze turns slowly toward the guest.

He hastily says, "These strawberries are delicious. Nohi is right."

Rachel and Fanya

The three speakers are women.

The mother was once a partisan—as was the father, a builder today. But now she has the look of a dowager; as she sits sedately in this apartment in the prosperous Yadeliahu quarter of Tel Aviv, it is not easy to picture her roaming in the forest of Sobibor, armed and dangerous.

The older daughter, Rachel, who is twenty-four, is extremely pregnant. "The baby is coming tomorrow," she says. "Really. It's due tomorrow." She is in her last year at Tel Aviv University, in Middle Eastern studies. Something wild has its lair in Rachel's head, just behind her eyes; she has a way of throwing her head back and barking out a bad girl's laugh, her fierce eyes scouting around the room. Her complexion is slightly broken out; her lips are dry.

Fanya, who is nineteen and in the Army, though she is in civvies now, is elegant, quiet, and conventional. She is wearing dark glasses, which in this darkish room give her face a far-away cool, modish, controlled look.

RACHEL: My mother. Well, let's take the kitchen—she cooks in her way, and I cook in mine.

FANYA (*seeming to apologize for Rachel's crude way of putting things*): There are differences in approach. Because Mother's past affects her attitudes toward people. And Mother's not naïve—she saw people showing their worst side. We younger ones haven't met the worst in people.

RACHEL: Here we are in Israel, and Mother cooks Yiddish.

MOTHER (*smiling, very sure of her cooking*): Gefilte fish. Chicken soup with the chicken cooked in it. Noodles ...

RACHEL: Whereas I like Oriental food more. Different dishes. Kebab. Lots of pepper! I would have chips at every meal.

FANYA (*clarifying*): This country has many nationalities. The cooking of younger people expresses this mixture of races. Anyway, Rachel, Mother also experiments.

RACHEL: She experiments. (*To the guest*) You can't compare our lives. Mother stays home; I'm out all day—working, studying. Look, I'm still her daughter. I'm a daughter of the Holocaust. I *hate* the Germans, maybe more than my parents do. Once when I was in the Army, I was hitchhiking, and a VW stopped to pick me up, and I said, "Go on. I won't get in that thing."

FANYA: For my part, I respect my parents' feelings. I try not to hurt their feelings. All my friends know what my parents went through. I'm proud that they revolted against the Germans.

RACHEL (*glowering, perhaps still thinking about the VW*): I can't say I hate the *Arabs*, though.

FANYA: My ideal Israeli woman would be one who has a household and works as well. Some people might have an aim of being public servants—

RACHEL: Politics doesn't interest *me*. We can't do anything in this situation. Not I, not she (*nodding toward Fanya*)—we can't do a thing.

FANYA (*untracked from what she had been saying*): People can join together and influence things if they organize.

RACHEL (*scornfully, but laughing, too*): She's a simple person. You can't just go out and organize.

FANYA: As I was saying, I aim to have an occupation, raise a family, and be happy. Not just be a housewife but also work outside.

MOTHER: Not like her mother.

FANYA: I'm not reacting against you, Mother.

MOTHER: To be a housewife is also to be a working woman.

FANYA: Every woman has to have a wide scope, has to be a woman of the wide world. She should be able to take part in discussions and not just be a listener to men.

RACHEL (*the wild look in her eyes*): My landing craft in the Navy was named for a woman—Sheba.

FANYA: Maybe Mother wanted to be something and didn't have a chance to be.

RACHEL: Of course she had no chance. The years she should have been studying, she had to sit in bunkers and forests. I sit in a good room with a good table and good books, and nobody disturbs me. Then why am I always behind time? Why am I always so tired? Before I was married, when I had more time, I was always around the university, I talked to more people, I read all sorts of things that interested me. The situation today is that you want to get places *fast*—if my parents reached such-and-such a level of apartments when they were forty, I want to reach it when I'm twenty-five. Next year! I have a constant quarrel with time. They ought to lengthen the day. I can't remember when time dragged. Oh, maybe once in a while when my husband was late coming home, and one hour seemed like ten. (*Her head goes back, and she laughs.*)

FANYA: Army time is always slow. I'm in the Army, and that's all. You know, this country doesn't put women in a trench with a telescope watching to see if an Egyptian is moving. I'm a secretary. I do my work and wait for the day to end.

RACHEL: You always did what you were supposed to do. Mother had to push me. She always pushed me. I hate to read books. *I don't like books.* (*Head back, bad laugh.*) "Have you done your homework?" "What mark did you get?" She didn't have to ask Fanya! (*She pats her stomach.*) I'll send him to my mother if he's lazy like *his* mother. If he doesn't want to study, I'll send him to his grandmother. She knows how to push!

MOTHER: Rachel never understood that she was studying for her own sake, not mine.

RACHEL: All those great things—ambition, will, poetry, gazing at the sunset beyond the sea—they're all cold noodles for me. I have many small problems to solve. Solve them and I'll be happy. (*The laugh, the eyes looking around the room.*) We have a door that was never properly finished in our apartment, we can't get a carpenter. Now the baby will be in the room, the door open, a draft. And at the university I have one professor who is an unbearable person! Ambition? I want my husband to succeed. If he reaches his goal—he's a psychologist, he doesn't want to teach, he wants to be a consultant in the public field, he feels that if he teaches he'll just repeat things over and over—if he can reach his goal, I'll be very happy.

MOTHER: The past isn't forgotten, and it seems alive even today. Time didn't affect it at all. Just today, I was sitting together with Fanya, and she was asking about her family. Her aunts. There was one who was just like her—Brandele.

FANYA: We were talking about when I was a little girl and Mother used to call me Brandele.

Nitsana

Everything the historian says about himself moves him inexorably—though along a zigzag path—toward an account of a certain day in his life. He is bald but youthful-looking. His apartment on Tchernichowsky Street is full to brimming: a friend's family, the foreign guest, his own wife and two daughters, some classmates of the older daughter. He speaks quietly, calmly, of shattering experiences. The fragments are not chronological—illegal entry into Palestine; his partisan unit clearing Germans out of Vilna; a message from the poet-leader in the forest, about the best way to get to Eretz Yisrael; work for the N.K.V.D., rooting out collaborators; life on a kibbutz; roles in five wars; years of nightmares; a Ph.D. at the Hebrew University; street work for a Zionist youth movement in Chicago; the modulations in his life from social worker to sociologist to historian. Then, abruptly, he arrives at the day.

October 26, 1943. Kovno. He is eighteen years old. In the

morning, a courier comes with a message from underground intelligence: the Nazis have planned an "action" for this day in the streets near his family home. He takes refuge in an underground hiding place in another part of the ghetto. But at the height of the day he is irresistibly drawn out into the open, and toward his home and danger, by a force he can neither resist nor understand; perhaps it is the burden on him of the Fifth Commandment. But as he walks quickly toward his house he sees his mother and his father (whom he does honor, to this day) and his twin brother, his other self, in a huddle of Jews on the sidewalk; German and Jewish policemen are also standing there; the roundup is still going on. His mother sees him. She gives a decisive signal with her eyes—get away from here! He thinks of an underground commandment: *Stay alive to fight another day*. He turns and runs . . .

Nitsana is now exactly the age her father was on that certain day—eighteen. She is a beautiful teen-aged child in a dark sweater and faded blue jeans, and if she tries to put herself in her father's place, as he was on that day, she says, she has to admit she feels young, very young. Up to now, she has known the life of a carefree middle-class child: swimming, tennis, hikes, movies, scouting, the accordion. Listening to the Rolling Stones, Joan Baez, Cat Stevens, the Beehive. Reading all sorts of authors: Dahn Ben Amotz, Graham Greene, Irving Stone. And drawing—especially drawing. She has just broken up with a boyfriend. The age eighteen, she says, is the dividing line. She is going into the Army in six months. "Before the Army," she says, "we follow our parents. After that, the ways part." She also sees certain vague possibilities for the time after the Army, beyond the parting. She thinks of going to the Israel Academy of the Arts. Of marriage, of having children. But she thinks, too—for, though she is still a child, she feels, in some

respects, more mature than many of her contemporaries, and
perhaps this fact also has its place on the zigzag path leading
back to October 26, 1943—of ways in which she can work for
peace. She thinks that one absolute requisite for peace with the
Arabs is a healthy, exemplary internal society in Israel. She has
thought of the possibility of joining a Gar-in Nahal—a social-
welfare unit—after the Army, and going to live in one of the
depressing settlement towns: Dimona, Migdal Haemek, Yeru-
ham, Qiryat Shemona (in the last, a gruesome Arab massacre
had just taken place). These towns, she says, are where the
most underprivileged people in the country—poor Oriental
immigrants—have been forcibly settled. "The money problem
is not the only problem for them," she says. "They need spiritual help. They live at the end of the world. They need things
to do, they need to feel someone needs *them*. Maybe," Nitsana
says, "besides giving two or three years to the Army for defense, every young person should give one additional year for
other kinds of work, to make a contribution to peace. There's
a lot of talk about this among my friends."

Shlomit, Yonat, and Yehuda

In the book-lined kibbutz room the poet speaks of the ele-
ment of time in Israeli literature—of a tension between an
urgent present, in which every moment counts, and the long,
long, long Jewish past. "American writers can go back to the
time of Washington, Lincoln. But our history in this land
stretches back one thousand, two thousand years. . . ."

The poet grew up in Vilna; he was a sculptor before he was
a poet—and now, he proudly says, the pattern repeats itself:
his son is in New York studying to be an artist. The poet commanded the 1943 resistance in the Vilna ghetto, and when it
fell, and some fighters managed to escape to the forests, he
commanded the Jewish "Vengeance Battalion." Here in the
room with him today is a woman who was one of his deputies

in that partisan organization, now a teacher in the kibbutz school. Also here with the poet are his wife, who is a child psychologist, and their seventeen-year-old daughter, Shlomit, who is in the kibbutz high school, and the teacher's husband and twenty-two-year-old son, Yehuda, an Air Force pilot, and their twenty-two-year-old daughter, Yonat, who is in the Army.

These people all sound very sure of themselves, sure of their place among the country's élite. They live like kings and queens. Thanks to good management, and to a shrewd choice of the kibbutzniks of products to manufacture that are much needed in the nation's economy—metal and plastic kegs, barrels, and other containers—this left-wing kibbutz, not far from the sea on the coastal stretch from Haifa to Tel Aviv, is rich. On its grounds, glorious now with many varieties of flowering trees, are a luxurious library; two clubhouses, one exclusively for the young; a biology lab worthy of a university; a painters' studio; a huge, blue-bottomed swimming pool, set in a wide lawn; tennis courts; and even a miniature golf course. The poet has been awarded a private building in which to create; his wife also has a separate little building for her consultations.

In the case of the poet—a slight-bodied man with curly gray hair and piercing eyes—the self-assurance has manifestly been earned. He is one of the foremost poets writing in Hebrew. In the transactions with time in Israeli literature, he sees himself as having helped to fill in the previously "empty" space between the ancient past and the present. He has written long, dense-textured epics, which weave memories of ghetto and forest and recent wars into the long continuum.

Yehuda says, "Yes, as an aviator I experience time in strange ways. I move over and through it—very fast. When I fly over the Judean desert, or over a weird place like St. Catherine's Monastery, way down in the Sinai, over what looks like dead terrain—or, anyway, a very distant past—and then in a few minutes over the green coastal lowlands, where I see so many new things being built for the future, it's as if I'd plunged through centuries in no time at all.

"I know a lot about the European past from my parents, but I can't completely identify with the people in the Diaspora. I feel secure, and they felt helpless. I understand their predicament intellectually but I can't connect with it emotionally.

"Or something from the immediate past. When I heard about the Qiryat Shemona massacre on television, my first reaction was intellectual. I tried to analyze it. But then something deeper hit me—I wanted revenge. Not abstractly. Revenge on those specific terrorists—on men who could throw babies out of upstairs windows.

"You see, I consider what I feel more important than what I do. The latter's all routine. Wake up. Fly. Go to a bar. My friends are all fliers; that means they're all top quality. The books I see them reading when I walk around are real literature, not trash. Last night, we had a party here at the kibbutz for people who'd just been released from the services, and we read poetry aloud to each other. We read Amichai—I like him because he uses simple words. Shlonsky—rich language. Altermann—the words jump right off the page. At the airbase, we sit around and talk and talk about everything. Politics. Points of view. Women—the flavor of life!"

Yonat says, "I'm at a tankists' camp in the Negev Desert." The guest at once hears in her Hebrew, more than he had heard in the others', a bold lilt, and he is told that this is characteristic of kibbutzniks' speech. "My job is as an instructor for Gadna, the outfit that prepares high-school students to come into the Army. Each week, we get a new group; mostly they come from the bottom of society—many Orientals. We do get some who are educated, but the others—they aren't used to encountering sympathetic guidance. If you could see some of their teachers! They aren't much better than the pupils! We have discussions on the Jewish heritage and on Zionism"—like most of her contemporaries, Yonat cannot help loading that word, which stands for worn-out passions, with irony—"and on the Yom Kippur War. And there they meet for the first time the Chekhi rifle. It's the famous one that was used in the War of Independence. Girls train with it nowadays. The men fight with the Uzi, that sawed-off thing you see them carrying when they're on leave—they fire it from the hip. And I take the kids on tours there in the desert. That's where you *see* time. Sde Boker, where we put pebbles on Ben-Gurion's grave; you can feel his presence. Then we go down from there into this huge cleft, and there we're at Ein Avdat—in a gorge—layers of chalk and slate—millions of centuries—a waterfall in the desert! And then Avdat itself, with Nabataean, Roman, and Byzantine ruins—it was on the ancient trading routes. And then Nahal Tsin. And then Ein Mor . . ."

Shlomit says, "When I was a little girl, I read books and accepted the Holocaust as a fact, but now I understand why people want to put it out of their minds—and so convince themselves that it won't happen again. I do, myself. I want my life! I'm involved with creative dancing. I hope my Army training will be near Haifa, so I can go on with my lessons in the same studio there. Here in the kibbutz, besides going to school—Yonat's mother teaches me history—I'm an assistant in the children's house. I don't read poetry"—she smiles tauntingly at her father—"but I do read some novels sometimes; I just finished Heinrich Böll's *The Clown*. But I'd rather just watch television. I like detective shows and old movies. I know they're not on a very high level, but they're what I like. Then, I'm in a youth movement, and our age group plans to go to a city for a while; there's an organization, Va'ad Hapoalim, that knows which industries need workers, and they'll place us temporarily, and we'll have a chance to see how the common people live." There is a trace of a smile on her face as she gets off this bit of kibbutznik snobbery. Yehuda explodes with laughter and makes a thumbs-up sign. "So, anyway, I don't think the Holocaust could recur—not in the same way. There is a State of Israel now, and if anything happened to Jews abroad, they could come here. If the Arabs try to push us in the sea, and even if the Russians help them—I know that's what the Arabs want—we feel we'll be able to resist them. But if we're talking about patterns repeating themselves, the same thing could happen in the world again—"

The poet, her father, says, "You notice Shlomit didn't say 'Germany.' She said 'the world.'"

Shlomit says, "Yes. What I mean is, if it did happen again, one thing would be the same. The world would stand by and watch again."

Lillian Hellman

Lillian Hellman has long been known as a moral force, almost an institution of conscience for the rest of us—but my view is that her influence, and her help to us, derive rather from something larger: the picture she gives of a *life* force.

It is the complexity of this organism that stuns and quickens us. Energy, gifts put to work, anger, wit, potent sexuality, wild generosity, a laugh that can split your eardrums, fire in every action, drama in every anecdote, a ferocious sense of justice, personal loyalty raised to the power of passion, fantastic legs and easily turned ankles, smart clothes, a strong stomach, an affinity with the mothering sea, vanity but scorn of all conceit, love of money and gladness in parting with it, a hidden religious streak but an open hatred of piety, a yearning for compliments but a loathing for flattery, fine cookery, a smashing style in speech and manners, unflagging curiosity, fully liberated female aggressiveness when it is needed yet a whiff, now and then, of old-fashioned feminine masochism, fear however of nothing but being afraid, prankishness, flirtatious eyes, a libertine spirit, Puritanism, rebelliousness. . . .

Presentation of the MacDowell Medal, the MacDowell Colony, Peterborough, New Hampshire, August 15, 1976; "Lillian Hellman, Rebel," *New Republic*, September 18, 1976.

Rebelliousness above all. Rebelliousness is an essence of her vitality—that creative sort of dissatisfaction which shouts out, "Life ought to be better than this!" Every great artist is a rebel. The maker's search for new forms—for ways of testing the givens—is in her a fierce rebellion against what has been accepted and acclaimed and taken for granted. And a deep, deep rebellious anger against the great cheat of human existence, which is death, feeds her love of life and gives bite to her enjoyment of every minute of it. This rebelliousness, this anger, Lillian Hellman has in unusually great measure, and they are at the heart of the complex vibrancy we feel in her.

But all the attributes I have listed are only the beginnings of her variousness. She has experienced so much! She has had an abortion. She has been analyzed. She has been, and still is, an ambulatory chimney. She drinks her whiskey neat. She has been married and divorced. She has picked up vast amounts of higgledy-piggledy learning, such as how to decapitate a snapping turtle, and I understand that as soon as she completes her dissertation, said to be startlingly rich in research, she will have earned the degree of Doctor of Carnal Knowledge. This is in spite of the fact that during a long black period of American history she imposed celibacy on herself. She will admit, if pressed, that she was the sweetest-smelling baby in New Orleans. As a child she knew gangsters and whores. She has been a liberated woman ever since she played hooky from grade school and perched with her fantasies in the hidden fig tree in the yard of her aunts' boardinghouse. She is so liberated that she is not at all afraid of the kitchen. She can pluck and cook a goose, and her spaghetti with clam sauce begs belief. She can use an embroidery hoop. She knows how to use a gun. She cares with a passion whether bedsheets are clean. She grows the most amazing roses which are widely thought to be homosexual. She speaks very loud to foreigners, believing the language barrier can be pierced with decibels. She scarfs her food with splendid animal relish, and I can tell you that she has not vomited since May 23, 1952. She must have caught several thousand fish by now, yet she still squeals like a child when she boats a strong blue. I know no living human being whom so many people consider to be their one best friend.

She is not perfect. Her chromosomes took a little nap when they should have been giving her a sense of direction. "We can't be over Providence," she said, flying up here this morning. "Isn't Providence to the south of Martha's Vineyard?"

I told her it was to the northwest of the Vineyard.

"But when you drive to New York, you go through Providence," she said, "and New York is to the south of us."

I said that the only way to drive directly to New York from Martha's Vineyard would be to drive on water, and that I could think of only one person in history who might have been able to do that.

She said, "You mean Jews can't drive to New York?"

God gave her a gift of an ear for every voice but her own, and when she tries to disguise that voice on the telephone, as she sometimes does, the pure Hellman sound comes ringing through the ruse. "No, Miss Hellman is not here," the voice will say. "Miss Hellman is out." The only thing you can be sure of is that Miss Hellman is in.

She is, I believe, the only National Book Award winner who can claim to have had a father who cured his own case of hemorrhoids with generous applications to them of Colgate's toothpaste.

I am fairly certain that she is the only member of the American Academy of Arts and Letters, female or male, who has thwarted an attempted rape by staging a fit of sneezing.

She also has the distinction of being the only author at or near the summit of the best-seller lists who has publicly stated that she has always wanted to go to bed with an orangutan.

She is surely the only employee of Sam Goldwyn who ever

refused to attend two conferences with the great mogul because of being too busy rolling condoms. (Perhaps I should
add, in case you are wondering why this activity was taking
place, that it was in the interest of a practical joke.)

M iss Hellman has changed the lives of many people, as
teacher or exemplar or scold, and a few people have
changed hers. Among these, two stand out.

The first is Sophronia, her wet nurse and the companion of
her childhood, and, her father would say, the only control she
ever recognized. "Oh, Sophronia, it's you I want back always,"
Miss Hellman cries out in one of her books. As a kind of
pledge of her debt to Sophronia, Miss Hellman sent her the
first salary check she ever earned. There is a photograph of this
remarkable figure of pride in *An Unfinished Woman*, and, looking at it, one sees the force of what Miss Hellman writes: "She
was an angry woman, and she gave me anger, an uncomfortable, dangerous, and often useful gift." Once, when the child
Lillian had seen her father get into a cab with a pretty woman
not her mother, Sophronia counseled keeping her mouth shut,
saying, "Don't go through life making trouble for people." We
all know the stern and dazzling resonance of that advice in
Miss Hellman's appearance before the House Un-American
Activities Committee in Joe McCarthy's time.

The other person was Dashiell Hammett. With that handsome, sharp-minded, and committed man she had a relationship, off and on, for over thirty years, one which, as she has
said, often had "a ragging argumentative tone," but which had
"the deep pleasure of continuing interest" and grew and grew
into "a passionate affection." Hammett was—and he remains
to this day—*her* conscience. He was her artistic conscience, as
ruthless with her as he was with himself in his own work, for
ten of her twelve plays. She still makes many a decision by

HELLMAN AND HERSEY AT THE MACDOWELL COLONY

"Anger, an uncomfortable, dangerous, and often useful gift."

asking herself, sometimes out loud: What would Dash have wanted me to do about this? Death took Hammett and became her enemy.

I have spoken, she herself has spoken, of a religious streak in her. It is hard, perhaps dangerous, to trace or describe it. She is profoundly yet also skeptically Jewish—more in culture and sensibility, obviously, than in faith. She tells of an indiscriminate religiosity that her mother had, dropping in on any house of worship. Hers is certainly not like that—yet there is a weird ecumenical something-or-other going here. She writes somewhere of Bohemia bumping into Calvin in her. Calvin! When anything seems unspeakable to her, she will shout "Oy!" and cross herself. When all her beliefs and rituals, serious and playful, are rendered down to their pure state, just this remains: she insists on decency in human transactions.

This places her—a lonely, lonely figure—at the nowhere crossroads of all religions and all politics.

She is a moral force, but take a firm grip on your hat!—for the moment will come when the force, operating at high pitch, will suddenly go up in smoke before your eyes, and in its place will stand pure caprice. This is sometimes a mischievous thirteen-year-old girl.

Nothing gives this girl greater pleasure than to be shocking. She knows I was born in China and love and respect the Chinese, so whenever I'm around, her universe is suddenly thronged with Chinks. Niggers, kikes, and idiot WASPs crowd tales told to prim folks. Bad food—even if it is bad lox and bagels—is always "goy dreck." She incessantly offers TLs— "trade lasts," compliments spoken by absent parties and offered on a barter basis (there was one in *The Children's Hour*)—but again, be wary: what she gives in exchange often has an ironic barb in it.

If she says, "Forgive me," my advice is to back away. This is a signal for the final blunt blow in an argument. In Vineyard Haven, she and my wife and I have a mutual neighbor, a willful lady whom I shall call, as Miss Hellman calls all women who should be nameless or whose names she has forgotten, Mrs. Gigglewitz. Miss Hellman met Mrs. Gigglewitz downtown one day, and the latter began to complain about the noise certain neighborhood dogs made. One of them, she said, was that awful Hersey dog. The fact of the matter was that our dog could bark—but seldom did. Miss Hellman's powerful senses of loyalty and justice were instantly mobilized.

"I don't think you hear the Hersey dog," she said.

"Oh, yes," the woman blithely said. "It makes a hell of a racket every morning."

"No," Miss Hellman said, "their dog is exceptionally quiet."

"*Quiet?* It barks all day."

"I think you're mistaken." Any ear but Mrs. Gigglewitz's would have heard the sharpness in the voice.

"I'm not mistaken. It makes a terrible racket."

"Forgive me, Mrs. Gigglewitz," Miss Hellman then said. "I happen to know that the Hersey dog has been operated on to have its vocal cords removed."

Miss Hellman's powers of invention are fed by her remarkable memory and her ravenous curiosity. Her father once said she lived "within a question mark." She defines culture as "applied curiosity." She is always on what she calls "the find-out kick." How long is that boat? How was this cooked? What year was that? All this questioning is part of her extended youthfulness. More than three decades ago she wrote, and it is still as fresh in her as ever, "If I did not hope to grow, I would not hope to live."

We must come back around the circle now to the rebelliousness, the life-force anger, with which Miss Hellman does live, still growing every day. There was a year of sharp turn toward rebelliousness in her, when she was thirteen or fourteen. By the late nineteen-thirties or early forties, she had realized that no political party would be able to contain this quality of hers. Yet the pepper in her psyche—her touchiness, her hatred of being physically pushed even by accident, her out-of-control anger whenever she feels she has been dealt with unjustly—all have contributed in the end to her being radically political while essentially remaining outside formal politics. Radically, I mean, in the sense of "at the root." She cuts through all ideologies to their taproot: to the decency their adherents universally profess but almost never deliver. "Since when," she has written, "do you have to agree with people to defend them from injustice?" Her response to McCarthyism was not ideological, it was "I will not do this indecent thing. Go jump in the lake." Richard Nixon has testified under oath that her Committee for Public Justice frightened J. Edgar Hoover into discontinuing illegal wiretaps. How? By shaming.

In her plays, in her writings out of memory, above all in her juicy, resonant, headlong, passionate self, Lillian Hellman gives us glimpses of *all* the possibilities of life on this mixed-up earth. In return we can only thank her, honor her, and try to live as wholeheartedly as she does.

She and I share a love of the sea. We fish often together. Coming back in around West Chop in the evening light I sometimes see her standing by the starboard coaming looking across the water. All anger is calm in her then. But there is an intensity in her gaze, almost as if she could see things hidden from the rest of us. What is it? Can she see the years in the waves?

Appendix

Sources of materials in four essays in this book which draw in part on published writings:

HENRY R. LUCE

Robert T. Elson, *Time Inc.: The Intimate History of a Publishing Enterprise, 1923–1941;* and *The World of Time Inc.: The Intimate History of a Publishing Enterprise, 1941–1960* (New York: Atheneum, 1968, 1973).

John K. Jessup, ed., *The Ideas of Henry Luce* (New York: Atheneum, 1969).

John Kobler, *Luce: His Time, Life, and Fortune* (Garden City, N.Y.: Doubleday, 1968).

W. A. Swanburg, *Luce and His Empire* (New York: Charles Scribner's Sons, 1972).

JAMES AGEE

James Agee, *Agee on Film,* vol. 2 (New York: McDowell, Obolen 1960).

——— and Walker Evans, *Let Us Now Praise Famous Men* (F Houghton Mifflin, 1941 et seq.).

Letters of James Agee to Father Flye, 2nd ed. (Boston: H Mifflin, 1971).

Laurence Bergreen, *James Agee: A Life* (New York: E. P. Dutton, 1984).

Mark A. Doty, *Tell Me Who I Am: James Agee's Search for Selfhood* (Baton Rouge: Louisiana State University Press, 1981).

Genevieve Fabre, "A Bibliography of the Works of James Agee" (*Bulletin of Bibliography,* 24, no. 7, May–August 1965: pp. 145–48, 163–66).

Robert Fitzgerald, "A Memoir," preface to *The Collected Short Prose of James Agee* (Boston: Houghton Mifflin, 1968).

Dwight Macdonald, "Death of a Poet" (*The New Yorker,* November 16, 1957).

David Madden, ed., *Remembering James Agee* (Baton Rouge: Louisiana State University Press, 1974).

Genevieve Moreau, *The Restless Journey of James Agee* (New York: William Morrow, 1977).

Alma Neuman, "Thoughts of Jim: A Memory of Frenchtown and James Agee" (*Shenandoah,* 33, no. 1, 1981–82: pp. 25–26).

Ross Spears and Jude Cassidy, eds., *Agee: His Life Remembered* (New York: Holt, Rinehart and Winston, 1985).

William Stott, *Documentary Expression and Thirties America* (New York: Oxford University Press, 1973).

John Szarkowski, "Introduction" to *Walker Evans* (New York: Museum of Modern Art, 1971).

Lionel Trilling, "Greatness with One Fault in It" (*Kenyon Review,* 4, 1942).

————, "An American Classic" (*Midcentury,* 16, September 1960: pp. 3–10).

JANET TRAIN

Francis Galton, *Inquiries into Human Faculty and Its Development* (New York: E. P. Dutton, 1908).

Charles Spearman, *The Abilities of Man* (New York: Macmillan, 1927).

Lewis M. Terman, *Genetic Studies of Genius,* vol. 4 (Stanford, Calif.: Stanford University Press, 1926).

————, *The Measurement of Intelligence* (Salem, N.H.: Ayer, 1975).

———— and M. A. Merrill, *Measuring Intelligence* (Boston: Houghton Mifflin, 1916).

L. L. Thurstone, *Primary Mental Abilities* (Chicago: University of Chicago Press, 1938).

ERSKINE CALDWELL

Kay Bonetti, "A Good Listener Speaks" (*Saturday Review,* July/August 1983).

Erskine Caldwell, *With All My Might* (Atlanta: Peachtree, 1987).

Edwin McDowell, "Fifty Years of Successes for Erskine Caldwell" (*New York Times,* December 1, 1982).

————, Caldwell obituary (*New York Times,* April 13, 1987).

PERMISSIONS ACKNOWLEDGMENTS

Some of the essays in this collection were originally published in the following periodicals: '47, Hotchkiss Alumni Magazine, The New Republic, The New York Times, The New Yorker, and an article on American education from The Woodrow Wilson Foundation.

Grateful acknowledgment is made to the following for permission to reprint previously published material:

American Academy and Institute of Arts and Letters: Commemorative tribute to Erskine Caldwell, published in the Proceedings of the American Academy and Institute of Arts and Letters, Second Series, Number 38, December 4, 1987. Reprinted by permission.

The Curtis Publishing Co.: "A Life for a Vote" by John Hersey, published in The Saturday Evening Post (September 26, 1964). Reprinted by permission from The Saturday Evening Post, copyright © 1964 by The Curtis Publishing Co.

John Hersey: "Introduction" by John Hersey to the new edition of Let Us Now Praise Famous Men by James Agee, published by Houghton Mifflin Company, Boston, 1988, and originally, in a different version, as "Agee," in The New Yorker, July 18, 1988. Reprinted by permission of the author.

Alfred A. Knopf, Inc.: "Alfred A. Knopf's Love Affair" by John Hersey from Alfred A. Knopf at 60. Copyright 1952 by Alfred A. Knopf, Inc. Reprinted by permission.

Life magazine: "Prisoner 339, Klooga" by John Hersey, published in Life magazine (October 30, 1944). Copyright 1944, © 1972 by Time Inc. Reprinted by permission of Life magazine.

PHOTOGRAPHIC ACKNOWLEDGMENTS

page

15 Sinclair Lewis: Estate of Carl Van Vechten, Joseph Solomon, Executor

31 Henry Luce with Chiang Kai-shek: Courtesy Life Picture Service

49 James Agee: 1945 © Helen Levitt

81 Lieutenant Kennedy in the Solomons: Elliott Erwitt, Magnum

125 Hersey and Father Morse: Dmitri Kessel, *Life* magazine © Time Inc.

147 Capa with Gerda in Paris: © Fred Stein

171 Baruch on His Park Bench: Walter Sanders, *Life* magazine © 1943 Time Inc.

193 Alfred Knopf in Paradise: Harry Ransom Humanities Research Center, University of Texas, Austin

235 Harry Truman on a Morning Walk: Marie Hansen, *Life* magazine © Time Inc.

261 The Living Room of Jessica Kelley's Winsted Home: A. E. Barnes

325 Erskine Caldwell on Tobacco Road, 1936: Margaret Bourke-White

371 Hellman and Hersey at the MacDowell Colony: Bernice B. Perry, courtesy of the MacDowell Colony

ABOUT THE AUTHOR

John Hersey was born in Tientsin, China, in 1914 and lived there until 1925, when his family returned to the United States. He studied at Yale and Cambridge universities, served for a time as Sinclair Lewis's secretary, and then worked several years as a journalist. He has had published fourteen books of fiction and eight books of nonfiction, as well as writing the many profiles and sketches that are now collected in this volume. John Hersey has won the Pulitzer Prize for fiction. He is married and has five children and four grandchildren. He divides his time between Key West and Martha's Vineyard.